W9-AUU-888

COYOTES

*A Journey Through the Secret World
of America's Illegal Aliens*

Ted Conover was born in 1958 in Okinawa, Japan.
He left Amherst College in 1980 to ride freight
trains with hoboes, returning in 1981 to graduate
summa cum laude in anthropology. *Rolling Nowhere*, his first book, is an account of that travel.
He has worked as a reporter, ski instructor, and
in a sausage factory in Pamplona, Spain. As a
Marshall Scholar at the Centre of Latin American
Studies, Cambridge University, he did graduate
research into the journals of the first European
explorers of the Americas. He lives in Denver,
where he is currently writing his first novel.

COYOTES

ALSO BY TED CONOVER

Rolling Nowhere

Ted Conover

COYOTES

*A Journey Through the Secret World
of America's Illegal Aliens*

HEINEMANN : LONDON

William Heinemann Ltd
Michelin House, 81 Fulham Road, London SW3 6RB

LONDON   MELBOURNE   AUCKLAND

First published in the USA by Vintage Books 1987
First published in Great Britain in this edition by William
Heinemann Ltd 1988

Copyright © 1987 by Ted Conover

This book is sold subject to the condition that
it shall not, by way of trade or otherwise, be
lent, resold, hired out or otherwise circulated
without the publisher's prior consent in any
form of binding or cover other than that in which
it is published and without a similar condition
including this condition being imposed on the
subsequent purchaser

British Library Cataloguing in Publication Data

Conover, Ted
    Coyotes: a journey through the secret
    world of America's illegal aliens.
    1. United States. Illegal Mexican immigrants
    I. Title
    325'.1

    ISBN 0 434 14082 1

Author photo © 1986 by Richard Larson

Printed and bound in Great Britain by
Richard Clay Ltd, Bungay, Suffolk

For Judy

Thou shalt not oppress a stranger,
for ye know the heart of a stranger,
as ye were strangers in the land of Egypt.

—EXODUS 23:9

Acknowledgments

Without the help of the following, this book could never have been written. Thanks to: Scott Lankford, Jay Leibold, and Eric Green, for manuscript suggestions. Dale Appelbaum, Elizabeth Krecker, the Richard Mallery family, Lupe Sanchez, Joaquín Lira, Laurie Martinelli, Nadine Wettstein, Matilde Martinez and family, Josie and José Ojeda, Francisca Cavazos, Phil Decker, Dr. Raymund Tanaka, Rita Goodman, Don and Niomi Devereaux, and the good people of the Arizona Farmworkers Union. Brad Segal, Katie Conover, Jerry Conover, Jacquelyn Wonder, Pamela and Jay Kenney, and Ross McConnell, in Colorado. Jim and Joey Christiansen and families, René Flores, "Dogie," Christie Evans, Rick Larson, Teresa Keenan, Simon Boughton, Marvin Stone, William MacDougall, and John Crewdson, in various states. Hilario Pacheco and family, Peter Copeland, Joe Keenan, Richard Meislin, Patricia Morales, Marcia and Victor McLane and the people of the Casa de los Amigos in Mexico City, Lic. Eduardo Chávez Padilla, and Jorge Fragoso and family, in Mexico. Bob "Roberto Grande" Boorstin; Seth O. Lloyd; Peter Engel; David Rosenthal, my editor; and especially Jack Rosenthal and Sterling Lord, my agent, in New York City. Elizabeth and David

Acknowledgments

Beim and Janet Conover, belatedly, for aiding and abetting an errant nephew.

Much of my research/travel in Mexico was made possible by an Ernie Pyle Fellowship from the Scripps-Howard Foundation and the Inter American Press Association (IAPA). Small portions of this work may have appeared previously in short articles published by IAPA member newspapers and in *Grassroots Development*, the journal of the Inter-American Foundation.

Most of all, my thanks to those Mexicans brave enough to entrust me with their story.

A Note on Translation

The translation of Mexican voices in English-language literature and movies too often makes them sound folkloric or like simpletons. *"Sí, señor. The horse, she is very big, yes?"* Obviously, in their native tongue Mexicans sound as natural to each other as we do when we speak English. I have tried to recreate this ease of communication when translating the words of Mexicans here.

A difficulty has been the richness of Mexican slang and profanity. Sometimes it can be translated, but often too much is lost: *"¡Ay, cabrón!"* has a completely different character than "Dammit!"; *"hijo de la chingada"* is but a distant cousin to a "son of a bitch." Because of this, I have let some slang go untranslated. I believe readers will pick up the meanings of some of the more common epithets as they read along; those desiring more background might consult the works of Octavio Paz or Alan Riding.

Much of the book's dialogue is between Mexicans or between me and Mexicans. To indicate that we were speaking in Spanish, translated dialogue appears in italics. Dialogue that took place in English is not italicized.

The word "Mexican" in this book always means a Mexican national. American citizens of Mexican extraction I refer to as Mexican-Americans or Chicanos. "Illegal alien" and "undocumented worker" I also treat as synonyms, though I try to avoid both labels, as the former makes them sound like outlaws from another planet, and the latter is unwieldy.

Contents

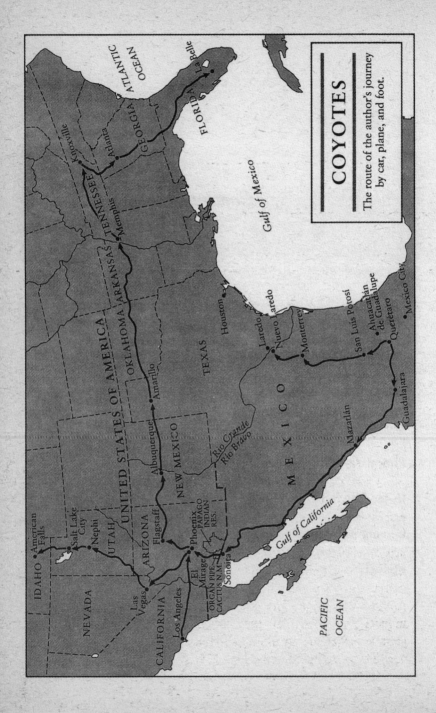

COYOTES

The route of the author's journey by car, plane, and foot.

Foreword

I met my first "illegal alien" while researching an earlier book on American railroad tramps. Both of us were sneaking through the Southern Pacific yards of Bakersfield, California, having ridden into town on different freights. When he appeared between two boxcars and asked me simply, "Mission?" I knew we were looking for the same thing, the local rescue mission, the "Jesus Saves." My Spanish then was not great, but we could communicate; and, over the next couple of days, Enrique Jarra and I became friends.

From that meeting I realized that many Mexicans rode the freights—it was a way of getting around while staying out of the public eye—as well as something else: that, much more than the tired, aged tramps I had been sharing camp fires with, these people were the true present-day incarnation of the classic American hobo. Unskilled, single (or traveling alone, at any rate), immigrant, they were here to work their tails off in the finest American tradition. The skin was darker, the faith Catholic, but in most other particulars they bore much resemblance to my late great-grandfather, an immigrant from Norway, here to make a new life by doing America's work.

By later traveling and working with Mexicans for more than

a year, I caught a glimpse of the United States from the underground perspective of an immigrant group that may profoundly change our country. Lacking here is a good account of the experiences of female immigrants: while it was a challenge for me to earn the trust of Mexican men in the States, it was nearly impossible to gain the confidence of Mexican women. This is a project which I hope will be undertaken soon, and best by a female researcher. Also, though several of my companions asked me to use their real names (and spread the legend of their exploits), nothing has been revealed that would make it easier for the Immigration and Naturalization Service to apprehend "aliens." The INS, I was surprised to discover, often knows where they are and how they move, even if it doesn't always act on the information.

What *La Migra* does not know—what it perhaps cannot afford to know—is the more human side of the men and women it arrests, the drama of their lives. That's what this book is about. It is not a policy book, but a story. It relates to policy only insofar as I hope through it to flesh out a missing perspective in the immigration debate: the perspective of those whom the whole thing is about. My belief is that few of the authors of the many books and articles written on immigration would recognize an "illegal alien" if he came up and offered to shine their shoes—much less share a word or two. That is a problem, the main reason, I think, that the terms of the debate have tended to dehumanize the Mexicans, turning them from people into "illegal aliens." But because we as Americans control their destiny in so many ways, it is urgent that we know more about these people who ask little more than to wash our dishes, vacuum our cars, and pick our fruit.

How to know them? It seemed important to move beyond newspaper coverage. The truly meaningful things about a people are not learned by conducting an interview, gathering statistics, or watching them on the news, but by going out and living with them. To get to know Mexicans you need to speak their language, be willing to put up with living conditions less comfortable than our own, and, especially if you look and were raised as differently from them as I was, you need to believe in the subversive idea that a human is a human, and that human beings everywhere, with a little effort, can come to understand and even like each other.

This is not the whole story, but I have tried to make it their story.

Ted Conover
Denver, Colorado
May 1, 1987

COYOTES

Chapter 1

The Gringo and the Mexicano

SUN SLIPPED through the cracks left by poor workmanship, providing the shack's only light. A space around the plywood slapped across the window, a slit between the corroding sheet-metal door and its jamb, tiny arcs between crumbling cinder blocks and the corrugated tin roof: if you stood in the right places the rays hit your shoes, surrounded by cigarette butts, everything dusty on the dry dirt floor.

Alonso, squatting down to give his legs a rest, surveyed the scores of butts. *"Lots of wetbacks waited here, eh?"* I thought of the minutes of worried waiting represented by each butt, the cumulative anxiety of them all. Already, since the *coyotes* had left us here, we had waited two hours; my cigarettes, now, were gone. No one but the *coyotes*—the smugglers—knew exactly where we were. If things were going according to plan, we were somewhere near the Rio Grande, and would soon be ferried across to the United States. But, if they disbelieved the story I had invented and still suspected I was an undercover cop, then . . . anything could happen.

I was an unlikely wetback. Blond haired and blue eyed, I was in Mexico as a journalist, researching what illegal immigration to the States means to Mexicans. It had not been my plan, when

I boarded a northbound bus in central Mexico, to cross the Rio Grande this way. But then I met Alonso. He was on his way to the border. Sitting next to him I realized that, with a partner lined up, I too might sneak across the border. *"It is better to see once than to listen many times,"* a Mexican farmer had told me a week before, when I was asking him about crossing. The words echoed in my brain. Alonso and I seemed to get along. The only remaining obstacle, it seemed to me, would be to convince smugglers that they ought to take me.

Intoxicated with the possibility of experiencing a crossing, I became possessed of a crazy confidence that somehow I could make it all happen. Now, exhausted and edgy from hours of tense negotiation, breathing the close, hot air of the shack, I felt I had ignored my better judgment. I had narrowed my options to one—there was no turning back. Yet too much could still go wrong. And the wrong move, in this sort of situation, could end your life.

The floor of the shack, slightly larger in area than a king-size bed, was really the only thing to look at. Scattered around it, besides cigarette butts, were a couple of planks, an old wash-basin, a barrel, a quart beer bottle, and other trash. The bottle caught my eye. If worse came to worse, I thought, I could grab it by the neck, knock off the bottom against a wall, and have a fairly good weapon.

I joined Alonso at the window cracks, which afforded a view of the cooking area of an adjoining shack. A teenage girl was out there, trying to cook over a smoky wood stove while a teenage boy, one of the smuggling crew, tried to fondle her. He would reach from behind for the front of her body and, smiling, she'd hit him with a spoon. She was maybe fifteen, and very pretty. A group of prostitutes we passed outside a store on the morning's drive out here had been pretty too. Somehow, I had not expected to find beauty in this town made of planks and corrugated tin.

Tired of spying, we returned to our respective walls to sit and wait. Alonso whistled a tune through his teeth for a while. *"El Gringo y el Mexicano,"* he announced finally, reminding me of the popular *corrida*—or Mexican ballad—we had discussed the night before. *"Remember what happened to the gringo?"* The gringo of the title was a Texas rancher. He admired the young wife of one of his Mexican ranch hands, stole her away from him, and killed the Mexican for good measure. She was already pregnant with the Mexican's son, however, and the boy, learning of his father's fate, waited only until he was big enough to fire a gun to shoot and kill the Texan. Alonso was grinning.

"Very funny," I said to Alonso, who, with his perpetual good spirits and high energy, was as fine a person as existed for breaking the tension in a situation like ours. *"By the way, when are you going to introduce me to your girlfriend?"*

"Ha! Never! One look at the size of your North American wallet, and you'll have a wife." Thus reminded, I moved my roll of cash to my shirt pocket, inside my sweater, because the *coyotes* had seen it in my sock.

"They told me not to trust you," he said, *"back when you left the restaurant to get the money."* This was nothing new—other Mexicans, seeing a countryman traveling with me, had issued him similar warnings: *"He may seem nice, but he'll fuck you over. That's how gringos are."* This was, in fact, the first of three warnings Alonso would receive while we were together. I looked at him closely in the dimness, listened for more, to see how he had taken it. But he was silent. Finally I had to prompt him.

"And? . . ."

"And nothing," said Alonso. *"I'm here, right?"*

"Yes. You and I are here." Silently I thanked God he was there. I'd be going crazy if he weren't. A long silence.

"My God," he exclaimed suddenly, *"who ever would have thought I'd find myself in a coyote's shack with a gringo? My parents'll never believe me!"*

Alonso and I had been traveling partners for only three days, but in the difficult circumstances of those days, trust had proved necessary for survival. We met for the first time while waiting to board a northbound bus in San Luis Potosí, in central Mexico.

Besides us, only one other passenger, a middle-aged businessman, waited on the platform outside the nearly empty *Tres Estrellas de Oro* coach from Mexico City that afternoon. *"And where are you two young men going?"* the businessman asked politely.

Alonso, young and slight, was smartly dressed in jeans, a light blue snap-up cowboy shirt, and a sturdy leather belt that widened in the front to form its own buckle, interwoven with lanyard and lots of studs. His black, pointed-toe cowboy boots had the Mexican-style heel that angles rakishly forward, sometimes giving the wearer a peculiar rolling gait. He looked about twenty, and had jet black hair and strong Indian features—except for the very un-Indian grin, with which, nodding, he invited me to answer first.

"I'm going to Monterrey, to talk to some people at Radio XEG— do you know it? 'La Ranchera de Monterrey?' "

The men nodded. It was one of Mexico's—probably North America's—biggest radio stations, beaming 100,000 watts of *ranchera* music to AM listeners twenty-four hours a day. *Ranchera*, with its accordion, bass, and guitar, is Mexico's country music, especially popular in the north. I had tuned it in a couple of times on my car radio while driving across the American Midwest at night. *"I'm a writer, interested in ranchera songs about the indocumentados who travel north to work in the United States."*

"Ah, los mojados," said the businessman—the wetbacks. *"And you, young ma—"*

"Well, hey, that's me," interrupted Alonso, beaming. *"Yo voy de mojado."* I'm going as a wetback.

I couldn't believe it. In the States you had to know a Mexican for weeks before he would make an admission like that. The older man looked uncomfortable. *"Are you serious?"* I said. There seemed to be no coyness about Alonso, no irony.

"Sure. I'm headed for Texas. Got to stop off in Monterrey first to see if some friends want to go."

On the bus Alonso and I sat across the aisle from each other. I gave him my card, which he placed in his wallet with great care. Maybe if I was a writer, he said, I could help him learn to speak

English. He had already crossed into the States *"three or four times,"* he said, and picked up a little: "plees, fren'," "no got money," "no speak Engliss," "you got beer?" "one momen, plees," "money order," "house." He knew some of the numbers from one to ten but had great difficulty with the others, his tongue and lips contorting into awkward, impossible shapes.

Did he spell it A-l-o-n-s-o or A-l-o-n-z-o? I asked. *"Whichever you like,"* he reassured me. *"It's the same either way."*

"But which way do you spell it?" He shrugged and looked out the window at the desert.

All afternoon we talked. I learned that Alonso had only finished fifth grade, and was just a beginning reader. His parents, small farmers, gave him money to go away to secondary school, *"but some friends and I used it to get to Texas. We wanted an adventure."* He was fourteen at the time. He and his friends crossed the Rio Grande at Reynosa, skirting its sister city of McAllen, Texas, and avoiding apprehension in the dangerous border zone by walking four days over the hills and desert to Pharr, Texas, carrying only water bottles, a few sandwiches, and a compass. *"The only time I made it without getting caught,"* said Alonso glumly.

From his accounts I judged Alonso to be clever and resilient. Like most Mexicans who cross, though, he was not book-smart. His ignorance of science and geography was astounding—but not, for him, a cause for shame. *"Why does it snow up north, but not here?"* he asked. I tried to explain about the tilt of the earth and the angle of the sun, but didn't really believe I'd made him understand. Texas itself, he believed, was larger than Mexico. Big cities confused him; he would much rather live in the country, where the air is clean. The *"negros"* in places like Houston, where he worked last, scared him—much more than the *gabachos* (whites), whom he told me were nice. Just about everything about America, Alonso was convinced, was better than Mexico—the economy, the law-enforcement system, the general way of doing things, the *people. "English is a better language, isn't it?"* he asked me.

I was the first *gabacho* he had ever had a real conversation with; he stared at me as I spoke to him, as though amazed that we were actually talking. It occurred to me that, having finished college, I was perhaps the most highly educated person he had ever met. But I didn't want to seem like a professor; I was here to get an education from him.

We stared out the window at the arid Mexican northeast, and he named for me the passing cactuses—the *palmas, garambullos,* and *nopales carbón,* the tall, thin *ocotillos* that some desert villagers plant close together in rows to grow into green fences around their small homes. The bus had the inevitable flat tire of any long haul on a Mexican coach, and noisily hobbled off the highway at one of the thousands of *vulcanizadoras,* or tire-repair shacks. Taking refuge from the harsh sun in the shade at the side of the bus, Alonso and I watched the driver and the thin man from the *vulcanizadora* change the tire. Alonso bought us Pepsis. Cars shot past on the narrow two-lane road, and we squinted to avoid the dust. A few of the vehicles had the foreign license plates of my country: tourists, heading down from Texas. We caught brief glimpses as they passed: inside the big cars they looked cool, relaxed, sometimes blond.

I talked cars with Alonso. Yes, I told him, I did have one, though not a very good one. Any car would be okay with him, he said, but a Corvette was his first choice. That, or a pickup truck. We stood there for a long time, in the shade of the bus, watching the cars and not talking.

"The dreams we have here can be reality there," said Alonso suddenly.

"What?" The remark seemed to come from out of the blue.

"You asked why I go to cross the river."

"Yes."

"Well, that's why."

"Oh, I see. You're still talking about cars."

"No, it's not just cars. It's not just money. Look, it's everything. Cars, jobs, women, music. Everything. Everything you've got is better. If you can make it in El Norte, you've got it made."

Shiny cars sped past. Meanwhile, the driver and his thin

assistant were battling with a huge, nearly bald spare tire that seemed reluctant to be put back into service. Infuriated, the driver blamed the problems on the thin man and recruited a couple of passengers to help position the tire on the rear axle. Still it didn't fit. With a great rumble of profanity the driver landed his boot on the tire, raising a small cloud of dust. Why, he asked the Virgin, why him?

All night we sat in the Nuevo Laredo bus station. Scores of earlier arrivals had claimed the available benches for sleeping, and the floor was too dirty to stretch out on. Two cups of coffee were our excuse for occupying a pair of molded plastic chairs in the cafeteria section of the big room. Blasts of cold air whenever anyone entered or left the station reminded us of how chilly the desert nights could be in springtime. With the steam from my coffee cup warming my face, I looked out over all the prone bodies.

"*Guess not too many buses leave at night, huh?*" I surmised to Alonso. "*All these guys waiting for connections in the morning.*"

" '*Mano* [brother], *they're not waiting for other buses,*" he said. "*These men have arrived. Would* you *want to cross the river in this cold?*"

"*What—all these guys are going to cross? How do you know?*"

"*Well, they're not on vacation. See how they're dressed? They're going to work.*"

On closer examination I saw that the men were farm men—with straw cowboy hats, canvas pants, dirty feet in worn *huaraches* (sandals), tough-skinned hands and weathered faces. No luggage to speak of, just fiber *costales* (woven sacks) and sometimes a blanket and a coat. But I was not convinced. Such a massive concentration of about-to-be fugitives allowed to congregate here in this obvious way? Couldn't they be going to work in Mexico?

"*I don't think so,*" said Alonso, who knew no other way to convince me. "*Look tomorrow and you will see.*"

But his point was proved before then. Less than half an hour after we had sat down at the small cafeteria table, a skittish, uncombed man with a flushed face sat down in the seat next to Alonso. "Where are you going?" he asked, and his breath smelled of liquor.

"Oh, just here," said Alonso, trusting no one.

"Aaah," said the man, lighting a cigarette. He took a few deep puffs and sent his exhalations my way. Apparently I was not meant to be a part of this conversation. "Well, if you meet anyone who wants to cross to the other side, I have some friends who can take them there."

My heart leaped; but I tried to effect a look of boredom. This was the sort of encounter I was always hearing about. Bus stations like this were supposed to be a principal recruiting ground for *coyotes*, the smugglers who helped aliens across. Somehow, though, I had expected someone who looked not only sneaky and shifty eyed but, well . . . competent. I didn't want to miss a word, but tried hard not to stare at the smelly, hairy man across the table from me: any inordinate attention on the part of the *gringo* would surely kill the deal. In fact, I was surprised that anyone was approaching Alonso with me along. That evening, however, four more would be along—probably only half, said Alonso, of the number that would've come by had I not been there. Business must have been lagging.

Alonso, for his part, reddened as the man made his intentions clear; I too felt uncomfortable. This man was exactly what we had been looking for, was the sort of connection we would need in order to cross. Yet, besides being an opportunity, this was also a threat: to say you were interested was to say you had the cash. To say you had the cash was to make yourself a target for robbery. At 3:00 A.M. in a border-town bus station, no one should know how rich you are.

"*They can get you to Houston for five hundred dollars,*" said the man. "*San Antonio? Four hundred fifty. L.A., seven hundred dollars.*" Apparently it was normal, in this trade, to deal in a foreign currency.

Alonso stared at the table. "*Isn't that awfully high?*" he finally asked.

The man pretended offense. *"High? Look, things here are hot. We take a lot of risks. Anything could go wrong. You might not pay us, we might get caught. If you get caught, they just send you back. But if we get caught—"* He drew his index finger across his throat. *"How much you got?"* The man pointed at the bulge in Alonso's pocket.

The directness embarrassed Alonso further, and he began to withdraw. *"Very little,"* he said, looking away. For a long time we sat in silence.

"Okey," said the man finally, in hip border English, getting to his feet. *"I'll be around if you find you have the dough."* He nodded good-bye and left.

Dawn seemed to have little effect on the cold, but by 9:00 A.M. we felt the day was slipping by. Shoulders hunched, we set off on foot toward the city center and the Rio Grande.

The neighborhood was industrial, and wind from around the bleak buildings added to our chill. Alonso was nevertheless interested in the different warehouses and factories, and peered in any open door to see what was going on inside. The sight of the place seemed to cheer him. *"If I can't get across with the dough I brought, I'll be able to find work here,"* he said. *"Look—there's things happening everywhere."*

Though there was also great poverty, the Mexican side of the border did seem a relatively prosperous place. Here American corporations, taking advantage of cheap labor and few unions, had recently constructed a large number of *maquiladoras*—assembly plants, for the most part, using materials brought in duty-free from the United States (such as textiles and electronics components) and then exported back to the States with duty levied only on the value added by the work done in Mexico. The relative ease with which a Mexican, male or female, could find work in the border towns was a main reason that these towns, contrary to popular American opinion, were not large generators of illegal immigrants to the States. Those who crossed, as studies have shown, typically began their journeys in poorer regions far to the south.

"*What if you can't find a job, though?*" I asked. Alonso seemed to me to travel on distressingly slim resources, without a great deal of forethought, with faith in what seemed the questionable belief that something would turn up. "*What if nothing turns up?*"

Alonso shrugged, unconcerned. "*Something always turns up.*"

"*But, like what?*"

My lack of faith in providence was curious to Alonso. "*Something, anything,*" he tried to explain. "*See, I go to where the rich people are. Maybe a hotel, or a restaurant, or parking lots. Maybe the bus station. I offer to carry their bags, or open the doors—I see what they need. Sometimes I wash cars. I find a rag—*"

"*But where do you get water?*" I interrupted. "*What about soap?*"

"*You borrow things. You knock at the back of the restaurant, and borrow a pail. Maybe they lend you a sponge, a chunk of soap. If they don't, you go find a rag. If they like you, people will help.*"

The spirit seemed so enterprising. It reminded me of stories I'd read in school of the days when America was a developing country, when ordinary kids would hit the streets to sell newspapers, shine shoes, shovel a walk for a few pennies. If there were no jobs to be had, they would invent them. Kids still work hard in America, but the relative prosperity of modern times means less scrambling. America's poor, young and old, take little interest in work so poorly paid it seems tantamount to begging. In Mexico, though, where work is tantamount to survival, the lowest job is still an opportunity.

We came to a fast and dirty boulevard leading downtown and had to turn into the wind. Collars up and faces toward the sidewalk, we didn't notice the policeman until we had nearly walked into him. "*¡Ven aquí!*" he said, turning on his heel and motioning for us to follow him. His cruiser had been parked down an alley, hidden until now behind a hedgerow. Leaning casually against it, looking the other way, was his plainclothes partner. Startled, Alonso and I glanced quickly at each other. My instantaneous reaction, that of an American tourist used to being treated like royalty in Mexico, had been a feeling that the cop must have something important to ask us, that perhaps he needed help in solving some crime. But as we approached the car and were ushered into the backseat without a word, I sensed something very different was happening.

The cops slammed shut the doors. Turning around in the front seat, they began to fire questions at us: Where were we from? What were we doing in Nuevo Laredo? Where were we going? Did we plan to cross the river? On their demand, I turned over my wallet; they were angry to learn that Alonso had left his identification at home.

Ironically, he had left it out of fear of getting caught on the *other* side—if the Border Patrol discovered he had been deported several times before, he might face jail instead of what they called a "voluntary departure." A similar fear had prompted me to talk with him in the bus station about the risks should American Immigration catch us together and suspect me of smuggling him across. We had already come up with a story. I was a journalist hoping to interview *mojados* fresh from the river, and Alonso had just arrived. We knew no more about each other than that. Caught sooner than expected—though for what crime I had no idea—I knew the story would have to be quickly adapted to new circumstances.

Fortunately, the cops gave me a chance to begin revisions while Alonso was present to hear them. *"Where do you know this man from?"* they demanded.

"I met him in the bus station," I said calmly. *"I am a journalist learning Spanish and he seemed interested in learning English. We had time to kill so we started talking."*

One cop whispered to the other, and then the plainclothesman ordered Alonso out of the car. I felt certain he was going to beat him. When the door was shut, I could hear Alonso being questioned aggressively, and then the other cop began to do the same to me. No, I insisted, I have no idea whether he plans to cross the river. No, we have no arrangement to smuggle out drugs.

I know very little about him—but is it a crime for a Mexican to leave his own country? Is it a crime for an American to get to know a Mexican?

After about fifteen minutes, the policemen traded positions and, as I would learn later, asked each of us the same questions he had asked the other. Then Alonso was pushed back into the rear of the car, the cops got in, and we pulled out.

The policemen's questions as we drove revealed that they had learned nothing, that Alonso knew how to keep his mouth shut, that he kept cool under pressure. *"It's very dangerous to cross the river,"* they told Alonso. *"You might drown and never be seen again. Then, if you had no identification, how could we notify your parents? We're checking on you for your own good. Tell us the truth."*

Alonso had no more to add. Neither did I. Yet the cops kept driving. We had both said we were heading for a coffee shop to get some breakfast, which was true, and the policemen continually pointed them out as we drove by. Once they came to a stop beside one, tantalized us with the prospect of release, and then drove on.

"I think we are going to have to take them to interrogations," said the uniformed cop to the other, who nodded emphatically. This response, along with the way the cop addressed his friend instead of us, lent what could have been a truly terrifying statement an almost melodramatic air. It occurred to me then, for the first time, that perhaps the truth was not necessarily what they were after. My next question was overdue.

"Um . . ." I volunteered, *"uh, isn't there any other way we might be able to take care of this?"*

One cop glanced at the other. *"What did you have in mind?"*

"Well, isn't there maybe . . . some sort of fine we could pay?" There was a brief silence.

"How much did you have in mind?"

I looked at Alonso. He mouthed, *"Five hundred."*

"Five hundred pesos."

"Apiece, or for both?"

Again I glanced at Alonso, trying to avoid the driver's eye in the mirror. *"For both,"* I replied.

He shook his head and turned another corner. This time I conferred more openly with Alonso. *"Apiece, then,"* I announced. *"A thousand total."*

"Two thousand," said the cop. It was just like bargaining in a Mexican marketplace. I swallowed hard and took a chance: *"Fifteen hundred."* The cop took off his hat and laid it upside down between them on the front seat. *"In the hat."*

Alonso and I dug deep into our pockets. Alonso then reached over the front seat to deposit the dirty, crumpled one-hundred-peso notes in the cap. Perhaps purposefully, however, he chose an inopportune moment to do so—just as the car was passing through an intersection crowded with pedestrians. *"Not now!"* hissed the uniformed driver.

Moments later, and 1,500 pesos poorer, we were deposited outside a restaurant on Nuevo Laredo's main plaza. Upon slamming the door, Alonso let loose the most virulent stream of Mexican profanity I had ever heard. (Later, perhaps ashamed, he declined to translate specifics for me.) The police had significantly depleted his dwindling cash reserve. I, too, was furious, but the more I thought about it, the more pathetic the incident seemed. We had been driven around in the police cruiser, and occupied the time of two men in blue, for nearly an hour, and they had extracted the princely sum of four dollars! As my adrenaline subsided, it all seemed funnier and funnier. Amazed but not depressed, I offered to buy Alonso breakfast.

The border may be the only place in Mexico where things can happen quickly. Partway through our meal I left the table briefly. Returning, I noticed that a man had taken my seat and, in between bites of my pancakes, was talking to Alonso. Wondering whether I was perhaps ignorant of some fine point of Mexican etiquette—were pancakes fair game if left for more than a couple of minutes?—I presented myself cautiously at the table. Alonso's face was slightly flushed, as it had been after talking to the first bus station *coyote*. The man glanced at me, took another large bite of pancake drenched in butter and syrup, and scooted over in the booth to make room.

He was large and heavy, with shoulder-length hair and a thin mustache. His trousers were dark; his shirt was of the silk, disco/ black light variety. *"He has an offer,"* said Alonso to me.

"Two hundred fifty dollars to San Antonio. Houston, four hundred," he volunteered. I stared at him. *"Where do you want to go?"* he asked Alonso.

"Does a person who goes with you to these places have to swim the river first?" I interrupted.

"Of course not. The river here is a city block wide. It is fast, and there are many weeds and branches in it, and eels. Almost no one swims. There is a lancha."

I did not know this word, *lancha,* but it sounded very much like the English word "launch," a speedboat. Getting across the river was our main goal, and to cross the Rio Grande in a smuggler's speedboat—now, that would be something. From Laredo, Texas, Alonso had said he knew ways to get to Houston cheaply— there was no need to pay an expensive smuggler.

"How much just to cross the river?" Alonso asked.

The man considered this for a moment. *"A hundred fifty dollars,"* he replied finally. Alonso and I excused ourselves and moved to a nearby table to discuss things. The price, we agreed, was too high, and probably negotiable. A sense of unreality swept over me as we returned to sit with the *coyote.* Was I really in a Mexican border town, negotiating the price of an illegal crossing into my country, via speedboat, with a stranger who was eating my pancakes? It was all so far from any situation I had ever imagined myself in—and yet apparently I was capable of going ahead. My heart was pounding hard for the third time that morning.

My jump off the high board continued. *"A hundred and fifty is too high,"* I told the man. *"One hundred—for both of us."*

"Wait a minute," said the smuggler in midbite, staring at me, *"you're going, too?"* He turned to glance at a man standing behind him whom I had not noticed before—a slighter man who

also had long hair—and let out a short, incredulous laugh. The man standing smiled, revealing a gruesome collection of withered teeth. But I was in too deep to find it funny, and, besides, now I had to lie.

I nodded. "*But* why?" he demanded. The two of them watched me closely.

"*I've had some problems with the law. That's why I'm in Mexico. I can't cross on the bridge.*" Criminals, I thought, would relate to the problems of being a criminal.

"*Aaaah,*" said the big man. "*I see!*" That seemed, in his mind, to settle everything. "*Hermano,*" he said, smiling, "*I don't care if you killed your own mother with a pitchfork, for one hundred and twenty dollars we can do business.*" Capitalism, I thought, in its starkest form: no moral considerations. Alonso and I agreed to the price. My fists, my shoulders, my legs relaxed a degree. With arrangements for a rendezvous shortly in the plaza, Alonso and I left the warm restaurant.

It was not either of our contacts who approached us half an hour later, but a third man. Cautiously we followed him down some side streets, Alonso whispering that I was about to learn about a "*mafia de los coyotes*"—one of the large smuggling organizations that controlled the illegal traffic in humans across the border. Several blocks from the restaurant, along a nearly empty street, the man pointed to a car and told us to climb in back; then he disappeared. Presently our two restaurant contacts climbed in front. The car was an old Chevrolet, its body trashed but the interior, oddly enough, luxurious, with crushed velvet upholstery, chrome trim, felt dashboard, and an excellent stereo. A plastic crucifix dangled on a chain from the rearview mirror. Saying nothing, the *coyote* with bad teeth revved up the car, adjusted the seat, and cranked up the stereo. Over this came loud music from an American rock station. As we pulled out it seemed clear that these men made a lot of money, but took pains not to look like they did.

Within about three blocks the shiny veneer of the tourist zone began to fall away, revealing a side of Nuevo Laredo unknown to people like me. Streets ceased to be paved, sidewalks disappeared, and the number of cars dwindled. At the same time the numbers of dirty kids, stray dogs, and broken windows grew rapidly. We passed a legless man on a scooter. The smell of sewage hung in the air. We were asked for the first half of our payment, and Alonso passed it over, as agreed.

Bad Teeth drove very arrogantly, making an old man on a bicycle nearly fall to avoid hitting the car, and rapidly braking in order to draw up alongside a shapely woman walking alone. As his disco-shirted partner rolled down the window to reach for her buttock, the car radio was blaring a romantic hit song by the Spaniard José José. *"¿Y qué, si nos llaman de todo, Y qué, si vivimos felices, tú y yo?"* ("So what, if they call us names; so what, if we're happy—you and I?") As he missed the grab, the *coyote* recouped by picking up the song just as it reached the refrain. *"¿Y qué?"* he sang plaintively to the woman, in perfect unison with the radio. Bad Teeth howled. Even the *contrabandistas* had time for a pretty girl.

We continued on to poorer and more remote parts of Nuevo Laredo. The town can't go on much farther, I thought to myself, searching for landmarks along the nondescript roadside that would help me to find my way back—if it ever came to that. Bad Teeth was casual, not looking worriedly in the rearview mirror or over his shoulder. I had the feeling he had done this hundreds of times.

We turned off the main road into a dusty area sparsely dotted with little groups of houses of adobe, cane, and cinder block, through which the road ran a bumpy, indefinite course. *This*, I thought, is what you think of when you think of the worst of Latin American poverty. No trees, nothing green: all was dust, junked cars, mean dogs, naked kids; all was ramshackle. Everyone stopped to stare at the car, evidently an unusual sight. A big turkey was standing in the road; Bad Teeth gave it a little bump, but it managed to land on its feet. More laughter from the front seat, and Disco Shirt lit up a joint.

Presently the radio was turned down, and I caught snippets

of conversation from the front seat. Eyes in the rearview mirror began looking at me.

Suddenly the driver turned around. *"You're not a pinche* [fucking] *rinche, are you?"* I wasn't sure how seriously he meant it, and besides I didn't know what *rinche* meant, so I asked, *"What's a rinche?"* and laughed a little. Experience had taught me that an ignorant question—asking the meaning of some slang word—always seemed to get a chuckle from Mexican guys. I tried to make it all a bit funnier by adding, *"If I don't know what a rinche is, I guess I couldn't be one, right? Ha, ha!"* That did spark some laughter, and at least stalled out that line of questioning for a moment. I turned to Alonso and quietly he told me that *rinche* is border slang for a cop, usually a Texas Ranger.

Bad Teeth began to make a number of turns, some to avoid bad stretches of road, once to avoid an official-looking car parked ahead. There were, of course, no street signs, and I became disoriented. But I wasn't really scared until we pulled up in front of a mean, run-down house fronted by a half-collapsed picket fence. Our escorts climbed out of the car without a word and slammed the doors.

Evidently, the house was the *coyotes'* hideout, or headquarters, because scattered around its porch or "lawn" were about ten men, standing or lounging or sitting. Some were drinking and talking, one was whittling a long piece of wood. One was cleaning a pistol. All had watched the car pull up, and, after the big man in the disco shirt had said a few words to those near the front door, all seemed to stare long and hard through the open car window at Alonso and me. It was the same feeling I had had for a split second once in Panama City, when, strolling down a dead-end street I had been tricked into taking, I turned around to see five or six guys walking in formation just a few steps behind me: outnumbered. The guys around the house *looked* as tough as the Panamanians, but seemed to enjoy slightly better circumstances. Their watches reflected the sun, you could still see the pleats in their slacks, their tequila was the good kind. This, I thought, is where they're taking me to rough me up, to find out if I'm really a *pinche rinche*, and, if they extract a confession, to make me wish I weren't. As four of them sauntered over to the car window, bits of phrases drifted over: *"¿Es un gringo, no?" ¡Mira al güero!"* (Look at the blondie!) *"Pinche gabacho."*

A guy poked his head in the door. *"Eres un gringo, ¿verdad?"*

"Cien por ciento," I replied, smiling grimly. A hundred percent. The man smiled back, a cryptic smile that I didn't know whether to be relieved or terrified by.

In an intimidating fashion, he and another man climbed in back on either side of Alonso and me. The friend had a bottle of rum, and smelled like it. Alonso they ignored like any other *pollo* (literally, chicken; in border slang it refers to the client of a *coyote*, who is also known as the *pollero*, the handler or seller of chickens). But I was a strange kind of *pollo*: *un pollo* gringo, a contradiction in terms! They were aggressive in their questions, but underneath seemed uncertain, ambivalent about exactly the sort of creature I was. Suspicion seemed to mix with fear, respect, and perhaps a strange sort of thrill at having an American client—a citizen of that powerful, enviable, arrogant country to the north—here at their mercy.

"What are you doing here?"

"Problems with the cops [*rinches*, I say this time].*"*

"What kinds of problems?"

"My own problems." The *coyotes* smiled at one another.

"Why are you so nervous?" asked one.

"I . . . I don't know what waits for me over there . . . what problems. Across the river."

"Give us some money."

"We gave you some money. We'll give you the rest of it at the river."

The *coyote* sat and glared at me. He pointed vaguely toward some trees, without moving his eyes. *"There's the river,"* he said. I couldn't see it, and started to say so.

"Why don't we give them another quarter of it?" muttered Alonso to me, producing thirty dollars more. I said nothing. The *coyote* took it, still glaring at me.

About fifteen minutes later four new guys piled into the front seat, and, now loaded with eight of us, the car pulled out slowly. I couldn't imagine—or didn't dare to imagine—what so many were needed for, but it was not in the nature of the enterprise to ask questions, or to answer them. I was finally offered rum by the man next to me, a man who, judging by the way he stared, had never spoken with a *gringo* before. At first I declined, wanting very much to keep my head clear. But then I thought, what the hell? *"Coca-Cola?"* he asked, handing me the other ingredient of the *Cuba libres* they were drinking. *"No, gracias."* I took a slug straight, hoping that would look macho, and passed the bottle on to Alonso.

He had been very quiet through all of this, probably glad not to be the center of attention. Perhaps he was praying I wouldn't goof up, assuming that, if they decided to dispose of me, they would probably dispose of him as well. But it was out of his hands. Having constantly to imagine the possibility of being attacked, I wished Alonso were a bit larger than five foot three, 120 pounds or so. And I wished we could talk, but somehow it didn't seem appropriate—either not properly submissive, or else unwise, should they overhear some detail we wished to keep private.

The *coyotes*, however, were very talkative, especially one who had just been ripped off on a run to Houston. It was a large group he had taken, and apparently the fee had been lowered to $200 apiece. But some hadn't had it, and there hadn't been anything he could do. Apparently he was a complainer, for after a few minutes two of the others told him to shut up. Then they talked of other things—such as the two Salvadoran girls they had hidden away in another house. *"What, can't they pay?"* asked one *coyote*, laughing in an unpleasant way. *"They'll pay. They'll pay as soon as I get back,"* said another, making a gesture to indicate how the girls would pay.

One of the men turned and mentioned to me that recently they also had helped a Japanese man across, as well as a group of four Koreans, who'd successfully caught the bus to Houston.

They hadn't trusted the Koreans, though, because they couldn't understand what they were saying to each other.

"*Have you taken other gabachos?*"

"*You're the first.*"

We arrived at the shack in a swirl of dust. The *coyotes* in the backseat with us—the ones with the rum—walked us through a small settlement of shacks, pushed open the broken door of one that looked abandoned, and told us to wait inside. After collecting the final $30 of the $120 we were paying—this time I didn't object—they shut the door behind us. The bright midday sun rendered me blind inside the dark shack; I was still unable to see Alonso when we heard the cars doors slam and the *coyotes* drive away.

Three or four hours after the *coyotes* left us, a trio of teenage boys came through the door, blinding us again. As my eyes adjusted, I recognized one as the guy we had spied on earlier, making passes at the girl; the two others bore a resemblance to the *coyote* with the rum, and I guessed they must all be brothers. They chatted tentatively with Alonso, who was bending over backward to be pleasant, and stared at me when they thought I wasn't looking. They weren't filling the gaps in conversation with Alonso very effectively, and I was not helping. There were silences.

Not many Americans passed through these parts, said one finally. No, I wouldn't guess so, I agreed. Then they, after a silence: Why are you crossing this way? Why not use the bridge? What are you in trouble for? You're not a cop, are you? . . . questions like the ones that had been shot at me for the better part of the day. With the first barrage I had realized that, if I didn't feel like talking about it, there was no reason they could expect me to answer. This was purely a business deal; they had agreed to take me, and that was that. "*Amigos, es asunto mío,*" I told the kids—my business.

They frisked Alonso and checked through his ditty bag for weapons, but left me alone—or so I thought, until one of them

"discovered" a long loose thread coming out of his jeans. "*Perdón,
would you cut this off for me?*" he asked me.

"*Sorry, no knife,*" I answered.

"*Then what is that in your belt?*" he demanded angrily.

He had noticed the form of a tear gas canister I had carefully
hidden there. I glanced down—my sweater hadn't caught on it;
it wasn't immediately visible. Yet somehow, this street-smart kid
had seen it.

"*It's something else, not a knife,*" I said.

"*It's a cuete,*" offered another kid. That was tough talk for
"pistol."

I let that one sit for a second. "*No, it's not,*" I said firmly.
They glared at me, but then the kids finally left, possibly more
respectful and certainly more curious than ever. I had won a
round.

One Mexican I had met told me he was ferried across the
Rio Grande in the overturned hood of an old car. Others floated
across on inner tubes. Expecting a shiny speedboat, hidden under
the branches of a weeping willow, I was a bit chagrined when
the kids dragged an old inflatable yellow raft in through the door
of the shack.

"*First, we need to blow it up,*" explained one. All of us took
turns, and I was glad, because the deep breathing helped get rid
of some of my nervousness, and finally being able to *do* something
helped alleviate the complete sense of helplessness I'd been feeling. Meanwhile, one of the kids rummaged around the floor of
the shack and dusted off a couple of the planks, which I now
noticed had been carved into crude paddles. We squeezed the
thing out the door, and suddenly were being led quickly toward
some trees which Alonso realized must line the banks of the river.

"*We're there!*" he said excitedly. "*La línea divisoria!*" It was
a shock to realize we were so close to the river and a surprise, at
least, to see that we were going to cross in broad daylight. We
had to negotiate two broken-down barbed-wire fences to reach
it, but the kids showed no caution until the river itself was visible.

Then they crouched low, surveying the opposite bank through the trees. Alonso, farther behind, took the opportunity to visit a nearby tree. *"My last pee in Mexico,"* he explained with a grin.

The banks of the river harbored a world different from that of the dusty shacks behind us—one of greenery, cool breezes, and dancing shadows. Somehow, though, the murky waters of the Rio Grande beyond did not exude the epic quality that I had expected after talking with Mexicans for so many weeks. It looked too tame and weedy, too mundane to serve as the great symbol of division between two cultures, two economies. Though apparently deep, it could not have been more than fifty yards across. And the U.S. side, grassy and treeless with a couple of junked cars visible: this was the promised land?

From where we crouched, a steep and muddy slope dropped to the brown water. The three boys negotiated the mud with the raft, looked around again, and then signaled that the way was clear. Alonso and I skittered down the bank to the water line. As the small raft was placed in the river, we were told to take our shoes off—*"so that they won't damage the bottom."* Alonso, meanwhile, noticed a rapid stream of big bubbles emerging from underneath one side of the raft. One of the kids smiled sheepishly. *"We'll have to hurry"* was all he said.

Knees to our chins, Alonso and I packed ourselves in between the two paddlers, someone gave a push, and we were off into international waters. As the current was strong, the boys paddled furiously. The tiny raft bobbed and twisted. About halfway across I spotted the trampled spot on the opposite bank for which we were aiming, some twenty yards downstream. The front paddler was slow, and we almost missed the landing spot. Then, all of a sudden, we were there, and Alonso was out—*"careful! careful!"* hissed a kid, as the raft lurched—and then me, both of us scrambling up the bank barefoot, shoes in hand, heading for a patch of tall grass. It felt like a war movie, guerrillas penetrating enemy lines. *"Did you see anybody? Did you see anybody?"* I asked Alonso.

"No! Relax!" he said, tightening his laces.

The kids had given us directions to downtown Laredo, and cautiously Alonso led the way, through the grass and shrubs of the floodplain, past larger trees and then a house. Some of the reports on the "flood" of aliens entering the United States had led me to think the path would be well worn, but instead we had to pick our own way, deciding which routes would be least likely to have one of Immigration's motion sensors—devices which detect the vibrations of footsteps and transmit the information to a main computer—and which ones offered the best concealment. Onto pavement, then past two stop signs and a traffic light, a right-hand turn and . . . downtown Laredo lay before us, about two miles ahead.

Strangely opposite emotions swept over Alonso and me as we walked those streets of Laredo. I suddenly felt a great excitement and wave of relief, a joy at being home again after so many weeks, out of the hands of the *coyotes*, away from Mexican law enforcement, back in a place, I thought, where I could explain myself out of most predicaments I might find myself in. A joy, in other words, at being *alive*.

Alonso, on the other hand, was now out of the frying pan and into the fire: suddenly an "illegal alien," subject to arrest, almost alone in a foreign land where he didn't know the language. His nervousness grew perceptibly with his vulnerability. When we crossed the path of two uniformed deliverymen at an intersection, for example, Alonso walked to the other side of me and whispered, *"Stay between so they don't see me!"* Then, perhaps in some sort of habitual deference to the *gringo* on his own turf, he began to walk behind me, as though he were my manservant. The confidence with which he had led the way in Mexico evaporated. It looked very conspicuous. I was about to point this out when down someone's front steps walked a postman also in uniform and with a cap. Alonso seemed to hop a foot in the air, and the postman looked startled.

We continued our afternoon walk down the wide, warm, quiet, and *paved* streets of Laredo. It was probably the poor side of town, but worlds away from the poor side of Nuevo Laredo.

People watched us from their porches, probably wondering more about the connection between us—Were we gay? Was I some kind of a smuggler?—than whether Alonso had just crossed over, which no doubt they already knew.

The sun was beginning to set when we reached downtown, and our first priority was finding a place to spend the chilly night. We walked side street after side street, looking for some warm and inconspicuous spot, and ducking more than once into an alley or doorway to avoid being seen by the omnipresent, light green vans of the Border Patrol. Finally, in a park, we met an old Mexican-American drunk who, in exchange for sharing our quart of beer, told us in Spanish the location of a parking garage. In the back of this garage was a grating through which warm air was ventilated. And there Alonso and I passed our first night back in America.

The next day Alonso spent alone, figuring out his course of action. From other Spanish-speaking people he learned that finding work in Laredo was next to impossible. The risk of getting nabbed by Immigration was great. Smugglers' rates for rides away from the border zone were nearly as high as they had been in Nuevo Laredo. The Trailways bus station was hot, but, according to at least two people, the Greyhound station at night was not. This information Alonso shared when we reconvened in a park that afternoon; it was the sort of intelligence, we had agreed that morning, that having me along might make hard to discover. I had spent the day exploring a different side of Laredo. At a fashionable department store, I told Alonso with surprise, I had eaten lunch in a cafeteria where no employee, including the cashier, spoke any English at all.

"*Maybe* they *would give me a job*," he said, hopefully.

"*I think it's all women down there*," I replied.

"*I think I'm going to take the bus then*," he said after a while.

"*To where?*"

"*Well, maybe Houston. I worked there two years ago. I was on*

a lawn crew, and I worked for some cement pourers. Here—see?—
Larry gave me his phone number."

Alonso showed me the inside cover of a matchbook, where,
after a few beers on the last night of work, Larry, the cement
boss, had penned his number for Alonso.

"*He said he would give me my job back if I wanted. Would
you call him for me? Larry said to call collect.*" Alonso explained
that Larry spoke very little Spanish, communicating with his
workers via those who spoke some English.

"*Okay, sure.*" Houston, I remembered, was well known for
its heavy reliance on undocumented labor in the construction
industry. It might be a good tip—and Alonso said Larry might
even have a job for me, which would be a good way to be able
to stick together for a while.

From a pay phone in the park I reached Larry. I explained
that I had just met Alonso, that I spoke Spanish, and that I was
calling for him as a favor.

"I'm trying to remember," said Larry. "Is he a little short
guy?"

"Yes."

"That's the one. He wasn't here too long, but he worked
hard. Yeah, you can tell him there's a job for him here." We
worked out the particulars of how Alonso would find Larry, and
I made some small talk about Houston.

"Business pretty good right now?" I asked offhandedly.

"Oh sure, I got more than I can handle," said Larry.

"Well, I tellya, I'm asking because I just got back into the
country and could use some work," I said. "I worked construction
a few summers in Denver and even poured cement once or twice.
Any chance you might put me on, too?"

There was a long silence. "Oh, I'm sure you wouldn't want
this work. The hours are real long and I can't pay you as much
as you'd want."

"Hmm. How much do you pay?" I knew from Alonso that
Larry had paid $6.00 and $6.50 an hour.

"You know," said Larry, sounding slightly agitated, "really I'd rather not say. Anyway, we just work with Mexicans."

Undaunted, I pressed on amiably. "Well, you know, Mexico is where I just came back from. I can speak Spanish pretty good and—if you're worried about having a white guy on the crew— I get along pretty good with Mexican guys. I really could use the work. Maybe I could help you ou——"

This time Larry interrupted. "I'm sorry, I just don't think it'd work out."

"Are you sure?"

"Positive," said Larry, and hung up. Slowly I hung up too. Seeing I was upset, Alonso asked if it were bad news.

"Well, not for you. Larry says you can have a job." Alonso was thrilled. He had already checked the Greyhound schedule, he said, and there was a bus leaving for Houston in just a few hours. If I could loan him ten dollars, he'd have enough for the ticket and could be there by morning. He wasn't quite sure where the street Larry mentioned was, but he thought . . .

Alonso went on. I had stopped listening. Slowly I was growing angry. For the first time I began to understand the frustration of a blue-collar American who really needs work. The work was there—at a living wage—but the Mexicans had it, Mexicans with no legal right to be in the country. A white on the crew could be disruptive—if he got upset about something, he could mess things up by notifying Immigration of the situation. But I thought about Larry. Did the guy feel no guilt? Probably he rationalized it by reasoning, "All the other contractors do it. If I didn't, I'd go out of business." And probably there was some truth to that. But that didn't mean it was right . . .

Alonso was looking at me worriedly. *"What's wrong?"*

"Oh, it's just that Larry wouldn't give me a job too." I didn't want to ruin Alonso's happiness by going into why not.

"It's only because he doesn't know you. If he knew you, he'd give you the job for sure. Why don't you come along? I can introduce you."

At first I said no, but then slowly I reconsidered. He had

been a good traveling partner, and I would miss Alonso. And maybe, I thought, there was something to be gained by seeing how he settled into life in Houston, how he found a place to live and who his friends were. Maybe this adventure was just beginning. I'd give it a try. I told Alonso, and his smile returned.

We boarded the Greyhound around 9:30 P.M. Though there was no sign of Immigration anywhere, Alonso and I boarded separately and took seats a couple of rows apart. You never knew if there might be an inspection along the highway, or in the next town down the road. A couple of minutes later, Alonso quietly got up and walked back to the lavatory. To create the illusion that no one was inside, he would not shut the door. Rather, he would stand quietly behind it until the bus had pulled out—just a precaution against a last-minute check.

I heard the station's final call for the bus to Houston, and saw the driver climb in. Right behind him was the Immigration officer. He strode unostentatiously down the aisle, glancing to his left and his right, and asked two people for their papers. Both apparently had them. With my racing pulse and the lump in my throat, one might have thought he was looking for me. But quietly he walked by . . . to the empty back of the bus, to the lavatory. Out of the corner of my eye, I saw him push open the door . . .

I didn't turn around to watch my friend leave the bus; he did me the favor of not looking over as he followed the officer down the aisle. The bus door groaned shut as they stepped out, and the Greyhound shifted into gear. Alonso was crossing the street to an Immigration van as the coach lumbered out of the station and away to Houston.

Chapter 2

Deep into the Orchard

SPRAWLING PHOENIX is a city wrested from the desert. Its existence is made possible by dams, canals, some very deep wells, and the refusal of its inhabitants to accept that Nature made the land for jackrabbits and Gila monsters. Air conditioning has also played a part; only in cold, northern climes do so many drivers keep their windows up. The main streets in the daytime have the stark, dusty, commercial look of a Nevada gambling town. But Phoenix neighborhoods boast jealously kept green lawns, small shade trees, and swimming pools. The occasional palm or fountain evokes an overblown oasis; decorative citrus trees ("reach right out the window and pick an orange") remind one that for many, Phoenix is a long-awaited retirement paradise.

Retirees are everywhere. Even a middle-aged person can feel young, and out of place, in a suburban subdivision like Sun City. Traffic, mostly large American-made cars, moves cautiously. Personal golf carts, instead of bicycles, hug the far right-hand side of the road, their red traffic flags flapping in the breeze. Shopping bags often occupy the nook meant for golf clubs; every day a whole fleet of the carts converges on the parking lot of the local Safeway, competing for spaces with the cars. But the occasional traffic accident is blamed less often on this oddity than on another, the "snowbirds" who migrate down from the West or Midwest just for the winter, perennially unfamiliar with the roads. Across Grand Avenue from the Safeway, a banner on a high school stadium informs us that here is the "Winter Home of the Milwaukee Brewers." Nearby, huge Boswell Hospital, the largest building in the area, suggests that Sun City's main industry is keeping people alive. Retirement culture here is in full bloom, something new to comfort the old.

Beyond Sun City's split-levels the desert begins. It is cut into huge squares by a loose grid of county roads; driving out into these spaces, on old pavement and dirt, across viaducts and over canals, you notice with surprise that much of the desert is cultivated. Here, on the city's periphery, ingenious water engineering has turned barren sand into a verdant garden. A checkerboard of irrigated tracts, never lacking for sunshine, produces cotton, flowers, melons, and a variety of green vegetables. The dominant produce, however, is citrus: oranges, grapefruit, and lemons.

Almost no one appears to live on this farmland, but the empty look is an illusion. In the orchards and around the fields exists a culture as strange in its way as that of the retirees. It is composed mainly of a sort of "snowbird" who does not wish to be seen. He is here not on vacation but on business. He lives with other men about his age doing mainly the same thing. He picks the oranges that retirees buy at roadside stands, that processing plants turn into frozen concentrate, that monstrous ships transport to Japan. The work is not illegal, but the man, by definition, is— and for that reason the vast majority of his retired neighbors have no idea he exists. But pull off the county road next to any orchard, walk far enough into the rows of citrus trees, and you'll find them: *cuadrillas*, teams of up to twenty Mexican citrus pickers, ladders on their backs, bags around their necks, shirts drenched in sweat. Look quickly, because if you're white and unacquainted, they'll have fled deep into the orchard in a matter of seconds. At night, if you're quiet and a good spotter of camp fires, they may reappear, around the fires, even deeper in the trees. The work is backbreaking, the conditions are mean, but many Mexicans prefer orchard work to any other. The reason is fairly simple: where it is difficult to be seen, it is also difficult to get caught. Invisibility and an unlimited supply of free oranges are the dubious perquisites of orange picking.

On a cool, golden evening following close on a sizzling day, I found myself shooting across the desert checkerboard in the white pickup truck of one of the area's major personalities. As the pickup turned west onto a dirt road, we pulled down the sun visors, and dust dropped swirling into my lap. Long clouds of golden dust shot out from behind the pickup's rear wheels like a contrail. No matter how I positioned myself on the seat cover, I couldn't manage to get comfortable. Finally, I reached under the cover to see what the problem was . . . and pulled out Lupe Sanchez's 9-mm Browning automatic pistol. "Ummm, Lupe . . . ?"

"Oh, sorry," said Sanchez, putting his cigarette in his mouth to free his right hand, opening the glove compartment, and tossing in the pistol. No explanation was offered, so I asked: "Find yourself using that very often?"

"Oh, not so much these days," said the labor leader, swerving in order to hit a snake creeping out from the side of the road. A naturalized American born in Mexico, Lupe Sanchez retained the snake hatred of his motherland. It crunched like a stick under the tires. "Back when we had a lot of strikes going on, it came in handy. But you never know."

Bane of the local growers and hero/strongman to hundreds of local Mexican workers, Sanchez was something of a legend in the citrus orchards of El Mirage, just beyond Sun City. He was also a legend in the tiny rural towns of several Mexican states from which the 300 members of his union were drawn. Through cunning and persistence, Sanchez and his associates had succeeded where established unions and conventional wisdom had insisted they would fail: they had *organized* illegal aliens. The Arizona Farmworkers, the first organization of immigrant labor since the Wobblies at the turn of the century, believed that immigrants should expect the same rights in our country as other workers, and that farmworkers deserved the same protections as industrial workers. "A worker," Sanchez was fond of saying, "is a worker, is a worker." Because I was interested, he had agreed to take me to a ranch where the AFW had recently won a contract. The workers wanted someone to teach them English, he explained; as time permitted I might also have the chance to see what picking was all about. It seemed a good place to continue my research.

Farmland spread out on both sides: to the right, shriveled cotton plants, waiting to be collected and taken to the gin; to the left, fields of dense, colorful roses. Wading through these, looking not unlike Dorothy and her friends on their approach to the Emerald City, were Mexican workers, dressed in leather chaps, gloves, and armguards as protection against thorns. The pickup flew over some railroad tracks at fifty miles an hour, and then the left-side view became a citrus orchard.

"Where does everybody live?" I asked Sanchez. "Do they all go back to El Mirage at night?" You sometimes saw farm buildings out here, and an occasional trailer home, but almost never the dwellings of workers.

"Some do, the established guys with cars," he said. "But the rest stay out here. You've got to remember, most of them don't want to be seen. They don't want to live by the road, in plain view. The growers know that—they don't want them to get caught either. So where there's a house, it's usually hidden away somewhere in the orchard. And where there's not a house, that's still where you'll find 'em—if you know where to look."

He slowed, and then turned left into the orchard on an unmarked dirt road. Between the trees it was dark and cooler. Sanchez turned on the headlights after an unseen bump in the rough road launched us off our seats. Eventually the road widened into a clearing containing a barn and a ramshackle white frame house. Three dogs, two of them lame, ran up barking as we stopped and climbed out; Sanchez ignored them completely, so they concentrated on me. There seemed to be people about, but in the gloom and the commotion it was hard to say just where. Finally a voice cried out in Spanish: *"Shut up!"* A flying stone narrowly missed the dogs, and they slunk away.

The stern face of the young man throwing the rock brightened into greeting as Sanchez approached him on the porch. *"Hola, 'mano. ¿cómo estás?" "¿Qué hubo, qué hay?"* The two men shook hands, and I watched carefully: it was the first two-thirds of the American soul handshake, first the normal grip and then the interlocking thumbs.

"How's the picking?"

"It's okay."

"They worked you today?"

"Most of the day. Maybe twenty guys."

"And how many are here now?"

". . . mmm, ayy, hard to say . . ."

Sanchez was an unbelievably busy man, but they spoke without hurry, the pauses between questions an important part of rural Mexican etiquette. A quick visit to a ranch, Sanchez had advised me, was impossible.

As they spoke, a file of men emerged from the orchard carrying large containers of water. Plastic milk jugs, pails, jars— they seemed to have used anything they could find. Perhaps half of the dozen men carried the containers on their heads, two of these using no hands. They acknowledged Sanchez with a smile, a nod if possible, or a quiet *"Don Lupe"* as they passed, en route to the kitchen door. *Don*, in Hispanic cultures, is a title of respect reserved for aristocrats or others of importance.

Sanchez directed the group inside. I fell in behind; the screen door with no screen was held open for me, and as I crossed the threshold the foreign tableau widened. It was the sort of scene that, coming from my side of America, one only imagined. The main room—once a living room, but that now seemed a misnomer—was full of Mexican men, young and old. Most of them, just in from work, were streaked with sweat, hair mussed, clothes rumpled. They were poor men, country men, in dirty clothes,

with crudely cut hair, crooked and missing teeth. Many wore
dark leather sandals—*huaraches*—practically indistinguishable from
their feet. Darkened by sun and heredity, they looked much more
Indian than people I had met in Mexican cities; in their midst I
felt albino. The room buzzed with Spanish-speaking voices. I
shook a few hands and tried to look relaxed, but ease eluded me.
Meeting another's eye appeared to cause a sort of mutual embarrassment, so I stood, tried not to stare, and had the sensation
that I was stammering . . . even though I hadn't opened my mouth.
The crowd parted for Mariano, the thin, sheepish man with whom
Sanchez had spoken, as he left the main room to round up other
residents.

I looked at inanimate things. The room held only three pieces
of furniture: an old couch, a steel-frame bed, and a chair. The
day's last sunlight, passing through a window missing its pane,
turned one of the stained walls orange. The men filed into the
room, talking softly. The couch filled immediately. The chair,
everyone knew, was reserved for Sanchez. Other men found places
on the floor. I stood uncertainly, until one of the men gestured
at the bed, conspicuously unoccupied. I was to sit there. I politely
declined, but he insisted, and, when others joined in, I sat down.
The bed could have provided a seat for three or four, but no one
else, it seemed, would touch it. When the room would hold no
more, Sanchez rose to his feet.

"*How many are you?*" he asked no one in particular. Men
looked around, counted.

"*I think maybe forty-five.*" "*Fifty.*" "*Yes, fifty.*" "*Twelve more
arrive tomorrow.*"

"*From where?*"

"*Guanajuato,*" said one young man.

Sanchez paced for some moments in silence.

"*Compañeros,*" he began, "*there are too many. The contract
calls for twenty-five or thirty, that's the maximum. We may have
double that—even triple—by the end of the week.*" He paused and
lit a new cigarette, savoring the taste and, it seemed, the drama.
"*Has anyone heard of other work? Raise your hands.*"

A few hands went up.

"*If anyone knows of other places to go, then please go there. Some system will have to be arranged to decide who can stay. Volunteer to leave if you have a place to go, a friend somewhere.*"

He moved on to other business. "*What about the house? The water pump?*"

"*Still no pump,*" said young Mariano. He gestured toward the men in the back of the room who had just carried in the water. "*We have to carry it in twice a day, half a mile . . . you know, from down by Smith's.*"

Sanchez was visibly annoyed. "*I'll talk to Pete again tomorrow,*" he said grimly. Pete, the ranch foreman, was the owner's son. "*How about the rest of the place?*"

"*We'll fix it up if he'll just give us the supplies,*" said Mariano. "*It's cold at night with that window broken. And what about paint?*"

"*I'll ask him, but you'll have to talk to him too—I mean, the ranch committee will.*" Sanchez, still speaking in Spanish, discussed the election of the ranch committee, and then came to the last item on the agenda.

"*My compañero Ted*"—he didn't even need to gesture at me—"*is going to be your teacher. He will be staying here. Didn't one of the guys from Guerrero work in the literacy program down there?*"

A shy, thin, young man named Victor nodded to Sanchez that he had.

"*And doesn't your cousin speak some English?*"

A bolder, rounder fellow piped right up: "Yehss, I do espeak some Engliss!" The other young men all around him on the floor laughed in embarrassment. "And how are you today?" he continued, addressing Sanchez.

"*Muy bien, Carlos,*" responded Sanchez, with a smile. "*You will be his assistants, okay?*"

"Okay!" the two responded in unison, causing the Guerrero contingent to fall to pieces once again. This, I had a feeling, was going to be more fun than I had expected.

I and several others accompanied Sanchez out to his truck,

and soon he was gone, leaving me with only my sleeping bag and a "good luck!" I dreaded what I expected to be the awkwardness of being back in the main room, alone with the men. But this was egocentrism. Most, I was relieved to find, were quite capable of ignoring me.

The exceptions were the guys from Guerrero, the poor state in southern Mexico perhaps best known for containing Acapulco. Our introduction had been a bit more specific, and they now invited me to share in the supper they had prepared—flour tortillas filled with a sauce of tomato, green chilies, and ground beef. There were six of them in all, four besides Victor and Carlos. Imitating Lupe Sanchez, I shook hands with each one, the Mexican way. All of them were friends or relatives, or both, from a *rancho* near Iguala, where most of their fathers had something to do with raising avocados. It was the first time any of them had crossed to work in the United States—though Carlos, the one who spoke some English, had actually spent a semester at Oregon State University on an agronomy scholarship from his government.

"You did that, and there was no job for you back home?" I asked, surprised. Carlos shrugged. *"The situation in Guerrero is pretty bad,"* he explained, and the others nodded. *"There are no jobs for anyone."* More sauce was brought from the camp's single kitchen, and Carlos spooned some onto another tortilla for me. Besides a couple of pocketknives, the spoon was the group's only utensil. Nor was there other dinnerware: the tortillas served as plate and napkin. The skillet was commonly owned.

I looked at Carlos. Either his bearing or his receding hairline conveyed an air of responsibility; though not fat, he had a build that let you guess where he might put on weight—you could imagine him in middle age. But he was friendly and earnest, his seriousness tempered, it seemed to me, by a share of the mischievous streak that ran through the group.

"How is it you ended up at this ranch?"

"We met Lupe Sanchez last spring," explained Victor. *"Our fathers were interested in joining a cooperative he's involved with in*

Mexico, and he came to talk. When he said there might be work, we knew we'd come. It was just a problem of deciding how many could come with us. Everyone wanted to."

They had rendezvoused with a more experienced group of the camp's workers—including Mariano—in a neighboring state, and traveled with them to the border. *"None of those from our town knew how to cross,"* Victor explained. *"They helped us."*

I looked from our seat on the porch back into the main room. The other men were now eating, lounging about, or even sleeping. Carlos pointed out the group that had brought them. *"From Querétaro,"* he explained. *"So is that group, but from a different part. And see those guys there—they're from Sinaloa. We don't have much to do with them."*

Instead of a solidary group, it now dawned on me that these men were very different from one another. They were all Mexican, but their home is a big country, with limited travel and communication between regions. It is much more regionally oriented than the United States: the gap between a Guerreran and a Sinaloan, for example, is probably wider than that which separates a U.S. Southerner and a New Yorker. The men were brought together by language and life in a foreign land, but not, it seemed, by a great deal else.

Sunset yielded to darkness, and we on the porch to yawns and shivers. The bulb on the living-room ceiling gave the room an illusion of warmth, but wind had begun to blow in through the jagged borders of missing windows. Four older men, seated on the couch, were already asleep, jackets on their laps, pressed against each other, bodies leaning to one side, necks, jaws, and hands at rest. Others, including a father and his twin sons, were spread out in a corner of the wood floor, each curled up in his own blanket, jackets for pillows. No one, I noticed, was yet on the single bed.

"We sleep out here," said Carlos, stepping through the tiny kitchen and out the back door. *"See you in the morning."*

"What? You sleep outdoors?"

"Well, not exactly. You want to see?" I followed the group to

a barn not far from the house. The big doors on its side were open; again a single exposed bulb, hanging from a rafter, dimly lit the interior. What appeared to be a small refrigeration room, with metal door and thick walls and ceiling, was set against one of the corners. *"The ranch doesn't use this anymore,"* explained Carlos, *"and it's pretty safe, because they'd never imagine anyone was here."* "They," I had been around long enough to know, didn't mean anyone associated with the ranch. It meant thieves or Immigration.

The last place I would have chosen to keep warm was a refrigerator. Yet it was quiet, fairly windproof . . . even cozy in its way. But Carlos and the others insisted I return to use the bed. They were very concerned when I seemed uninterested: I didn't want special treatment, I explained. *"But it's been set aside for you. Everyone discussed it."* I vacillated, worried I might offend but not wanting to set myself apart.

Ismael, lanky and the most direct of the group, finally broke the deadlock. *"Fuck, if he doesn't want it, I'll take it,"* he announced, laughing and picking up his blanket. The others looked on with great disapproval, some of them embarrassed. This was all going the wrong way.

"No, I guess I'll go after all," I said quickly. The favor was too great to be declined. *"But just for tonight."* I shouldered my bag and headed back out across the moonlit clearing, the orchard black and forbidding around its edges.

It was 7:00 A.M., and already Nate the tractor driver was in a bad mood. He had the throttle of his small John Deere wide open, and the tractor rolling in high gear down the bumpy orchard road. This would have been his own business, or at least a matter between him and the ranch mechanic, had he not been pulling a small, flat trailer piled with sixteen ladders and as many of us pickers. Already this morning we had picked three rows of Valencias; where we were headed now, and why in such a homicidal hurry, was anyone's guess.

Making the workers travel on the same trailer as their ladders was, I had first thought, simply an economizing move. Why do in two trips what you can accomplish in one? After a few rides I had realized that, the way *tractoristas* like Nate drove, the ladders wouldn't arrive unless there were workers on top of them. To keep from bouncing off, we held on to the ladders, and each other, like crazy. We were the ropes that should have been there, lashing the ladders down, the inadvertent glue. And, with every backbreaking bump and jolt, we were praying.

Dust kicked up by the tractor quickly replaced the sleep in my eyes. All I could see, looking forward, was the outline of Nate's dirty shirt. But I pictured him in my mind's eye. Some fifty years old, Nate had the look of a man who had been yelling at Mexicans under the Arizona sun for most of his productive life. The skin on his face and forearms was brown, wrinkled, and folded. His jaw muscles flexed continuously, as though he were chewing on an old piece of gristle. Short white hairs bristled from beneath his "Cat Diesel" cap and from around his chin. His body was lean and dusty, strong but desiccated, raisinlike. During the day his attention was occupied mainly with counting bags of oranges, and with spotting abuse by workers: the idle moment spent wiping dirt and leaves from one's face, the tiny orange left behind in the far reaches of some tree, the picking bag not filled to the top.

Nate braked to a halt a short time later and pointed to four rows of trees across an irrigation ditch. We jumped off the trailer, and the race was on again. None of the ladders was assigned to anyone in particular; the idea was just to grab a good one and get picking as soon as possible. With everyone pulling, the pile disintegrated as though it had hit a major pothole. As the senior, more cunning men shouldered their ladders and rushed airborne over the ditch, I found myself, as usual, embattled with two or three other junior pickers for the worst, bent and battered ladders. We tugged and maneuvered and, finally, arm through the middle of my sorry ladder and hand trying to keep its weight off my tender shoulder, I was off and toward the ditch. This time I landed successfully on the other side, but, with my impact, the front of the ladder nosedived into the dirt, halting my forward motion with a blow to the shoulder. Recouping in silent agony, I hefted it again and started down the rows toward an unclaimed tree.

Over the past few days I had absorbed much of the technique of citrus picking—and been thoroughly disabused of the notion that this was some kind of unskilled labor. Most any individual in reasonable shape could pick a few oranges, of course. But to do it all day long, at the lightning pace of the Mexican professionals—fast enough, in other words, to avoid getting fired—was something else again. It required a vast store of special knowledge and dexterity. Not only did you need to know the optimum position of the ladder against a given tree, for example, you also had to be able to get it there fast and deftly. Men half my size could manipulate the twenty-foot ladders as though they were balsa wood, but in my hands the ladder was a heavy, deadly weapon. I had bruised a friend's arm with my ladder one day and had nearly broken my own when, with sixty pounds of oranges in the bag around my neck, I had slipped from its fifth rung and been grazed as it followed me to the muddy ground.

Handling the fruit itself was a further challenge. To be successful, you had to pick with both hands simultaneously. This meant your balance had to be good—you couldn't hold on to a branch or the ladder for support. And you had to *twist* the fruit off: pull hard on a Valencia without twisting and you're likely to get the whole branch in your hand. Planning was also important: ideally, you would start with your sack empty at the top of the tree and work your way down. Oranges would just be peeking out the top of the sack when your feet touched the soil, if you did it right; you topped off the bag by grabbing low-hanging fruit on your way to the tractor.

Nate, if you had chosen your tree wisely, would be no more than fifty feet away, having substituted the ladder trailer for two long trailers of large wooden crates. Standing next to this rig with cap and clipboard, he looked something like an airline baggage handler who had taken a wrong turn. He would watch while you hoisted the big bag up over the edge of a crate, dumped its contents, and then claimed your ticket. He would holler out a warning if you were falling behind. And, especially, he would holler if the fruit was not to his liking: if it had brown sunspots, or was too small or too big (a leftover from last year), or was bumpy with a superthick rind—*gordos*, these grotesque misshapen fruits were called. Sometimes he would dig out the offending fruit and throw it at you, though, of course, if you were moving at the proper speed, you would be back at your ladder and picking before he succeeded.

To my distress, I discovered that the new rows of trees were not oranges but lemons. The Mexicans, of course, would be pleased: the rate per bag of lemons was higher—$1.15 as opposed to $0.63 for oranges—since the bags weighed more and it took longer to fill them. With harder work, they could make more money. My ambition, however, was merely to survive, and lemon picking was killer work. For one, the full sack of lemons weighed upwards of eighty pounds, more than half my weight and nearly sufficient to pull me off the ladder. If there was any question about whether the lemon was big enough, you had to size it with a ring provided for that purpose—and, for me, there was almost always a question. Lemons all looked alike to me. On your way to the lemon, you had to watch out for inch-long thorns the shape of pencil ends. Perhaps worst, lemons could not be twisted off—they had to be clipped, with special clippers that looked like wire snips. My friend Carlos had showed me how to keep the clippers ready by connecting them with a length of tape around my fingers—but there was nothing he could do to toughen the tender muscle in my palm, the one that registered arthritislike pain with every clip.

I found a tree, muscled the ladder up, climbed it, and began to clip. I knew I wasn't too far off the pace, because from my perch I could see several of the other guys in my *cuadrilla* still atop their trees. The view from on top of the ladder, when I had time for it, was one I loved: here, above the press of trees, you were out of view of the boss, bathed in sun between blue sky and the mass of green below. I called out to Carlos, a couple of trees away, and got a smile in return. Step by step, the bag slowly filling, I made my way groundward.

It was as I was circling the bottom of the tree, crouching under branches to find the lemons I hoped would finish my bagful, that I noticed movement in the branches on the other side of the trunk. Normally this was something you had to live with: other pickers, on their way to the tractor, often pinched an easy ground-level lemon or two from someone else's tree. The savvy victim usually compensated by discreetly snagging a couple from *his* neighbor's tree in turn. "Borrowing" easy fruit from trees that weren't yours was known as *coyoteando*, from the noun *coyote*. Coyotes, as everyone knew, are sneaky, slinking loners, out to make it on their own in an inhospitable world. It was selfish and underhanded, but you lived with it. Indiscreet borrowing, however, amounted to stealing and required a response. I became angry as I noticed the branches continuing to shake, moving around the tree toward my ladder. Obviously the thief thought I was off emptying my bag at the trailer. I unshouldered my bag and stepped out from under the tree.

"*Hey, what do you think you're doing?*" I demanded.

The culprit was a picker known as Raúl. Along with a man named Pancho, he was an outstanding picker, one who usually ended the day ten bags ahead of most. I was somewhat in awe of his speed and endurance, though perhaps because he made the others look slow, he was generally disliked.

He looked startled to see me, but quickly recovered: "*Ah, I didn't know this tree was yours,*" he lied, turning to continue with his now-full bag toward the trailer.

"*Bastard! Keep to your own tree!*" I shouted after him. Raúl didn't look back. "*Pinche coyote,*" I added under my breath. Of course, it was just another test. My first had come a week earlier, when a man had placed his ladder against the heavily laden tree I was already on. "*There's room for two on this one,*" he had assured me when our eyes met. I might have fallen for it, had not Carlos and company warned me previously: there's never room for two.

The tree you pick is your own. My loud protests had provoked some laughter from other men in the vicinity—I think they were laughing at him—and the man had finally left. It had not happened again. The orchards, at times, were a very *macho* world.

Some time around noon Nate decided he would break for lunch and we, by necessity, did the same. Carlos and I, our legs dangling into a dry concrete irrigation culvert, pulled off our gloves and unwrapped the foil around the *burritos* we had made that morning from the tortillas and sauce of the night before. Nothing was said for a long time, as we caught our breaths and restoked our stomachs. I was staring blankly at my gloves, lying on the dirt, when I realized that the palms were reflecting the sun. Suddenly I focused. "What the . . ." I began in English, reaching over to pick one up. The inside of the leather work gloves, the part that touched the fruit, had a dull gray gloss, the color you get when you blacken paper with pencil lead.

I held the glove up and looked quizzically at Carlos. *"What's this stuff?"*

"Pesticidas," he replied. I thought about that for a moment. The tree leaves were all covered with a flaky white residue. When you reached into a tree, you almost always got snowed on by a small shower of dusty white flakes. Some stoical pickers wore bandannas over their mouths, banditlike, in order to avoid breathing the stuff. But most of the others, hot enough already, resigned themselves to inhaling it. These substances, I had been told, were dropped on the orchard by airplanes on Sundays, days "when everything stinks," as they put it. Good days, I supposed, to be somewhere else. *"That's why we wear gloves,"* Carlos added.

These pesticides, I had noticed, affected more than just gloves. Among the trees you never saw things you might expect to see: bees, spiders, mosquitoes, flies, never a single bird or nest. Not even any snakes or ground animals. This was convenient, as none of these things could bother you. But, the more you thought about it, the creepier it seemed. These orchards, oases in the desert, were gardens where every thing but one was killed. They seemed strangely dead.

For me the afternoon began like any other: fatigue came more quickly and bags filled more slowly; my eyes didn't focus quite as sharply as they had in the morning. But for Nate it seemed to be going worse. Turning the tractor-train too quickly, he tore two big branches off trees at the end of a row—where the ranch foreman would certainly see it. With that gaffe, his mood, bad since the morning, reached new levels of sourness.

Ismael speculated that perhaps the dog he slept with had wet the bed the night before, or that Nate had been surprised during breakfast by a worm in his chaw. Whatever the reasons, Nate's bile was approaching intolerable levels, for when he saw Victor drop to the ground a grapefruit he was trying to empty into a crate, he started visibly. When Victor, unaware that he was being watched, playfully picked the fruit up and lobbed it into the crate behind his back, Nate exploded.

"*Pinche* Mexican! What the fuck do you think you're doin'? Think you can just toss these things around? Huh? Do ya?"

Surprised, Victor looked back at him blankly. Nate continued, ranting and baiting Victor. "Wassa problem?" asked Victor finally, feeling he had been unfairly singled out.

"Sa problem," said Nate, imitating the accent, "is that yer a slob! Slob! Know what that means?" The veins pulsed on his forehead. Those around stopped picking. Victor, hot and tired, did not know, but then again it wasn't necessary to grasp Nate's words to get his meaning. Reaching for a grapefruit off a nearby tree, Victor lobbed it high into the air. We watched it arc down into the crate with a thud. The *tractorista*, a certain candidate for a coronary, picked up his own fruit and hurled it at Victor, who successfully dodged it.

"Git outta here! I don't wanna see you again, you sonuva-bitch! You get your fuckin' ass outta here." Victor disappeared into the trees, later to arrive at camp two miles away, on foot.

Nate stewed and grumbled the rest of the afternoon. Everyone strove to be inconspicuous and not catch his attention, and only I failed.

"Yer his buddy, ain'tcha?" he asked, when I emptied my next bag.

"Mmm," I replied, uninterestedly. Being white, I had thought I might escape his wrath.

"Well, remember this." Nate spat. "All the guys we see like you, they're either drunks or fuckups. They don't last two weeks. This work's for Mexicans, and it's Mexicans know how to do it. I ain't seen one of you guys make it yet. And if you don't hurry the fuck up, you ain't comin' back tomorrow."

There was nothing Nate could have said to make me work faster—anger is a great motivator. But I was near my limit, and realized my days were numbered. Every night I stumbled into the house on the verge of collapse. My neck and shoulders ached dully and stung if they were touched; pulled muscles restricted the side-to-side movement of my head. My palms were so tender from squeezing clippers and grasping fruit that I had to do everything with my fingertips.

Carlos seemed to understand my desire to succeed, if only to prove a point. As insurance against Nate having the pleasure of seeing me fired, every day he slipped me a few of his yellow tickets, the kind you got for each bag of citrus picked. At first these tickets turned up anonymously, in the pockets of my jacket or the aluminum foil around my *burrito*—his way of letting me save face. Later he just handed me the damp things from his own sweaty pocket. Perhaps he felt that, through the rides I gave in the old Chevy Nova I had bought, and my contributions to the Guerrero grocery pool, accounts would be evened up. I also tried to help with food preparation, but was always rebuffed. At first I took this simply as a gesture of kindness. But one night, when I was more vehement about doing "my fair share" than usual, Carlos laid it on the line.

"Thank you, Ted, but the food you make, we cannot eat it." The differences between my Tex-Mex and their authentic Mexican cooking, apparently, were bigger than I thought. American food products, even those cooked the Mexican way, were taking

a toll on the new arrivals. Picking was interrupted countless times a day, as workers hustled off to do the American Two-Step.

The men's desire to learn far exceeded the energy I had left to teach. But two or three nights a week, with much help from Carlos and Victor, I set up an easel and tablet on the scrubby grass outside the house and began the call of *"¡Clase! ¡Clase!"* To my never-ending surprise, almost everyone would come, sitting in a large circle in the day's last light. I handed out pencils, paper, and pieces of cardboard to write on—though I quickly learned that the spoken word meant more to my students than the written; a good half of them were unable to write anything more than their names. Just the same, in a strange way the teaching reminded me of outdoor college classes in New England in the springtime. Real learning was going on. The more English a man knew, the better his chances of getting out of the fields and into the city, of making some real money. We started out with numbers, the English alphabet, and greetings. Those with experience had already picked up some interesting English ("How you doing, baby?" I was asked nearly every week), but even they had difficulty with subtleties of pronunciation. Our sounds of *j*, *th*, and *z* don't really exist in Mexican Spanish, for example. I emphasized the practical, the familiar, but these were not always the easiest words in English.

"Orange," I would say.

"Ornch," thirty voices would repeat.

"Three oranges."

"Shree ornchess."

Grammar was one of the most difficult things to teach, as few had studied parts of speech and English is so irregular. Some problems simply could not be anticipated.

"Victor, tell me in English how many grandparents you have," I said.

"I have four grandfathers," he replied earnestly, the Spanish word for "grandfather" signifying grand*parents* when used in the plural.

Probably because they were so gratifying, I somehow found

the energy for my English classes. How many other teachers are showered with Thank yous (in English, I insisted) after every class? What else that I know could mean so much to people as different from me as they?

The fabulous Darla Derringer writhed her seductive way over to our side of the stage, and the guys tensed. They didn't have this kind of thing back home. Darla, very close to naked, was a real dream *gringa*: natural-looking blonde hair, big white teeth, big white breasts, and pale skin, smooth all over. Also a dream was the way she seemed so attracted to the four Mexicans seated on the red-upholstered stools, seeming to dance especially for them, her stiletto heels tapping inches from Victor's trembling hands. Little more than a besequined G-string appeared to separate her womanhood from the yearnings of the four . . . nothing, perhaps, that enough dollars wouldn't cure. *"Tantas curvas,"* breathed Victor, *"y yo no tengo frenos."* (So many curves, and I've got no brakes.")

But alas, it was 2:00 P.M. on a Saturday afternoon, and the five of us constituted half the clientele of the Zebra Club, an establishment boasting "continuous dancing, round the clock." Decked out in their weekend best—clean slacks, shiny shoes, and colorful button-down shirts—the Mexicans were the only ones in the joint who looked like they might have a little cash. Well, besides me. And Darla had just tried me and not gotten her money's worth. Would her luck change?

Carlos pulled out his wallet. Grinding slowly his way, Darla leaned backward, spread her knees, and gave him "that famous Zebra smile," as the voice of the emcee, speaking over the music, put it. Taking a cue from a spectator at the previous set, Carlos folded a dollar bill in half the long way and set it on its end on the stage. Turning to show us her backside, Darla wiggled and then did a back bend—not easy in those shoes. Backward on all fours, blonde mane sweeping the floor, she opened her mouth, took the bill between her lips, and struggled back up to her feet. *"Gracias, amigo,"* we saw her say.

The other three all gave Carlos a visual ribbing as she danced
for him—*¡Qué chingón!* What an operator! He managed to take
his eyes off her for a split second to acknowledge this, and then
all of us watched as she wriggled away. Then the show was
over.

Over another round of expensive Budweisers, we debated
whether to invest in a "table dance." This was a "private" performance for which Darla descended to our table and danced for
the pleasure of whomever seemed to be laying out the bucks.
Twenty dollars was the minimum charge, and the emcee, still
invisible to us in his booth, was egging us on. Carlos was for it.
But the others, less enchanted, had their doubts. Finally, Carlos
decided to finance it himself. He found the performance so ex-
hilarating that he paid fifteen dollars more for what Darla called
a "grande finale": an energetic succession of shimmies and gy-
rations, of the shoulders and pelvis respectively, that had us all
captivated. So captivated, in fact, that when Darla suggested
champagne, there was general assent. But, feeling the responsibility of a tour guide and having been a victim of the champagne
scam before, I broke in.

*"You guys, for what we're going to pay for that champagne, we
could buy more than thirty beers at the Top Hat. And there's girls
there too."*

They paused. Darla, not needing to understand Spanish to
catch the drift, glared. Now that she had finished her dancing,
she looked more exposed—and chilly—than sexy. I felt like getting her a bathrobe. Carlos stood up to leave, and the others
followed. One thing I really liked about Mexicans was that, when
they decided something, they tended to follow through without
further debate or looking back. Carlos nodded at Darla and gave
a little bow—so politely one would have thought she had been
his date to the prom. Out the swinging door we went, and back
into the Nova.

The day had started with a movie—*The Horseman's Last
Revenge*—at Phoenix's only Spanish-language cinema. It was a
drama about an American horse breeder (played by a tall Mexican

wearing glasses and a ridiculous blond wig), his loose daughter (her wardrobe consisted of halter tops and cutoffs), and an undocumented Mexican, who was their stableboy. The daughter's lust for "a real man," someone "hotter, more passionate" than *gringo* guys, was satisfied by the unsuspecting Mexican, who was repeatedly seduced in the hay. Rescue was at hand when the Mexican's wife arrived on the scene, but was thwarted when the wife's brother, outraged at finding the lovers in the hay, killed the stableboy to satisfy the family honor. My friends liked it.

The six of us had left camp, the Nova almost skimming the road, as soon as we had shaken off our hangovers enough to move. You didn't want to spend too much time at camp on weekends. The life there—unrelenting toil, no women, separation from home and family—took a high toll of frustration. It reminded me of tales I had heard of work in the isolated oil fields of Prudhoe Bay, Alaska, or in the fish-processing plants of Canada's west coast. All week long, with every sack of oranges, the pressure grew; and on weekends it blew. Within an hour or two of the distribution of paychecks, the place was nearly empty. Those who had cars—often they were owned by groups of guys— left for town. Relatives of the carless, usually from nearby ranches, came by to pick up some more. A few small-time *coyotes,* often the *gente inmigrada,* or longtime Mexican residents, might stop by to offer a lift for a small price. The die-hard campbound, those who lacked either connections or a desire to leave the relatively safe, familiar confines of the orchard, usually scraped together enough money to send a couple of guys on a trek down the road. In half an hour they would be back, carrying overpriced cases of Hamm's from a grower who sold it from his back shed.

Carlos, Victor, Ismael, I, and an older Guerreran named Timoteo cruised back out of Phoenix to El Mirage. The Top Hat lounge, known to its Mexican patrons simply as *El Sombrero,* was a roadside honky-tonk with a black-and-white checkered linoleum floor, pool table, and a surly waitress with a heavily made-up face. But, in their deprived state, even she looked good to my companions.

"What's going on tonight, baby? Is there a dance up in Surprise?" asked Victor.

"That'll be five bucks."

"What? No dance?" He handed her some bills.

"There's only four bucks here."

"And only one of you, mamacita!"

It wasn't shaping up to be much of a weekend. We left the Top Hat, picked up some groceries, and went back to camp to wait and see if things might pick up later.

Camp, as it turned out, was where things were happening. Two of the car-trunk salesmen—locals who took advantage of the workers' isolation by filling up their cars with various consumer goods and selling them at the camps for a big markup—were parked outside the house. One was an aging Chicano who specialized in trousers, and in telling you how good you looked in them. The other was a quiet, thin man whose customized van was a regular duty-free shop on wheels. Stereos, liquor, jewelry, madonnas, sex aids, hats . . . if he didn't have it today, he would tomorrow. Nothing had price tags, of course. The worker feigned a passing interest in an object he savored, the salesman quoted an absurdly high price, the worker countered with a laugh and a ridiculously low price . . . and, if neither succeeded in offending the other, eventually a deal would result. This day Timoteo bargained again for a small ghetto blaster he had admired before; he finally got it when the salesman threw in batteries and several pirated pop music cassettes.

Everyone's inspection of Timoteo's purchase was interrupted, however, by hoots and hollers heralding the arrival of a dusty yellow Lincoln Continental. It was the camp's most celebrated sales team: Susi, Cándida, and Lágrimas—the prostitutes. Tiny disco purses in hand, spiky heels sinking deep into the gravel, they climbed from the front seat, eyeballed hungrily by all. Like the other vendors, they knew enough to come before the paychecks had been completely spent. The customized van man slammed shut his sliding door, recognizing that his sales for the day were over. The pants salesman pondered the women's undersized jeans, perhaps contemplating the chances of selling them three pairs that actually fit. Everyone else's mouth watered, which seemed to me peculiar since, if there was one feature of these women that really stood out, it was their utter lack of appeal. One, Susi, was grossly overweight; all three had that strange yellow-red color that results when Hispanic women try to become blondes; their natural complexions, thoroughly masked by various cosmetics, were impossible to discern; they exuded unhealthiness. This, truly, was the bottom of the barrel.

"What are you staring at?" demanded Cándida, moving her small, red lips at an admirer. *"Get me a beer!"*

They came inside, and Cándida and Susi sat on the couch and crossed their legs, trying hard to look bored and sexy at the same time. Lágrimas—the name means "teardrops" in English—moved toward the bathroom. It had been inoperative—and increasingly disgusting—since the water pump broke, but no one volunteered this information to her. Presently she could be heard muttering her displeasure. When she emerged the trademark mascara teardrops had been redrawn under the outside corners of her eyes.

Victor sat down on the bed with Timoteo's new radio in his lap and inserted one of the tapes. The room soon filled with Top 40 music, and runners were sent for more beer. *"I like your stereo,"* Cándida said to Victor, and the ice had been broken.

Guys took turns asking the prostitutes to dance; then, before long, the more senior workers invited one or another of them to *"go for a walk."* This translated into a quick stroll to the backseat of the Lincoln or out into the orchard; the charge was normally twenty dollars. The advantage of being senior, I supposed, was in having the women while they were "fresh." As the evening wore on, the idea of a quickie evidently became less appealing, because the prostitutes would have to wheedle and persuade to get the men out of the house. This reached a particularly pathetic level one night when, desperate for some business, Lágrimas virtually had to beg for someone to have sex with her. *"My grandmother is sick,"* she cried. *"I can't afford the bus ticket to California!"*

My Guerrero friends got the idea that it would be fun for me to have a go with big Susi, and there in the living room, between songs, Victor and Ismael suggested it. Susi herself took the initiative when I declined; but after we had danced, after much cooing and affection, I still could not be persuaded. Acting spurned, Susi angrily turned to my friends and asked, *"What is this guy, a faggot?"* Then, in English, "Hey, whatsamatter, Mexican girl not good enough for you?" I was reminded of the feigned anger of the Hispanic used-car salesman I had bought the Nova from when he thought the deal was falling through. To calm him down, I had finally bought it. Not again.

"You're too fat, too ugly," I said, returning the insult. It was a cheap shot, but my friends found it hilarious, and I was back in the fold. Later, I tried explaining to Carlos: *"For me, it's not like it is for you guys. I can meet girls here."* One night they had told me of a visit to some Acapulco whores, during which several lost their virginity. In Mexico that was often how it was done— prostitutes were a part of growing up, the first visit a rite of passage. *"The guys I grew up with, we're not so interested in that,"* I explained. Carlos said he understood, and I believed he did: if not the ways of Americans, then at least the allowances a friend makes for a friend.

One morning everyone's great fear came true: Immigration raided us. This particular raid, however, was an anticlimax. Due either to all the missing windows in the house or to the monumental ineptitude of the INS, ten agents succeeded in catching only six men. They arrived at about 5:30 on a Monday morning—an hour at which, because of their country upbringing, a good many of the men were already awake. *"¡Migra! ¡Migra!*—the alarm went out quickly. In less than a minute almost everyone had fled, by one route or another, deep into the orchard—there were escape routes that the INS hadn't anticipated. Asleep in the refrigerator room, we, of course, missed the whole thing. Despite the small number of casualties, people were quite upset. By Friday, however, it was party time as usual, due to the return from the border, by various devious means, of all but one of the deportees.

But the raid had a bad indirect effect. Pete, the ranch foreman, heard about it and, convinced the surplus of men at the camp was to blame for attracting Immigration's attention, announced that the day of reckoning had come. "Lupe, you gotta ship at least half these guys out of here," he announced at a meeting soon after. Privately, Sanchez blamed Pete's own reluctance to fix the water pump as well: the daily file of water carriers along the road to the camp caught the attention of other growers and was an embarrassment. Just the same, Sanchez agreed to abide by Pete's decision. The number of workers was fixed by the contract. As expected, the ranch committee elected to cut workers on the basis of seniority. Nervously, my friends made plans to leave.

Of course, I was cut too. For me it was a sobering time because my friends were nearly broke and unsure of where to go. Also, every day I continued to work now was a moral victory over Nate. But it was victory at a price: though I had met his challenge, I still felt little mastery over the job. Every morning at dawn, when my bunkmates began to rise, I still felt the dread of impending exhaustion. It was never clear to me whether I was getting weaker or stronger, but I suspected the former. And so, in this sense, getting laid off was a tremendous relief.

As news of the layoffs spread, *coyotes* began to show up at camp. They were, you might say, domestic *coyotes*, taking advantage of the fact that travel *within* the border states was difficult for Mexicans too. You knew it was them by the shiny, low-riding American sedans that cruised up to the house, by the radios blaring, by the guys in front wearing mirror shades and just dripping with hipness. Casually, they would light up a cigarette or joint and saunter around or just sit on the hood. The Mexican workers would humbly approach the cars, maybe offer their hands to be shaken, look down at the ground, and stand around for what seemed interminable lengths of time, until one *coyote* or another revealed what all had known since he arrived: that they could be hired to go to one place or another, that the prices were good but not cheap, that they could leave anytime.

Often, workers who had been around a while knew a given *coyote* or his reputation and would discreetly advise others when he left. Deals were almost never struck at once. Bartering was the game, as in Mexico, and not only was the price on the block, but the terms of payment—half down, half upon arrival; everything down; or some combination thereof. If a worker had the phone number of an employer who would pay at the other end, a hard-pressed *coyote* might call it to try and get some assurance of payment; if he were really desperate, it wasn't unknown for a *coyote* to take workers without charge and just "shop around" when he arrived at the destined farm area—if he knew the market well, he could sell his *pollos* for a handsome profit.

The *coyotes* were usually either Chicanos or experienced first-generation immigrants who really knew the score. Frequently they would pretend they were only representatives of a *coyote* to protect themselves. Savvy ones almost inevitably declined to say when they would come by to pick you up—they simply appeared, often in the middle of the night, and you had five minutes to get your belongings together and get into the car.

One day when I was gone, Carlos and his friends hooked up with a *coyote* who agreed to take them to L.A., where Carlos had an uncle, for $210 apiece, with payment in thirds. A third was due when they were picked up, a third when they were en route, and a third upon arrival. All were quite nervous because, in fact, none had more than $100. They were counting on the *coyote*'s investment of time, on stalling, and on their air of confidence about the solvency of Carlos's uncle to convince the *coyote* to keep going.

I considered asking them if I might come along, but the suspicious looks the *coyotes* gave me convinced me in advance that it was out of the question. Also, the financing arrangement seemed a recipe for disaster; as a rule *coyotes* carried guns, and did not like to be messed with. I got the address of Carlos's uncle and promised to visit once they had gotten settled.

I remember waking up when the *coyote* arrived. There was a mad frenzy of activity around the refrigeration room, all of it strangely silent and in the dark. Good-byes were hissed, and then, Carlos in the lead, they filed quickly out and into the *coyote*'s van. Heart pounding, I watched in sadness from the moon shadow of the barn's interior as the van's door slid shut, and the van slipped away.

Only a day and a half later I saw the van again. It came roaring up the dirt road and skidded to a stop in the dust outside the old house. Obviously unhappy, the *coyote* climbed stiffly from the driver's seat and slammed the door hard behind him. I retired discreetly to the back room. I listened carefully as he burst in through the screen door and began demanding answers to his questions about my friends. Where were they? Hadn't anybody seen them? No, they hadn't arrived in L.A. Who knew them? And what were their names anyway?

Later, through the grapevine, we heard that the van had been pulled over by a sheriff soon after crossing the California state line. While the *coyote*, driving, was being questioned in the front seat, another officer shined his flashlight through the rear windows to see what the van was carrying. Thinking they were about to be arrested by Immigration, Carlos and his friends jerked open the side door and bolted. They escaped; but the *coyote* was detained, questioned, and, went the story, avoided being sent to Immigration only by agreeing to part with the many crumpled ten- and twenty-dollar bills in his pocket. The last part sounded like the twist of a Mexican storyteller, but what was clear was that the smuggler, having discovered their lack of funds, felt robbed and betrayed by his fainthearted *pollos* and was eager to have a word with them. "I'll be back," he said as he left.

I tried to track down the source of this rumor—if it were true, then at least some of my friends must be around to tell it, because Mexicans fresh to the country almost never communicated by phone. The story had been introduced to the camp, I finally learned, by Rafael Sanchez, one of my students in the English class. He had heard it from his cousin at Bodine's orchard. "If I drive you over there, can you take me to him?" I asked. Because it was midweek, we would have to go at night, he said— and that would make it difficult, because Bodine's workers lived "in the trees"—out in the orchard, in other words. But he said we could give it a try.

It was very dark when we left on the twenty-minute drive to Bodine's. Other men came with us, taking advantage of the free ride to see their own friends. I had never been to Bodine's, which was said to have the most primitive conditions of any camp in the area, but was a bit surprised when they instructed me to park in the lot of a convenience store. *"From here, we walk,"* said Rafael.

Casually moving to the edge of the lot, the men wove through some decorative citrus trees and then, single file, descended a rocky slope to the dry wash of the seasonal Agua Fria River. Expertly they moved among stones, ditches, wires, and trash, through the dark shadow under a highway bridge. At the top of the far bank it dawned on me that, for reasons I didn't under-stand, this was a clandestine mission. One thing I was learning about Mexicans was that they weren't as committed to explana-tions as other people I knew. If you wanted to learn what was going on, you would just have to hang around. Asking too many questions was not done. Real men didn't need explanations.

A *"ssssssh,"* the same in English or Spanish, made its way back through the file to me; we were now crossing under some barbed-wire fence. A six-foot chain-link fence encircled a storage shed on our left; to the right, farm vehicles were visible under a mercury light. Rafael touched a spigot rising from the ground on the left and whispered to me, "It's the only fresh water they have." Another hundred yards and we were in the orchard.

We walked between many rows of trees, emerging now and then at a dirt crossroad, jumping the occasional irrigation ditch. Here, apparently in their element, the men were not so afraid of whatever it was they had been afraid of before. Always, though, they were watching, and when we stopped to take a better look at a distant flicker of firelight, barely visible through rows of trees, I understood one thing they were looking for.

"A campsite," said Rafael, meaningfully. *"La Migra never catches them out here."* For a long while the men debated whose campsite it was and then decided to keep moving. Fifteen minutes later we saw another one, and this time made our way to it.

"Yes, it's them," confirmed Rafael, and as we neared it he called out a greeting—important protocol when dealing with people who live outside. To a man around a camp fire, the surrounding darkness is a danger zone. The orchard dwellers, I had heard, often suffered at the hands of nighttime thieves.

Several men were seated around a fire; as we entered the circle of light one of them, Rafael's brother-in-law, rose and shook his hand warmly. Immediately, to defuse any nervousness, Rafael explained who I was. Though we had never met, several of the men around the fire nodded—they had heard of me. Easily three hundred men worked in the citrus farms this side of Phoenix, and yet it was a small world.

The beers we had carried in were passed around the fire, and for the next several hours the men talked and talked. After waiting a decent interval, I asked the brother-in-law about Carlos and his friends. It took only five minutes for him to relate the story I had already heard, and then share the information I'd been hunting for: they were staying with Fortino, a Bodine picker, in the town of Surprise, just north of El Mirage. Fortino, an excellent picker, earned enough to rent his own apartment and drove to work every day. The brother-in-law gave me directions.

I wanted to leave right then, but had no idea how to get back to my car. And, after all, I owed my guides a visit with their friends. I scooted up nearer the fire and resigned myself to look and listen. Really, this was an astonishing place—people *lived* here, right in the middle of this chilly, pesticided, artificial woods. Over our heads, just down the row from the fire, a large piece of plastic spanned the space between two rows of trees— the men's roof, sold to them by the owner, they said. This man,

I had read in the paper, had recently been named chairman of the board of the Western Growers Association, whose members "grow, pack and ship about 90% of the fresh vegetables, and some of the fruit, produced in Arizona and California." According to the men, he sold blankets too, which could be seen stashed by the trunks of the trees. Even with them, it had to be cold: this was, after all, the desert, disguised with fruit trees. Because the rows all had to be irrigated to survive, the men were periodically flooded out, often without notice. For bathing, and drinking, they had only the irrigation ditches. In the newspapers I had read of studies that claimed the wells supplying these ditches often were contaminated by pesticides leached from the agricultural soils above them. All of a sudden, my nook in the barn's refrigerator room seemed the lap of luxury.

Bodine's was the one citrus ranch in the valley that had never been unionized. The bad blood generated by strikes and organizing drives, I learned, was the reason we had to sneak in. Management had guards on the lookout for trespassing organizers; many of the workers, too, held grudges against AFW members, and you entered at your own peril. That was why it was important not to err in your choice of camp fire!

Most of the valley's citrus workers, I knew, were not from Guerrero but from Querétaro, a small, mountainous state just north of Mexico City. Years of labor and family connections had resulted in a traditional relationship between regions of Querétaro and the Phoenix citrus growers. Members of the AFW tended to come from a region around a town called Ahuacatlán; but Bodine's pickers came from around a town called Alejandría. Though neighbors, residents of the two regions were said to hate each other; their feud had its roots in the bitter labor disputes that had given birth to the AFW. Alejandríans, according to many AFW members, were nothing more than scabs. But those from Ahuacatlán, according to the Bodine pickers, were bullies and tyrants who didn't know how to mind their own business. It was only family ties between a few individuals that allowed us to sit around the same fire on this evening.

Testing the waters, I asked our hosts about a story that I had heard at camp about a Bodine foreman. When it came time to move his pickers from one side of the orchard to another, the story went, he would order all of them and their ladders into a large delivery van. Even with everybody standing, there were men who didn't fit, and so the foreman would jump behind the wheel, accelerate the truck, and then brake suddenly, compressing the passengers toward the front. This made room for more at the back. Others had been forced to travel with citrus in crates on the bed of a semitrailer, according to another tale. Yes, said one older man, those things were once true, but what of it? As I could see, life here was much improved. And why did I care about it anyway? Sensing a sore spot, I muttered that, really, I didn't care. And would he like another beer?

Early the next morning I drove to Surprise, just up the highway from El Mirage. The Hacienda Lounge had behind it a small motel with dirt parking lot and no amenities, residence for assorted American lowlifes and a few Mexican workers. I knocked on the door of Number 6, and a Mexican woman with a baby in her arms opened it a crack. Inside it looked dark; another baby screamed. *"¿Sí?"*

"I'm looking for some friends of mine, Carlos or Victor or Ismael . . ." I looked at her face: *Immigration*, she read me, fearfully. She withdrew almost imperceptibly from the light outside. *"I'm their friend. We worked together at the camp. I just—"*

"I'm sorry," she said, shutting the door. But suddenly there was another noise inside, sounds of men speaking quickly to each other. I heard my name spoken, and scuffling. Suddenly Carlos, sleepy looking and shirtless, appeared behind the mother. *"¡Hola, Teodoro!"* he said with a broad smile, opening the door wide despite her. He motioned me in, and before my eyes were Victor, Ismael, and Timoteo. Also shirtless, they had been laid out on the concrete floor, apparently engrossed in a very small television. Within a second we were shaking hands and slapping backs. The door closed.

Though wan and tired, all appeared to be in good health. Half of the fatigue, Carlos explained, came from sitting inside all day, avoiding the *coyote*. They had heard he was after them, and were terrified about it. The story, as recounted to me at camp, was basically true: they had run when the *policía* appeared, hidden in bushes and behind cactuses, and then regrouped when police and *coyote* left. There had been disagreement over whether they were close enough to Los Angeles to keep going, one way or another; or whether Phoenix was really closer and it was unwise to arrive in L.A. without a guide. Of course, there was no one around they could ask. Ten miles back down the road from Phoenix, Carlos's group had met a Hispanic convenience store clerk who, for cash, had driven them back to Surprise. The apartment, Carlos said, was that of Fortino, the friend who picked at Bodine's; the woman and children were Fortino's too. Though it barely had one bedroom—a large closet separated from the combination living room/kitchen by a sheet hung over the doorway—eight people were living there.

"Fortino's woman," Rebeca, fixed us beans, eggs, and tortillas while Carlos described their plan. They didn't have enough money left to pay a proper *coyote*, but between them they did have $300—enough to buy a car in which Fortino, in exchange for keeping it afterward, would drive them to California.

"*Sounds good,*" I said. "*When are you going to buy it?*"

"*Ah, we've already got it!*" exclaimed Carlos, opening the door a crack to reveal a shiny Toronado outside.

"*For three hundred dollars? What's wrong with it?*"

The group, as one, smiled sheepishly. "*We don't know yet,*" said Carlos.

It was great to see them all. We talked for a while, and ate, and then I went out and came back with more tortillas and a twelve-pack. I really didn't want to see them go again, and suddenly I decided:

"*Can I go with you?*"

Carlos looked puzzled. "*Where to?*"

"*To L.A., of course. To see where you guys end up. There's a cheap late-night flight back—I'll stay just a few days and then come home. Think they'll forgive me at the camp?"*

Everyone seemed for it, but agreed to ask Fortino when he came home from work. Late that evening Fortino, a tall, wiry man with long black hair and a U.S. Army shirt, pointed out that it would be crowded, but added that it was okay with him. We left the next evening, a Friday night.

Three-hundred-dollar cars always have something wrong with them. If they're at a dealership and can start up and run, that's almost worse, because then the defect is something not immediately obvious. Basically, Mexicans looked for a car they thought they could fix when it broke, and then they held their breath. The only problem with the Toronado that we could detect at first, as we got on the interstate highway on a remote ramp outside town, was that the seat-belt buzzer wouldn't go off. The noise, like a giant mosquito, threatened to drive me crazy, but I resolved that if the Mexicans could stand it for 400 miles, then so could I. For better or worse, I only had to endure for about 50: that's when the overheating light came on and we exited the highway, turning off the lights and ignition. When the steam cleared enough to take a close look by the flicker of a cigarette lighter, we discovered half-inch holes through two sides of the top of the radiator.

"Someone fucking shot this thing through with a rifle," commented Fortino, and it certainly looked as if he was right—though, to judge by the rust, it had happened several years earlier. That was at about 8:00 P.M.; it took us until 3:00 A.M. to drive the fifty miles back, all of them at about fifteen miles an hour, all on dirt roads to avoid having a police car stop and "assist" us. At every suspected bridge, hose, or irrigation ditch, we would pile out, fill up a variety of milk cartons, bean cans, and bottles we had found, and replenish the radiator. In the end, it was hardly worth the trouble: just blocks from Fortino's home the cylinders seized. The Toronado was no more. Unloading our few possessions, we abandoned it by the side of the road, closing the doors in defeat.

The next day was dreary and depressing. With my limited budget for the next several months, I couldn't afford to make my friends a loan that would entice any *coyote*. They had no relatives left at camp from whom they could borrow. The hard-pressed union couldn't make funds available for members to relocate. We were all lounging around on the concrete floor, breathing air that had already been breathed several times that day, when Carlos had an idea.

"How much did you say that cheap flight from L.A. to Phoenix costs?"

"Thirty-nine dollars."

"And does it fly the other direction too?"

I nodded.

Carlos took up a pen and began figuring, counting aloud in Spanish. *"If we bought your ticket, would you be our guide?"*

"What?" The others looked at him wide eyed.

"We've almost got enough money. I think Fortino would lend us some. It's just that nobody knows how to do it, how to go on a plane, how to be in an airport."

I was stunned, but intrigued. Illegal aliens flying in a jet—it was a novel concept. *"You mean, I would be your coyote? You guys, I can't! If I get caught, it's a felony!"*

"No, no," said Carlos. *"You're not helping us—we're helping you. You want to go with us to Los Angeles, right? You want to write about it, yes? Then you are the one who is being helped."*

With reasoning like that, I thought, Carlos was wasting his time being an illegal alien; he should be going to law school. I thought and thought. Victor went out to buy some beer, and with its help, I thought some more. We just might be able to pull it off. It would take some planning and preparation, though. *"When were you thinking of leaving?"* Today was Thursday.

"Sunday?"

I opened another beer.

"Sunday? Yeah, okay, Sunday."

Chapter 3

Welcome to L.A.

TIMOTEO LEAPT IN surprise as the electric doors behind him slid apart suddenly, with a hiss. Eyes wide, he turned warily around to see what was going on.

"*¡Tranquilo!*" I said. "*It's okay.*" Any other day this might have made for a good laugh. But the faces around me were grim. "*They're automatic. They use radar.*" I gestured toward the sensor above the doorway to the airport; Timoteo peered mistrustfully at its little red eye, blinking on and off. And a funny feeling lodged itself in my stomach as I wondered: What else had I forgotten to tell them?

It was like crossing the border again, though my friends were even more nervous. We were leaving one world, the sleepy, isolated *barrio* of El Mirage, with its orchards, dirt roads, and dusty cantinas, and heading to another—fast, urban, sprawling Los Angeles. The change itself, for these country boys, would be hard to get used to . . . but at least it would be from one mainly Hispanic environment to another. What had them really worried was the journey itself: to get to Los Angeles, we would have to pass through a place even more foreign, a terra incognita of video displays and moving sidewalks, a world with a different language and set of rules for behavior: the world of air travel.

There was no *coyote* to mistrust on this crossing, no cop to bribe. The sole requirement for success was not to appear like a foreigner, not to stand out. Failure could mean deportation for them, and a felony rap ("aiding and abetting illegal aliens") for me. As dependent as I was on them not to blow it, they were dependent on me to tell them what to do.

Between Thursday, when we decided, and Sunday night, when we left, I racked my brain: what did one need to know to operate in an airport? For me it was a hard question because it was almost second nature; but for them it was the United States at its most technologically advanced, its most intimidating. To reduce their fear of the unknown, I drew a map of the airport parking garage, the terminal building, and the route we would take through them to get to our gate. As we went over the map, I realized that educating my friends was in my own best interest, too—to succeed in this, I would have to be a tour guide who did not look as though he were guiding.

The main challenge, though, was to teach them how to *look* at home in an airport. Dress, of course, was very important: the work boots, jeans, and visor caps had to go. Victor and Ismael needed haircuts; Rebeca, Fortino's wife, was kind enough to oblige. Saturday we combed the flea markets—"swap meets," as they're known in Arizona—for other clothes. Carlos, a step ahead of the game, spotted and negotiated the purchase of four inexpensive nylon flight bags. At the homes of some Phoenix friends, I found more items.

But looking at home also meant *acting* at home, and dressing right would do no good if they didn't appear comfortable. They had to look as though they had been through the airport a hundred times, as though nothing for them was new or unusual—though, in fact, almost everything was. The worst giveaway, I thought, was likely to be the way they acted with each other. Their way of handling a public place in Phoenix, which I was familiar with through our weekend trips downtown, would never do. We couldn't cluster together in the customary way, the five of us sauntering elbow to elbow, talking with our hands, whistling, laughing, gabbing, stepping as one. Not only would I stand out, as usual—but they would be more obvious than a mob of Japanese businessmen. They had to be less gregarious, less animated, in more of a hurry. In short, they had to be more *American*.

In our coaching sessions in the tiny living room of Fortino's apartment, over the bawling of the babies, we sketched out a plan: Victor and Ismael would walk together in the lead. A few feet behind them, Carlos would follow. Taking up the rear of this loose procession would be Timoteo and me. In case of an emergency, I could direct Carlos in inconspicuous English; he could pass the information on, in Spanish, to the guys in front. By having Timoteo next to me, I could cover the weakest link. It had taken nearly three days of argument and reassurance to persuade Timoteo to come—the idea of airplanes terrified him. *"What if we crash? Wouldn't it be easier to take the bus? You know, I have heart problems. I think it would be safer for me to stay on the ground."* Slowly, though, he came to realize that the others were set on the trip, even a little excited about going, and that if he stayed he would be left alone. To a Mexican, that is arguably the worst fate on earth.

I dropped by the little apartment three hours before we were to leave, to reassure fainthearted Timoteo and see if everyone was getting ready. But when Rebeca opened the door, I was amazed by the sight. They had been ready for hours. Hair was neatly combed, faces cleanly shaved. Carlos wore beige slacks and a brown cardigan sweater, along with the good oxfords he always donned on weekends. Victor wore a Barnard College sweatshirt. Ismael had on a Pink Floyd T-shirt, which I was not satisfied with, and high-top Converse basketball shoes, which I was—real Mexicans almost never wore those. The pièce de résistance, though, was a seersucker suit and button-down shirt I had rounded up for Timoteo. At forty years old, he was the most rustic of the group, normally looking as though he might have stepped from straight behind an ox and plow. But the suit worked a miraculous transformation. It didn't make him look American, but it did nearly make him look professional—like a dentist, perhaps, from the provinces, a visiting Rotarian. Until I noticed the buttons.

"*Timoteo,*" I said, "*don't ask me why, but here it looks best if you don't button all those buttons on your jacket. Just the middle one. Yeah, like that.*" He gave me a look of great bewilderment—there's such a thing as buttons you don't button?—but adjusted the suit accordingly.

Motel neighbors dropped in to say good-bye—which left not even standing room in the apartment—and then it was time to go. "*¡Vaya con Dios!*" said Matilde, a kindhearted mother of nine. "*¡Que les vaya muy bien!*" May all go well for you! Carlos, Victor, and Ismael filed out and into the Nova, carrying the flight bags filled with their few possessions. These were men you didn't need to tell to travel light. And then, finally, Timoteo emerged. At his side he lugged his flight bag—but attached to it, with twine, were two rolled-up blankets and the ghetto blaster.

"*Timoteo, you can't take that. Men in seersucker suits don't carry blankets and radios with them on airplanes.*"

"*But I've heard you can check baggage, like we do on a bus!*" he protested.

I explained that we couldn't stand around the baggage claim at Los Angeles International Airport for half an hour, waiting for blankets and a ghetto blaster to issue from the carousel. No one seconded me, but neither did they support Timoteo, and, since I was tour guide, he had lost again. The "box" was left to Fortino and Rebeca, in thanks, and the blankets to their babies.

As the electric door slid shut behind us, we entered the terminal, passing rows of plastic seats and the shiny display windows of gift shops and newsstands. Victor and Ismael, taking my advice too literally, set off at nearly a run, quickly outpacing the rest of us. We caught up when they stopped at the first bank of flight monitors.

"*Hey, take it easy! We're not in this much of a hurry. Look, we need to go to the next set of monitors—those'll probably be the ones for our airline. I'll be right behind.*"

The airport was nearly empty. We had chosen Sunday night because, according to border-crosser superstition (which may have some basis in fact), that was when the least number of Border Patrol and other police was likely to be on duty. But what had seemed an advantage also made us look awfully vulnerable. Instead of lost in a crowd, we were practically alone.

One endless concourse after another broke away from the large main terminal, and I realized that the lack of other travelers wasn't the only reason the airport struck me as so vast. It was, simply, the largest indoor place we had been together. My friends' eyes were wide, and I realized that mine were seeing something new this night as well.

Besides all the space, there were the colors. The only bright ones came from colored electric signs; everything else—including my friends—looked pallid and ghostly, bathed in fluorescent light. From the textured walls to the hot dog cafés, everything was synthetic, plasticized. Even the wind, spilling cold and unnoticed from ceiling vents, was processed. The terminal was lined with restaurants and bars, but somehow the air carried none of their smells, no hint of cooking or consuming, no smells at all, really, except a vague, musty trace of air conditioning, and a whiff of disinfectant.

There were other sensations of a "nice," institutional environment, the likes of which hardly exist in Mexico. Our footsteps, for example—always, when we were out, we walked to the beat of our own shoes, hitting the pavement or the linoleum or the road, kicking up dust. Ismael even had taps on his boots. But the airport carpet gave no answer to a treading foot. Over the indistinct, nearly unnoted whoosh of cold air, I heard Muzak for the first time. Strange, I thought, that I hadn't noticed it before; though perhaps not, since not noticing it was exactly the point. Perhaps its subconscious message of relaxation had collided, this evening, with my conscious wish to keep alert and wary—in something like the way my friends' disguises, and physical distance from each other, collided with the way they really were; or the way this journey collided with what was customary and realistic for an illegal alien. For us, nothing was congruous in that airport; all was out of joint, trouble waiting to happen.

The next monitors indicated we would have to go to a terminal one level down. I nodded toward the nearest escalators. Victor and Ismael began to cross the floor, but suddenly halted, wide eyed, as an electric cart carrying elderly people beeped behind them and whirred across their path. Almost immediately following this, the room filled with a string of loud announcements over the public-address system.

"Wells, Mr. Brad Wells. Hart, Miss Ruth Hart. Waters, Mr. Todd Waters. Please come to a white paging telephone."

They stood there, stunned and seemingly paralyzed—had they been caught? It was an authoritative male voice, and the message had been delivered right over their heads. How were they to know it was broadcast all over the airport? How were they to know the phrases were merely people's names? Tense and apprehensive, Victor and Ismael looked back at Carlos, himself frozen, and then at me.

"There's nothing wrong!" I hissed to Carlos. *"¡Que sigan! Keep moving! Tell them to keep moving!"* Carlos passed the word, and slowly, like steam engines picking up speed, they began to walk again. As we continued across the wide floor, I thanked God there were no Krishnas about.

I might have been gaining some confidence as a troubleshooter, but things soon got worse. At the top of the escalator, Victor and Ismael balked, a panic-stricken look on their faces. Carlos immediately walked up to them and started talking. *"What's wrong?"* I asked nervously. *"What's going on?"*

"They've never been on one before," said Carlos, who, to my relief, had. He gave them a crash course in Spanish spoken so rapidly I had barely an idea what he said. *"Pónganse trucha,"* were his last words, slang which translated literally to "Make like a trout"—be alert, wary, quick. But Victor and Ismael made more like puppies. They took tentative steps onto the thing, grasping the railings tightly. Carlos stepped on next. Taking hold

of Timoteo's arm, I strode forward without hesitation. *"Put your foot on the first step,"* was all I said, as I dragged him on. The others looked back worriedly from several steps below; there now could be no pretense that we were traveling separately. *"Be careful at the bottom!"* I warned them, wishing fervently for some antacid.

Only Timoteo stumbled, but I was there to catch him. As the beginning of our concourse came into view, I felt a newfound respect for *coyotes*: maybe they did overcharge, but this line of work took years off your life.

Away we went. I breathed easier as we entered the long straight stretch toward the gates, dropping back as we got closer to the gate. They knew the number. We had plenty of time till departure. No wrong turns were possible. We wouldn't need to talk again until we had boarded the plane: the end of Phase I was in sight.

At that moment the security checkpoint came into view. How on earth had I forgotten it? For months I had been training to see situations through their eyes, and what I saw now panicked me. Two sets of sophisticated X-ray machines. TV screens for looking into them. Doorframes we were evidently supposed to walk through, and above them two more small red lights, like the one over the sliding door at the terminal entrance: invisible rays, I now could see, were going to be my downfall. Conveyor belts leading into the machines: were we to lie down on those? Worse than all this, behind the machines sat a police officer at a desk. And posted in front, large signs with red and blue letters, in English, and an official seal. If you read English, you would know, of course, that the signs warned of the consequences if you were carrying a firearm or joking about bombs. But if you were Carlos, Victor, Ismael, or Timoteo, these signs could seem to be a warning about anything in the world.

I could have killed myself for my shortsightedness at not having told them about this one. A hundred feet ahead of me down the concourse, Victor and Ismael probably shared this feeling. They were completely in the dark. But instead of balking, they continued to walk at a measured pace toward the machines.

It was too late to turn back, and possibly suicide to stop and discuss it.

I hurried to get there. I saw the woman working the X-ray machine tell them to put their flight bags on the conveyer belt. They, of course, had absolutely no idea what she was saying. She repeated. They put down their bags, and took out their wallets. They were looking for something . . . ID cards! The guys thought it was a police checkpoint, as exist all over Mexico, for which you have to show your papers. Victor handed her some card, and when she saw what it was, she began to get impatient. "No, no!" she said, handing them back and raising her voice, as though that way they'd understand. "Just *put the bags on the belt!*" The other attendants and the cop were all watching now.

Carlos, Timoteo, and I arrived at this moment. I had no choice. *"You guys,"* I said in Spanish, *"they don't care who you are. All they want is to see if you're carrying weapons. Put your bags on that belt there."* Flustered and anxious, they did. *"Now, walk through that doorway—yeah, the doorframe."*

One by one they did. And one by one each of them—every single one—set off the beeper. I could hardly believe it. The policeman now looked very interested. "Please empty your pockets," said the attendant, offering a basket. As one, they looked at me for instructions on what to do next.

Filled with a feeling of doom, I came through and took the basket. *"Does she want money?"* Timoteo asked me, probably reminded of the collection basket at church. *"No, no, she just wants to see what's in your pockets. You all must have metal things in your pockets. Put them in the basket."*

Everyone dug deep, and what emerged were a small penknife, a crucifix on a chain, a copied set of the Toronado keys, a fingernail clipper, three tire valves, a handbill from a Spanish-speaking clairvoyant, and probably two pounds of Mexican peso coins. It was the pesos, each as large as an American silver dollar, yet all together worth less than an American quarter, that had done it.

I held the basket, stony faced, as it grew heavy. They walked through again. This time nobody set off the machine. We picked up the flight bags and, eyes straight ahead, were off.

"Why the hell were you guys still carrying those pesos?" I whispered harshly, when we were two boarding gates away and out of sight. Carlos shrugged. *"We had nowhere to spend them,"* said Timoteo. They felt really stupid, I knew. They had been placed in an everyday American situation and had not had the slightest idea how to deal with it. It was a Mexican's nightmare. And then, as the adrenaline subsided, I recognized my culpability. *"I'm sorry, this was all my fault."*

"No, no," said Carlos, *"it's our fault. We should have told you about the pesos."* That was ridiculous, and I felt even worse. We arrived at the gate, and for a while all sat in silence. But then the boarding call came, and there were other things to think about.

Boarding was mercifully painless; the plane was only half full. The five of us took two sets of three seats, across the aisle from each other. I showed them about seat belts, about where to stow the bags, about how the seat backs and the tray tables worked. We had been provided with plastic headsets, and these were a big hit; everyone plugged in and listened until the flight attendant came to give her flight safety demonstration. Now here was something truly fascinating; they all watched in admiration, it seemed to me, without much concern about what she was saying. Finished with the spiel, she stepped gracefully by, checking all our laps for seat belts and tightening Carlos's when he couldn't seem to manage. Carlos, not the least bit nervous, thanked her and summoned up a big smile. *"She's pretty,"* he whispered, as she continued down the aisle.

Excitement grew as the whine of the engines increased and the cabin lights dimmed in preparation for takeoff. Victor peered out his window at the revolving red lights on the wingtips, the rows of deep blue lights that lined runways. Excited, he pointed them out to Ismael. Carlos glanced at me and smiled. *"Are we going to fly now?"* he asked. I nodded. Timoteo suddenly tapped me on the arm.

"*Teodoro, I shouldn't sit next to the window,*" he said. "*Can we trade?*"

"*Sure. Are you okay?*"

"*Yes, yes, it's just, well, you know, the view. Maybe you could sit over here and I could sit on the aisle.*" We traded places.

The big plane taxied down the runway. In the few moments before poor Timoteo asked me to close the window shade, I looked out the window and saw the terminal, the many lights, the tall fence that encircled the field. It reminded me of gazing through a window in the Mexico City airport a few months earlier. But something had caught my eye at the edge of that Mexican airport: a spot in the perimeter fence that had been modified, turned into a little visitors' cage, a grandstand for spectators. Since there were no cars nearby, and no easy access from the terminal itself, I had figured the fifteen or twenty people on the bleachers to be simply pedestrians from the working-class neighborhood adjacent—people interested in airplanes, in the miracle of flight. In the United States, where air travel is almost passé, observation decks went out years ago. In Mexico, where it is the privilege of only the very rich, where the vast majority of people will never see the ground from the sky, flight remains a fascination. The sight of those spectators, braving wind, noise, and exhaust at the edge of a sea of concrete, just to see airplanes leave the earth and return to it, said more than a thousand studies about the differences between our countries.

The whine of the engines suddenly grew to a roar, and the Boeing began to accelerate. I looked across the row: only Timoteo looked nervous. Expectancy and excitement tinged the faces of the others. The cabin pressure increased—I forgot to buy chewing gum!—and Victor placed his hands over his ears. The plane slowly left the ground. "*Are we there?*" Ismael mouthed to Carlos, and then to me. We both nodded, and I grinned. How had I forgotten the excitement of flight?

As the plane climbed above the clouds, we noticed that Victor still had his hands over his ears, and a concerned look on his face. I suggested he yawn, or swallow, to relieve the pressure, and that seemed to help a little. But then he asked Carlos, the only one among them who had finished high school, the recognized brains of the group, *"What's going on? What's 'pressure'?"*

"It's in the air," Carlos began, *"but it's not like sound, or light. Putting your hands over your ears like that won't keep it out. It's like there's . . . more air."*

"Because of the wind outside? Because we're moving so fast?"

"Well, not exactly. Look, it's like . . . inside a tire. Imagine yourself inside a tire. There's more air in one place." Victor didn't appear entirely satisfied, and Carlos looked over at me for help. But explaining atmospheric pressure was beyond my ability in Spanish. *"Just yawn,"* I offered. *"Eat something."*

The flight was the pay-on-board variety, and after a while the same flight attendant came by to collect our fares. I offered her our stack of $195 in small bills, with apologies. She laughed though, and asked where my friends were from. Mexico, I said, and they smiled and nodded. "Jes, we are from Messico," added Carlos, in his best conversational English. He did have a thing for her.

"On vacation?" she asked, smiling.

"Oh, they're soccer players," I said. "Up for an exhibition game."

"How exciting! Well, enjoy your flight."

"Jes, very much, sank you!" said Carlos, who received an elbow from Ismael as soon as she moved on to the next row, and lifted his eyebrows at the rest of us.

We listened more to the headsets and browsed through the in-flight magazines until she passed by again with the drink tray. "What would you like to drink?" she asked. Carlos and Ismael reached for their wallets but, assuming they were just going to order Coke or a Sprite, I told them the drinks were free, that there was no charge. Somehow, though, this point of information translated to mean to them that she was *buying us* a round of drinks . . . a bad goof. Before I knew what was happening, broad grins crossed their faces, and Carlos scooted over to make the aisle seat free for her.

"Lady, please, you would . . ." He didn't know how to finish the sentence. He looked at me.

"Ask her if she'd like to join us!"

I'm sure I looked very uncomfortable. This wasn't how it was done on airliners; we would stand out. I was trying to come up with a way to explain this quickly, when it occurred to me that I didn't need to be Carlos's guardian every second of the trip. Besides, she had probably figured it out herself. So I simply translated his request, as he had asked. She responded perfectly.

"Why, thank you! Please tell him that I would, but I've got a lot of passengers still to serve." Which I did. Carlos beamed.

Below, the Sonoran Desert was pitch black except for very occasional speckles of light. I calculated that we were just north of the border towns of Yuma, Arizona, and Mexicali, Baja California Norte. It was still Sunday night, a good time for crossing. The emptiness was illusory: there were people down there, walking.

The plane landed without incident, and we decided to get out of the airport as soon as possible; if there were Immigration agents out tonight, an international airport like LAX was where they were likely to be. Carlos's cousin, we hoped, could arrange for us to be picked up, but it wouldn't be wise to stick around until he arrived. We went downstairs to the cabstand.

I knew almost nothing about Los Angeles, apart from the names of a few of its suburbs—Pasadena, Hollywood, Santa Ana. And my companions knew *absolutely* nothing. As we stood there by the curbside, their apprehension seemed to grow, probably because I myself was hesitating. Where should we go? There were police around, directing traffic. The cabbies were aggressive, demanding to know our destination, telling us we couldn't all fit into one cab. They looked too hungry for a big fare, and it didn't seem a good idea just to hop in, completely naïve, and ask them to take us to a Denny's somewhere. Then I noticed a sign: SANTA MONICA, $19.00. HOLLYWOOD, $26.00. BEVERLY HILLS, $22.00.

DOWNTOWN, $24.00. A set fare seemed the way to go. Because I had no idea where any of these places were, I chose the cheapest: we would hit Santa Monica.

A Greek-American with a station wagon agreed to take all five of us, though of course we could have fit into any sedan. The station wagon, he informed me, normally cost double fare, but he'd give us a break—five dollars off. I said maybe we could ask a supervisor about that. Okay, okay, he said—ten dollars off. That, too, seemed a lot, but since the guys were already climbing in, I agreed.

The city glittered with lights and traffic and glass. Though it was almost midnight, everything seemed to be moving: elevators through the sides of glass buildings, planes overhead, cars on all sides, flashing signs. Reflections from glass and the glowing yellow aura of the sky made it seem the middle of a long twilight. The cabbie's acceleration when we hit the freeway reminded me of the jet's. My friends were quiet.

The driver was very curious about what a guy like me was doing with guys like them. I used the soccer story again, explaining that it didn't seem polite to ask our hosts in Santa Monica to pick us up at the airport at this late hour. We would find a place to hang out in Santa Monica, and call them to pick us up. The cabbie wanted to take us direct to their house. I said I only had a phone number. He wanted to look them up in the phone book— that way he could find their address and take us there. I said, just take us to some restaurant. He said, they're all closed by now. In that case, I said, let us off right here, and we'll find a cabbie who does know where one is. Well, come to think of it, he said, I think I know where there might be one—no guarantees, but I think I know.

We got off at McDonald's in Santa Monica. While Carlos found a telephone from which to try his cousin, the rest of us drank coffee. Victor asked me about the cab driver. *"Where was he from?"*

"Greece, originally."

"Do Greeks speak English too?"

"After they've been here long enough, they do," I said. *"Just like you will."* Victor smiled and looked at his coffee.

Carlos returned, unhappy; there had been no answer at his cousin's number. Half an hour later the manager told us we had to leave, the restaurant was closing. We stood in the empty parking lot and looked up and down Colorado Avenue: everything was closed except the Holiday Inn across the street. As the streets were empty and every conceivable outdoor waiting place was conspicuous, I walked over to the hotel to ask if we could wait in the lobby until our ride came. No one was at the desk, so I waved them in.

This time Carlos did succeed in reaching his cousin's house on the phone. His cousin was out, but someone else, apparently another, more distant relative, would try to round up a car and get us. We would have to stay near the phone, though, so that yet another someone who knew the city better could call back and see exactly where we were.

At this point, the black desk clerk appeared. If we weren't checking in, he said, we would have to leave. I tried to explain the situation to him, as one American to another: that they had nowhere to go, that they were just into town and out of cash, that it should only be an hour or so. He became very apologetic: if it were up to him, he said, we could stay, but he was new, and the manager . . . No doubt the manager, I thought, like the neighborhood, was white. He was in a tough spot too. "But why don't you go around the block to the doughnut shop?" he said. "They're open all night." As we got up to leave, he took me aside.

"Hey, man," he said, "are those guys hungry?" I said I thought they probably were. "Well, then, here," he said, slipping me a five-dollar bill, "buy 'em some doughnuts or somethin'."

When we got to the doughnut shop, I told them of the charity. They were surprised—the *negros* in L.A., they had heard, were *muy gachos*—bad news. At this moment, the desk clerk appeared through the door of the doughnut shop and nodded at us. "Telephone!" he said. Carlos hustled back to the hotel with him.

Perhaps in the daytime the doughnut shop could pass as a reputable place in calm, suburban Santa Monica. But the nighttime crowd didn't fit in . . . didn't fit in anywhere, that is, except maybe an all-night doughnut shop in Los Angeles. The gritty trio in the molded-plastic table-and-chair unit next to ours were dressed in denims and T-shirts, with long, stringy hair (one of them, bald on top, looked liked a hard-bitten Benjamin Franklin), dark glasses, and chains attaching the long leather billfolds jutting from back pockets to belt loops. One wore an overcoat, one was missing front teeth, two were sharing a cup of coffee, perhaps for reasons of economy. One was writing on the plastic tabletop with a pencil. Occupying three of the four seats on our other side were a bag lady and two of her bags. She was holding her coffee close to her face, both hands wrapped around it, as though it were the last source of heat on earth, and occasionally shuffling through old newspapers on the table. The counterman was a young Asian, serving two very expressive men, one black and one white, both wearing makeup. As far down the row of stools from them as he could be sat an old, bewhiskered white man in work pants, heavy black oxfords, windbreaker, and cap, probably just off the night shift somewhere . . . or about to begin it. All looked deathly in the wavering fluorescent light.

The time passed slowly. All of us were tired, and yet it was important to stay alert. From my seat I could see out the two large plate-glass windows of the storefront. There were few pedestrians, and no cars—the doughnut shop was about the only thing happening this time of night. I tried to keep something of a lookout but didn't know exactly what to look for. The police, I guessed—maybe this was where they took their late-shift coffee breaks. And, sure enough, the police would arrive in a short while—but not for any of the reasons we might have suspected.

For a long time we sat, saying nothing. Timoteo and I played a few games of tic-tac-toe, which he had never seen, on napkins from the dispenser. Then I taught them the game of dots, in which you draw a grid of dots and, by taking turns drawing lines to connect any two of them, you try to complete more tiny squares than your opponent. It was a simple game, which took a long time. We played a small demonstration match and then, encouraged by the response, I set to drawing a large grid for a lengthy game.

It was as I was involved in this absorbing task that the man apparently came through the door. I did not see him enter. The realization that he was there caught me in midsentence, as I was explaining to Victor that you could make the grid any size you wanted. When Victor looked up, I followed his gaze to a man standing at the end of our table, just inches from me. He was white, young, thickly built, with short brown hair. He wore a black leather jacket with lots of zippers and buckles, jeans, and heavy boots. He was swaying. The end of one of his lips was swollen, and he had a scar cutting through his right brow and down onto his eyelid. The area around his eyes was sort of puffy, and it was hard to see the eyes themselves. But from the way he held his head, he didn't seem to be focusing, or seeing too clearly. He didn't say anything, just stood there and swayed.

"Need anything?" I said finally, not belligerent but not too nice either.

His head sort of turned toward me. There was a long delay. When finally he spoke, his voice was slurred.

"White guy talkin' to some Messicans, huh?"

I stiffened. My friends all froze. "That's right," I said, still sitting. There was no reply. "You got a problem with that?"

"No, no, thassokay," he said, making a little wave with his thick hand, turning. In his somnambulant, doped-up way, he appeared to take in the room behind him. His slow operation, his sluggish response to stimuli, reminded me of a porcupine, or a big land turtle. He meandered about for a while and then plopped himself down behind me, in the empty seat at the bag lady's table.

"That seat's taken!" she snapped. "My friend's in the john

and he's coming right back!" The man leaned across the table toward her and said things in a low voice I couldn't hear.

"Waiter! Counterboy!" she called out, with strain in her voice. The Asian man appeared from the kitchen. "This man is insulting me! He's rude and does not belong in this establishment. Tell him to leave!"

The man in the leather jacket rose.

"You want coffee?" asked the Asian. The man in the leather jacket moved toward the counter.

Victor, Ismael, Timoteo, and I exchanged glances. *"Híjole, what a jerk!"* said Ismael. We all nodded. *"What did he say to you?"* Victor asked me.

"Nothing. Dumb things." No one else spoke. All, apparently, were scared. I should have been scared, too, but maybe it was the hour, or the fact I hadn't been hurt in a long time, or my refusal to take seriously someone so "gone" . . . whatever, my pulse was normal, and I thought it important to set a "cool" example. *"Let's play dots,"* I said. *"But do keep an eye open, okay?"* Since he was behind me, I couldn't see him. Victor, Timoteo, and Ismael nodded.

We resumed our game, and I discovered that I could see behind me, more or less, by looking at the reflection off the big front windows. The man had bought some coffee and was leaning against the restaurant's back wall, not far from the bag lady. Every few moments I looked up to check on him, but there was never any change.

The dots game, unlikely though it may seem, became quite absorbing as Victor and I neared its final moments, battling it out for the highest number of squares. At least twenty minutes had passed since the Neanderthal had left our table. My guard was down. I was scribbling a *T* in a square I had just completed, and handing our sole pencil back to Victor, when a tremendous blow landed on the side of my head, knocking me from my chair. From the floor, on my back, I curled up in defense against whatever might follow. It took a moment before I could see. When I could, it was blurry, and through just one eye.

The man was standing again at the end of the table. He had come up from behind me. I thought he had hit me with his fist, but I didn't know. My hand was up over the eye—there was nothing wet, it didn't seem to be bleeding. He turned and walked out of the doughnut shop.

"Hey, stop that guy!" I yelled. I tried to get to my feet and failed. The second time, with help from Timoteo, I made it. He held me up as I pointed to the door and yelled, in English: "Somebody get him! Somebody call the cops!"

I looked around at my friends. None of them were moving: all were just staring at me. Why weren't they helping? "Hey! You guys! *¡Oye! Hey, what's the matter? Aren't you going to get him?*" There was no response. The whole scene was beginning to seem surreal. The bag lady was at the counter, telling the counterman to get on the phone to the police. I saw him pick up the phone, and then I realized what the problem was.

The police. Commotion. Attention. This was exactly what our journey was designed to avoid. Probably to their dismay, they had not been the ones who ultimately had attracted attention— *I* had. The police were coming—what would that mean? If they gave chase—what would that mean? Either, probably, would mean questioning, the giving of accounts, the revelation of no English, the hard looks at appearance, and the recognition that these were not Mexican-Americans—these guys were wet.

But their problems weren't foremost in my mind at this moment. I still couldn't see with my punched-out eye. It was starting to ache and soon would swell. I didn't know what to do. I had absolutely no idea.

"*¿Qué hacemos?*" asked Ismael. "What do we do?" I felt like saying, "When your friend is attacked, you have to ask him what to do?" but the translation required too much effort.

I turned to the bag lady and asked if the police had been called. "Yes, sir, and they'll be right here!" she said, with an air of great satisfaction. I decided to wait for them outside, and suggested the guys just sit tight.

At this moment, Carlos walked through the door from the

hotel, looking cheered. The friend of his cousin's, he said, would be coming to pick us up. It might take an hour or two, but he would come. All we had to do was sit it out. "*¡Hijo de la Santísima Virgen!*" he suddenly exclaimed, at last noticing the disarray and my hand over my eye. "*What happened?*"

The patrol cars arrived less than a minute later—two of them. I walked over, still holding my eye, and explained that I had been struck by a man who apparently simply did not like the looks of me. I described him, and the direction he had gone, and they sped off.

Ten minutes later they were back—with my assailant, hand-cuffed, in the back of one car. He hadn't gotten very far. I signed a statement and thought that was the end of it until the cop began to open his door. "A few statements from witnesses will help make the charges stick," he explained, reaching for a clipboard.

"Well, umm," I stammered—this was the last thing we needed—"I don't think there *were* any witnesses."

"No witnesses with all those people? Are you sure?"

"Well, it happened all of a sudden, like, by surprise."

"If there's no witnesses, you know, they'll probably release him."

I thought about that for a moment. "Well, why don't I go in and check, just in case?" I entered the doughnut shop.

The bag lady came right up to me. "Let's get something for that eye!" she said, bending forward for a closer look. "No, not now—I'm just here for a second," I said. "The cop wants to know if there were any witnesses."

Nobody said anything; it all had been so sudden. "Well, if that's the case, then I saw it!" said the bag lady.

"You did?"

"Well, no, but I'll tell them I did!"

My heart went out to this woman. "Oh, ma'am, thank you. That's really nice. Thank you. But you'd have to go to court and swear on it and everything, and I'm not sure it would make a big difference anyway. Why don't we skip it this time?"

"It's your eye," she said.

"I'll be right back."

Soon the police cars had left and I was back inside. The bag lady had gotten a plastic bag filled with ice from the counterman and waved me to her table.

"Now, what you've got to do is put it on your eye for thirty seconds, and then take it off for thirty seconds. Guaranteed to keep you from getting a shiner," she said, placing one hand on top of my head and gently applying the ice pack with the other.

"Oww!"

"Well, okay then, you hold it on."

With my other eye I watched as she rummaged through one of her bags. "It's here at the bottom," she said, "I know it is." Eventually she produced a huge alarm clock, the windup kind with two bells on top, and set it on the table. And for the next half hour she watched it, telling me when to put the pack on, when to take it off. In between commands, she worked on the *New York Times* crossword puzzle, from the local paper. I was so unobservant I didn't notice this, until all of a sudden she asked me, "Do you know a river in southern Uganda?"

"Southern Uganda? No, ma'am, I don't think I do."

"Damn. I've got all the rest of them. Well, except for '————War (1899–1902).' "

I peered over in amazement. These puzzles were nearly impossible to complete. I wondered: Did she have the key somewhere?

" 'Course not! Those don't come out till the next week." It was Sunday's paper; she had done it, all right.

"You do crosswords a lot?"

"Well, Sundays I do."

I looked over at some of the clues she had solved. "Successful" (ONTOPOFTHEWORLD). "Geneva's lake" (LEMAN). "Swiss abstractionist" (KLEE). I pointed to the last two. "How did you know those?"

"Oh, I lived in Switzerland for some time. My husband and I moved over there when we were first married. He was in the diplomatic corps."

I kept asking; this was the sort of bag lady which I had thought, from living with the homeless, was largely mythical: the fallen princess–bag lady. She spoke some Italian and French. After she and her husband split up, "things just began to fall apart." She wore two coats and a sweater; her face was wrinkled, and her eyes were blue. I stood up after a moment to get some more ice. As I turned to go back to the table, I noticed that Carlos and the others were standing up, gathering their flight bags. Carlos looked at me and gestured toward the door. The ride was here. I walked back to my nurse. "God bless you," I whispered.

The others had piled into the sedan, parked in the alley, by the time I arrived, but they held open the door for me. The driver, spotting me in the rearview mirror, abruptly shifted back into PARK and spun around to stare. For a moment I was ignorant enough to think he was looking at my eye.

"*Who invited this gabacho?*" he demanded of Carlos, maybe assuming I didn't speak Spanish, maybe not caring if I did.

Carlos began to explain, but the man didn't listen. He just interrupted, vehemently. "*¡Chinga!*" he swore. "*You know what kind of idiocy it is to hang out with gabachos? Which one of you dragged me into this? You know what he could do to us?*" Patiently, Carlos continued to try and get a word in; the others fidgeted, looking worried and embarrassed. For my part, hearing this man object because of the color of my skin only aroused the rancor I had been unable to vent at the Neanderthal. They seemed to operate on the same racist principle. I wasn't going to budge, no matter what he said—not after what I'd been through. If it came to blows, this time I was ready.

Fortunately, Victor joined the fray, and even Timoteo put in a word on my behalf. Still agitated, the man at least quieted down. He eyed me suspiciously again in the rearview mirror, and then finally shifted into DRIVE without a word. We creeped from the alley onto the street, and within moments were back on an L.A. freeway, speeding away to yet another part of the unknown city.

It was a fairly long drive, and on the way the guys told him the whole story—of the aborted trip with the *coyote*, of the Toronado fiasco, and then, finally, of their journey through the skies. Carlos, now referring to the guys as *"los aeromozos"*—the jet kids, loosely translated—was almost boasting of their experience: desperate necessity, in a very short time, had turned into exploit. As the chapters unfolded, the driver glanced back at me again and again, and his glare seemed to soften and then even warm. *"Really?"* he kept asking the others. *"—him?"* When the facts were finally out I, the *gringo* guide, came out looking pretty good.

"But why did the cuate (slang for "cousin, Mexican guy") *punch you in the eye?"* he finally asked, his first words to me.

"It wasn't a Mexican that did it," I explained. *"It was another white guy."*

"What!"

"He saw me speaking Spanish with Mexicans, and I guess he thought I was some kind of traitor." It was the only explanation that made any sense.

It took a moment for this to sink in. Here was a racial warfare twist the driver had never considered: the enemy punching out one of their own! He had to confirm it with the others, and then broke into wild laughter. This was hilarious! Like the Russians blowing up one of their own tanks because of a squabble between commanders. He turned around, and to my surprise offered his hand and a greeting: *"¡Bienvenido a Los Ángeles!"* Welcome to L.A.! Welcome to the Hispanic team!

Acceptance is a wonderful thing, but I was pretty sure the man still had misunderstood. He liked me for the same reason the Neanderthal hated me—because, he thought, I had spurned my own kind and effectively switched sides. Nothing could be further from the truth; in my view, it was the team mentality, the whole idea of sides, that was flawed. But that, apparently, was going to be a hard message to get across in Los Angeles.

We left the highway and were soon in a dark neighborhood of small frame houses, most of them peeling and deteriorating, the kind of neighborhood where the front lawn is a parking lot for pickup trucks and low-riders, where trees are for chaining up dogs, where dust blows and babies play. It was evidently Hispanic, though it was hard to be sure in the gloom. We pulled up next to a house like any other, squeezed in between two parked cars, and climbed out. I couldn't wait for the couch or even the floor I imagined waiting for me inside; it had been a very long day.

We walked into the shadow of the house, and there for the first time I, and perhaps Carlos and the others, realized that this ride hadn't just been given as a favor. The man was a friend of a distant relative, not the relative. He expected to be paid—extortionately, as it turned out. *"How much does he want?"* I whispered to Carlos as he and the others conferred.

"Fifty dollars apiece."

"What!"

"Don't worry—we'll cover yours. That was the deal we made."

"But fifty dollars—that's ridiculous!"

They went about discussing how they could appease the man. Obviously, they didn't have that much apiece right now. He said he could wait for the rest, that he trusted them, that he knew their cousin Martín. As a favor, he said, he'd let them sleep in the van over there, until they could sort out other arrangements tomorrow. He pointed to a broken-down vehicle on blocks in what was once a backyard, but which now, scattered with metal objects and other junk, was resigned to some vague utilitarian purpose. *"Muchas gracias,"* said Carlos to the man, with no irony in his voice at all. I could hardly believe his stoicism. Welcome to Los Angeles, indeed.

The *coyote* entered his warm house and, as we walked into the yard, a cat shot out from underneath the van. Ismael and Victor, pulling together, opened the rusty door. We leaned in, lit a cigarette lighter, and turned up its flame to have a look. Two dirty blankets lay crumpled on the metal floor, around them a tire jack and cigarette butts—a real *pollo* way station, all right. What a way to end a glorious trip! Flight bags in hand, the five of us climbed in. A resounding clunk from the vicinity of Timoteo's head alerted us to the fact that two iron bars ran the length of the ceiling, making it even harder to maneuver inside. We guessed it must have carried garments, like a dry cleaner's delivery truck. Discomfort, however, was a state with which my companions were well acquainted. We lay down sardinelike on one of the blankets, spread the other blanket on top, and, for pillows, wedged the flight bags under our heads. My eye throbbed as the blood ran to it; just the same, I could have fallen asleep within seconds. Unfortunately, I happened to be in the middle, and everyone else was excited—they had made it!—and wanted to talk.

"*The door in the airport,*" said Ismael, "*did you see it? The one that slid open when we walked up to it? It was like a genie!*"

"*How about that music, through the little ear-speakers!*" said Carlos. "*And the waitress . . . ahhhh!*" There was laughing, ribbing, a mention of Darla Derringer, the stripper.

"*I didn't care for the moving staircase,*" said Timoteo.

"*We're just glad you didn't throw up on it,*" said Carlos, to laughter. "*Sssssshh,*" he then added, trying to control his own giggles. "*Shut up!*"

There was a long pause, as the mirth subsided. "*Hey, Victor,*" said Ismael.

"*Yeah?*"

"*Ever get that pressure out of your ears?*" The tittering broke out again, all the more inevitable for being supposedly ill advised. Finally they could make fun of his ignorance, which all but Carlos, probably, had shared, but which only Victor had admitted. I thought it was a low blow.

"*Sssssssh,*" said Carlos again, noticing my silence. "*Ted is trying to sleep.*"

"*If only I could,*" I said.

"*What's wrong?*"

"*My pockets are too full of these goddamn pesos!*"

It was nighttime again before we arrived at the home of Cousin Martín. Most of the day we spent in and around the van, waiting for the *coyote* to get home from his job in a plant nursery so he could take us to Martín's and finish the job. His wife, while we were waiting, invited us in for a meal and also let us use the phone; Carlos surprised me by ringing up two uncles of his who also lived in Los Angeles—Cándido and Esteban, both middle aged. They agreed to float him a loan to pay off the *coyote.*

"You know more people in this state than I do," I commented, and Carlos grinned. We picked up the uncles on the way to Martín's, and they paid the *coyote.* That behind us, we looked forward to a big reunion.

Our next stop was a strange sort of industrial-residential area which could only have resulted from a lack of zoning laws. Except for the large warehouses, everything was one or two stories, with lots of brick and concrete and very few living things; all the soil, it seemed, had been paved over. Those windows which were unbroken seemed clouded, dirtied by the air. The neighborhood, I was told, was San Pedro. We pulled up at a curbside along a busy avenue, just before a driveway closed off by a six-foot chain-link fence. The fence extended around a small lot containing an old school bus and other metal artifacts, ending at a squat, one-story building also set against the street. Behind the fence, a small dog snarled at us.

"What are we doing here?" I asked.

"¡Oso!" cried Uncle Cándido. *"¡Oso! Don't you recognize your uncle?"* *Oso* means "bear," a funny misnomer for such a small dog. It calmed down as Cándido put his shoulder against a section of the fence on wheels, a six-foot sliding gate which opened slightly for us to enter. Oso wagged his tail as we came in. It was dusk, and we were at the front door of Martín's place, which was to be our home for the next several weeks.

Flashes of light illuminated the old bus, parts of the fence, and cars in the driveway as we walked in. Martín's was, in fact, a welding shop outdoors, and a small windowless living area indoors. Resident in the States for several years, Martín, in his late twenties, was already a small businessman. His main product was custom decorative ironwork; most of his clients were interested in security gratings for their doors and windows. We walked past his pickup truck, outfitted with racks for transporting his creations, and past storage shelves for long iron bars and pipes. There was a small painting area outfitted with a spray compressor. And then, rounding a corner, we came upon the building's patio, its walls bright with the light of Martín's acetylene torch.

Sparks flew into the night as Martín, wearing a steel welder's mask and bent over his task, finished attaching a row of scrolls to a bar. One young Mexican was holding two bars steady for him, his eyes shut and head turned in the other direction; two more watched from a distance. We joined the two, and waited. Eventually, Martín straightened his stiff back and then lifted the mask to wipe his face and take a breather. It was at this moment that he saw us. Turning off the torch, he marched over, shaking hands with the uncles and looking the others up and down.

"*Well, well! Where did you get those ridiculous clothes?*"

Carlos and Victor turned a little red, and I laughed out loud. In the tension and excitement of our journey between two little Mexicos, we had forgotten how peculiar the clothing looked out of context. Carlos's cardigan, Ismael's high-top "Cons," and, best of all, Timoteo's seersucker suit, the jacket once again closed with all three buttons—I had stopped trying to change his habits— looked like a parody of Anglo clothing tastes.

"*We got them at the swap meet,*" said Carlos, with a grin, "*for the airplane.*"

"*What airplane?*" asked Martín.

"*The airplane we came on.*"

"*You came on an airplane?*" Martín glanced over at the uncles, gestured at the guys as though they were crazy, and swore amiably. He was an old U.S. hand, but still he was impressed. *Los aeromozos* were pretty cool. "*Come on in, let's eat.*"

The three other young Mexicans followed us inside. Already at the sink, doing the dishes, was a middle-aged, one-armed man. "*Supper?*" he asked Martín. "*Lunch,*" Martín responded—lunch, for Mexicans, is the big meal of the day and, though no one had complained of hunger, Martín had been around. He knew that when you traveled in the States, Mexican style, you went without. In fact, it had been twenty-four hours since we last ate. Martín brought out some beers, and the sound of the caps being twisted off mixed with the hiss and sputter of eggs on the stove.

The cook, I would learn later, was named Luis. He was in Los Angeles to try and take his younger brother, a man who had encountered only hard times and a drinking problem in America, back to Mexico, where their family were neighbors to Martín's. Luis had lost his arm in a tractor accident elsewhere in California when he was much younger. He wasn't much help around the welding table, but in the kitchen he made a great contribution. Quickly he cooked up a huge quantity of scrambled eggs, mixed with green and red peppers, corn tortillas, and beans, and set the table with a hot tomato sauce he prepared with a stone mortar and pestle, common in Mexico, and strong white cheese cut into little cubes. As usual, there was no silverware; we just scooped everything up with rolled pieces of tortilla. The food was gone within minutes, and Luis, who had been watching over us, re-stocking the stack of hot tortillas, cooked up another batch. The effect was pure euphoria.

As Carlos and the others spoke to the uncles and Martín about Phoenix, the journey, and me, I looked around. A living room and a bedroom branched off from the kitchen; down the hall was a small bathroom with shower. But it was questionable whether the space had ever been intended for habitation. The only see-through window was set over the kitchen sink and looked onto the patio/welding area. The other rooms had small opaque windows at ceiling level, lined with paper and sealed with bars; even with the lights on, the rooms were dark. The security bars and the nonhuman design of the rooms said a lot about the neigh-borhood outside: that it was rough, that it was industrial. They made you feel glad to be inside, as though the shop were a sort of sanctuary.

Under the sagging couch, behind the color TV, in the lower shelf of a bookcase, and in a closet were a wide assortment of well-used blankets, comforters, and pillows: the living room was not only for relaxing, it was evidently also a dormitory. Including us, nine men, I would soon learn, slept there most nights. Those who were able paid Martín some rent or bought groceries. Most left during the day; if they stayed around, they helped with the welding. I was a guest at Martín's Decorative Ironworks and Hostel.

Oso began to bark again, and Martín left the kitchen to see who was at the gate. He returned with Anabel, the laundry girl. This was definitely a step up the ladder: being able to *employ* someone to do the "women's jobs." The guys nodded their approval—Martín was doing all right. She stopped and stared at me as she came in. *"It's okay,"* Martín reassured her, *"there's no problem with him."*

But apparently that was not her concern. *"What happened to your eye?"* she said worriedly, coming over to take a closer look. I began to explain, but already she had gone over to Luis. *"Where's the salt?"* Getting punched out was turning out to be a great way to get female attention.

Anabel mixed the salt with a few drops of water in a saucer, and then came and leaned over me. *"I'm going to put this under your eye,"* she said. *"It will keep it from getting black."* She smoothed it on gently. *"Make sure you put on more if this comes off."* I promised I would.

As we sat, more of the other residents returned. Some stopped to chat, but others, looking exhausted from a long day, simply nodded, slipped into the living room, found their blankets, took off their shoes, and lay down. By the time we finally said good night to Uncles Cándido and Esteban, there were seven bodies around the perimeter of the living room, and the peaceful drone of slow, heavy breathing. We scrounged some extra blankets, staked out small plots from what was left of the floor, and joined them. I felt curiously at home: though we were strangers here, there was a great feeling of security, of safety in numbers, of the peace of routine and stasis. We weren't going to be moving for a while; we were in the company of future friends. I slept hard and long.

The next day we showered and hung around, resting, watching TV, and watching Martín work. He had the work habits of America's first immigrants—up at dawn, to bed at dusk, quick and efficient labor all during the day, which somehow he mixed with constant banter with those around him. He was my age, built like an acrobat, and, until I stood next to him one day, I would have said he was my size—but Martín was in fact two or three inches shorter. The illusion came from his commanding presence, and his dynamism. He had dark hair, over his ears, a black mustache, and glimmering dark eyes, always ready to size up the next task, return a gibe, or make a scandalous remark. His favorite winter shirt was a white turtleneck sweater—at least, it was white at the beginning of the week. That it was white again after the laundry girl visited every weekend was a tribute to another kind of industry.

Though the business didn't have a name, sign, or telephone listing, the phone was always ringing. Martín's reputation for good, inexpensive ironwork had spread by word of mouth over the years, first through the Mexican community and then, as Martín learned some English, into black and white areas. As "Dogie," Martín's oldest friend and trusted helper told me, they had taken English classes together for a while in the evenings at a local high school. Martín, who had not finished high school in Mexico, had studied furiously for six months. He would have studied a lot longer if the teacher hadn't made the mistake of telling him how good his English was getting. The compliment, to Martín, was as good as a diploma. *"What I don't know yet I am sure to pick up,"* he told Dogie. *"Now I know enough for business, so now I know enough."* Though perhaps three-quarters of the callers were Spanish speaking, Martín always answered the phone with "Hello." It was a courtesy to his customers-to-be— as well as, perhaps, a first-line defense against La Migra.

Those first few days the guys had little desire to go outside the gates; one of the other young men had told Victor there were *"lots of Negroes out there."* This caused much murmuring and consternation among the others; Carlos went so far as to verify it with his cousin. *"What's wrong with the Negroes?"* I asked, remembering their suspicions of the Santa Monica Holiday Inn clerk who had helped them out. They all just shook their heads. It had the vagueness of something conveyed, overheard, not the certainty of personal experience. I felt sure it was a superstition that firsthand dealings would dispel.

"Negroes" sometimes passed along the sidewalk outside the big gate and looked in to see what was up; Martín knew some of them, and occasionally waved. It was Friday, and that night Martín said he'd take us out. The five of us, his old friend Dogie, and one-armed Luis, all piled into his '69 Chevrolet Impala, four in front and four in back. This particular evening, desiring some personal space in the way Americans do, I was a little exasperated to see that, even though there was no need for it—Martín had another vehicle, the truck—we were going the sardine route again. I made some joke, dropped some hints, about the difficulty of breathing or something, but got no response. Deciding to be more blunt, I inquired: "Doesn't this make the police suspicious, an older car like this filled with so many people?" Dogie answered no, that in L.A. you don't worry about things like that—in a way that made me wish I had never asked. To the Mexicans, there simply was nothing out of the ordinary about this sort of travel.

We pulled into a McDonald's drive-in lane and up to the menu board. Martín did all the talking; he was no foreigner here. "Eight Big Mac, eight larch french fry, eight Coke, big." After a few moments the order taker repeated Martín's request, but it was all for naught: Martín was already pulling around to the pickup window.

Martín insisted on paying for everything; I was the only one to protest, perhaps because I was the only one with money, perhaps because I just did not understand. "Ted," said Martín in English, "my life is good now. I have lots of money, I have lots of work. Sometime, maybe I don't have money. Then, you buy the Big Mac!" The others laughed as they heard a phrase they recognized, and Martín smiled. "Lots of money," to Martín, was more like poverty level where I came from. His cash flow might be okay, but Martín couldn't have much to fall back on if problems arose. Certainly he didn't have health insurance; probably he would lose everything if the INS were to find out about him. And yet Martín was more generous—generosity considered in relative terms, the most meaningful—than 99 percent of the people I had ever known.

We drove a couple of miles down the boulevard to a crowded parking lot, where we parked and Dogie distributed the food. If you think a sedan filled with eight people feels crowded, try one filled with eight people eating McDonald's hamburgers, trying to balance their Cokes, trying to find a place for all the used wrappers. I experienced a small wave of claustrophobia, but it subsided. Perhaps it was Martín's jokes, or the bright *ranchera* music on the AM radio; but probably it was all these guys with uncertain futures, at the mercy of any powers that be, having such an unabashed great time, enjoying each other's company, possessed of nothing in the world but their hope and their friends, led by one of their own who had made it in this big foreign city. There was a lot to make you feel good in that old car.

Dinner finished, we climbed out of the Impala—not to take a pee, I realized, but because we were at our destination. I was a bit alarmed as we walked toward the squat little bar, with the old neon sign on top advertising "Rita's Elbow Rest"—there were a couple of pickup trucks in the parking lot, and it looked like a real redneck hangout.

"*I thought we were going to the 'El Paso,'* " I said to Martín.

"*This* is *the 'El Paso,'* " he said. "*They just changed the name. Didn't bother to get a new sign.*"

As we entered, I realized that the era of *gringos* in Rita's Elbow Rest had come to an end. It was rednecks now, not Hispanics, who would be worried upon walking into the dimly lit bar. There was not a blue eye in sight. A full-size pool table dominated the floor, illuminated by a light hanging directly overhead; everything else lay in its shadow: the bar itself, at the end of the room, the assorted stools along the walls, the doorway leading to the rest rooms. With our arrival, the place was very nearly filled.

"*Puros mexicanos?*" I asked Martín, who was at the bar, ordering eight beers.

"*Mexicanos y salvadoreños,*" he answered. "*The owners are from El Salvador, and there are a lot of Salvadorans in Los Angeles. But we're closer to a Mexican neighborhood.*"

Besides no *gringos*, there were virtually no women. Two waitresses helped to take beer orders and collect the empty bottles, but bars, for Mexicans, were places that men gathered, not women. Unless you were looking for a hooker, you met women somewhere else, someplace less sinful.

Carlos and I, leaning by the pool cue rack, assessed the female situation. One waitress was rather heavy, wearing vast synthetic slacks and a blouse of the sort once known as a muumuu. Because of the limited space, she brushed against almost everyone as she parted the sea of men, taking orders. She piqued a certain sort of interest. "*Mucho jamón por dos huevos,*" was all Carlos had to say—lots of ham for two eggs. The other waitress was slender, dressed in jeans and a soft blouse, with a pretty face and hair that looked authentically auburn. Probably, I thought, she was Salvadoran—there were fewer mestizos there and more direct descendants of Europeans, especially among those from the professional classes who had had the wherewithal to escape the civil war. She looked up and saw me watching her.

My friends were my passport, and I had no trouble with other patrons of the bar, though a couple came up just to chat and see what I was all about. Dogie challenged me to a game of pool. I beat him but then lost the next game to Martín. All the while, every time I looked up, it seemed I was meeting the glance of the pretty waitress. This was more than chance, as no one on earth seemed more adept at avoiding men's eyes than the Mexican and Central American women I had been around in the past few months—and with the men as aggressive as they were, it was a necessary survival skill.

But it presented a problem. The better looking of the two lone women in the crowded bar seemed to find me—an outsider—attractive, and the feeling was mutual. For months I had been walking a sort of sexual tightrope with my Mexican friends. I didn't want to show undue interest in females they had designs on for fear of awakening macho rivalry. And yet at the same time it was important to show some sort of interest—some wolfish hunger—to reassure them of my heterosexuality. The unaggressive man was likely to be the butt of the next Mexican faggot joke.

The kind of outsider I was—an American—complicated matters too. A Mexican man could be charismatic, physically attractive, influential, and even rich, but still he couldn't be as powerful—and, therefore, as attractive on the macho scale—as an American with the same qualities. Machismo is obsessed with rivalry, and to a citizen of that proud but very poor country to the south, northern neighbors could be powerful rivals indeed. I enjoyed a degree of acceptance at the bar—but I was worried, just the same, about the insecurities that might be simmering just under the surface of the camaraderie, awaiting a crisis to bring them out. As always, I had to watch my step.

And, of course, the final complication was that, after so many weeks of fraternal living, this woman looked very pretty. I swallowed hard when she came up and asked me if I wanted another beer, but managed a smile and a *"Sí."* The next time I looked up she was behind the bar, looking at me again and pointing to a bottle she had placed in front of an empty stool. I took a deep breath, moved to the bar, and took a seat. She had green eyes, wet-looking lips, a nice voice. She asked where I was from.

"Denver—do you know where that is?"

"No, but it must be nicer than here. Any place would be nicer than here."

"You mean Los Angeles?"

"Yeah, Los Angeles, the bar . . . I'm so tired of it."

"Are you salvadoreña?" She nodded. *"From the capital?"* She

couldn't have been from the countryside. I had read much about El Salvador, and was eager to learn more. But she didn't want to talk about El Salvador. She wanted to talk about me.

"Where did you learn Spanish? You speak it perfectly!"

That was a lie. *"Here and there. In school and in some other countries."*

"I'd love to go to some other countries! But, oh—my situation . . . I can't travel anywhere."

"Why not?"

"Well, uhh, you know—documents."

"Ahh." I looked around the bar to size up the reaction to our little chat. My eyes caught Martín's as he bent over the pool table to line up a shot. The quick wink and lifting of the eyebrows a couple times quickly was his equivalent of a thumbs-up, a "go for it."

"What's your name?"

"Ted. It's short for Theodore—'Teodoro,' *in Spanish."*

"Teodoro, te adoro," she said. This was a timeworn pun among Spanish speakers.

"I adore you, too," I said, laughing with the joke. *"What's your name?"*

"I'm Marisol."

"That's a lovely name."

"Are you American?"

The question caught me off guard; of course I was. *"What do you mean?"*

"Nothing. Oh, you know, a citizen."

"Oh, yeah, sure. Born and raised. Though, actually, I was born outside the country on a military base . . ." But something had caught her attention. It was Martín, holding up two fingers and pointing at his beer bottle and then at the two of us. She blushed slightly; it was becoming on her.

"What's he saying?"

"He is buying two beers for you and me," she said. I winked facetiously at Martín. Marisol opened two more beers and drank hers from the bottle.

"Do you have wishes?" she asked.

"What do you mean?"

"You know, things you wish would come true?"

"Well, sure I do." I take such questions too literally; I started giving it some thought, but she interrupted.

"I'll tell you what my wishes are. . . . You know what I would like? What I would prize most of all? A green card!" She beamed at me, at the thought.

But my bubble suddenly burst. Why had she said that? She had tipped her hand much, much too soon. I was disheartened, deflated. Instead of seeing in me the things I thought she had, she had seen in me a ticket. I wasn't a sex object, but something sexier: a green-card object, a hollow marriage object, a means to an end. I took another swallow of beer, and it tasted bad.

"Ted—isn't that your name? What is it you do?"

"I'm a writer."

"Ooh, a writer! You don't say! Someday, will you write me a poem?"

Someday, I said, I would do that. She would want a love poem, and that's what I would write. A sonnet, maybe, or something shorter, of an unexpected love in an unlikely place, of a poisoned circumstance.

The parts of Los Angeles we frequented were unlike any place I have ever been. Los Angeles, I had read, was after Lima, Peru, the largest Spanish-speaking city on any coast of the Americas. We always had a choice of several Spanish-language radio stations, we picked up Spanish-speaking television stations as clearly as the others, and we were offered Winston cigarettes and a host of other products on billboards in Spanish. There was no need ever, really, to speak English. Food stores carried everything they did in Mexico, and more. In a way, you could feel right at home.

The hospitability of Los Angeles caused problems for my friends, though. Word on the street was that it was so easy for a Mexican to blend in here, so easy for him or her to feel at home, that far too many had come. The labor market for undocumenteds was glutted. This observation was borne out by our experience: despite the many connections of Martín and the uncles, pavement pounding, and a willingness to do almost anything, my friends could find no jobs at all. Our first weeks in the city were a time of waiting, of killing time, of sloth. All morning, usually, we would watch TV—inane Mexican variety shows, breathless soap operas, gory news programs. It was one of the most difficult parts of my travels, much harder than picking oranges. I read welding manuals, English texts, old magazines, newspapers, the thick Mexican comic books known as *novelas*—anything to keep from watching TV.

To move outdoors was always a tremendous relief for me, as the welding shop had slowly become less a cozy sanctuary than a dark little prison. For the others, though, Martín's place remained a safe haven. The street still held dangers, premier among them a racial one. Martín lived right on the border between a Hispanic and a black area. The main grocery store and variety store were deeper into the Hispanic side, but the nearest convenience store was right on the borderline. None of the guys ever went there alone, which I thought was silly until the first time I joined them. Three men were lounging around the door as we exited, waiting to persuade us to part with our change. They started out friendly enough, even using a little Spanish: "*Hey, amigo, ¿qué pasa?* Got any change today for a hungry man?"

"No espeak Ingliss," Carlos said.

"Hey, that's all right, man. *Cambio. ¿Tiene cambio?*"

No, they said, and then the wolves got a little more threatening. These were not poor derelicts but healthy young adults, savvy to the fact that because Mexicans came to work, they usually made money; and that because they didn't trust or were unable to use banks, they tended to carry it with them. The wolves stood up, came too close, demanded instead of asked, felt the pockets of those who said they had no change and asked, "All I find?" We moved off as a group, keeping our money because we outnumbered them. But the tales of larceny in that neighborhood were many. Chicano gangs, as well, were known to prey on the poor Mexicans, though apparently they didn't operate near where we lived.

Besides visiting the convenience store, we went out to play basketball, to buy groceries, to visit acquaintances in other parts of town. They were surprisingly good at basketball, only slightly handicapped, like others from the south of Mexico, by their short stature. Never in my life, in fact, could I remember being the tallest person in a basketball game. We played on courts in public parks, in schoolyards on weekends, wearing street shoes and jeans, working up a sweat and having fun, putting together pickup games with other Mexicans we'd meet. Since we were in California, perhaps it makes some sense to think of these other Mexicans as a "support group": they would share job information, news of home (*"Where are you from?" "Michoacán. How about you all?" "Guerrero." "Heard of any jobs?" "Well, my brother said they might need help next week on his roofing crew"*) and tales of life in Los Angeles. It was networking, there on the grass after forty-five minutes on hot asphalt.

Grocery shopping was another diversion. As in Phoenix, it was an instance of men doing "women's work" by necessity. But there were decisions that didn't have to be made at home: do we buy Budweiser, or do we buy generic beer? Which brand of tortillas is the best? (At home, Mom made them by hand.) Are any of these *salsas* any good, or should we make one ourselves? Like many Mexicans I had met, they weren't big on fruit or fresh produce, so I usually did my shopping for those separately. One day, though, when Carlos had joined me in the produce section, I heard him exclaim in surprise. *"Híjole!"*

"What is it?"

"Look at this!" He held up a mango.

"What's wrong, is it bad?"

"No, no, it's from my state—look at the sticker." "Iguala, Guerrero," it read—*"that's only one hundred kilometers from my town. That's where I went to college!"* Carlos looked at the mango as though it were an old friend.

"Well," I suggested, *"let's get it."*

Carlos looked at the price. *"Seventy-eight cents!"* I told him that seemed about right to me.

"But at home, these cost—" he calculated the exchange rate *"—three cents."*

"You're kidding!"

Carlos shook his head slowly. *"My father sells them to the grocer for about two cents."*

Another good break was going to church. Though there were calendars of the madonna on the wall in Martín's, and Victor and Ismael wore crucifixes, they had never struck me as a particularly devout group. They were Catholics more by culture than conviction. But they learned of a bilingual church—the first service was in English, to blacks, and the second, in Spanish, to Hispanics—a short bus ride away, and began to attend every weekend. The white priest's Spanish was horrible, the sermons stock and trite, but toward the end of the first service I attended, our presence made a little more sense to me. We were here to meet girls. When the priest said it was time to "share the peace of Christ," my friends ranged up to five or six rows back to shake the hands of attractive young women. They had, I then realized, been scoping them out during most of the service. Church was the undocumenteds' singles scene.

On our way out the door that first Sunday, a deacon passed out printed invitations, in Spanish, to a dance the next Saturday night. The timing, I thought, was clever—give them out before the service, and by the end half of the young people would already have left. But to my surprise, the man did not hand me one. Probably, he had thought that I was coincidentally walking among the group of Mexican guys, and was not interested in a Spanish-speaking dance. I stopped and walked back up to him. He looked at me as I held out my hand.

"Could I have one, please?" I said.

"One of what, sir?" he replied with a confused look, perhaps startled to hear the Spanish.

"An invitation to the dance. Isn't that what you've got there?"

"You want one? Err, um, of course," he said, fumbling with the stack, trying to peel one off.

"Thank you."

Something similar occurred on the city bus later that week. I preceded the group up the bus steps and discovered the transfer I had in my hand was from the day before. As I began to dig around in my pockets for the right one, the bus driver grumbled at me to get out of the way so the "other passengers" could pass through.

"They're with me," I said.

"What? Who?"

And then there was the time I was with the guys in a liquor mart. Carlos, Timoteo, Victor, and I were standing near the door, waiting for Ismael to get through the checkout line. The only person near us was a white security guard. I began saying something to Carlos, and was surprised to hear the guard interrupt by saying, "Pardon me?" The only other non-Hispanic in the area, he thought I was talking to him.

And so it went in L.A., a city of races and racism. Later, back in Phoenix, I would relate the doughnut shop incident to a scruffy white farm hand I knew who was raised in Los Angeles. His words of consolation summed up the situation better than he probably realized: "Shit, you're lucky you wasn't with niggers," he said. "If you'da been talkin' to niggers, that guy that punched you woulda gone out and got his friends!"

One afternoon Martín spent on and off the phone, in long conversation with someone he apparently couldn't hear too well. He shouted, then spoke softly, and for once didn't pay any attention to us. That evening, as Luis cooked dinner, Martín came in, washed up with his dirty bar of Lava soap, snapped open a can of Bud, and leaned against the refrigerator with a big smile on his face.

"Well?" said Dogie.

Martín took a long swill, and then announced it quietly. *"They're coming. They're coming next week."*

"*Really?*" "*Who?*" "*They'll stay here?*" "*How old is the kid?*" "*How about her sister?*"

Martín's wife and son were on the way. It was a moment Martín had long awaited, a moment when he was secure enough in his business and his situation to send for his family. It had been six years in coming. He had left Mexico a year after marrying; his first son, whom he had never seen, had been conceived during a trip home three years later. Their firstborn, a daughter, had died of pneumonia soon after the marriage; it was frustration over his inability to afford a good doctor in the city and the transportation to get her there that led Martín to America in the first place, Carlos told me.

Dogie, with more than twenty border crossings to his credit, would take the truck down to San Diego to pick them up. He knew the Tijuana–Chula Vista area, its dirt roads and canyons, its reliable *coyotes*. The two would be in good hands. Martín handed out beers to the rest of us, but then Luis outdid him with a bottle of strong, clear mescal he had been saving. Ismael and Victor left to brave *los negros* of the convenience store and pick up some extra goodies for dinner.

It was a grand celebration. And there was an even grander one when, early the next week, the honking from Dogie's truck, waiting to be let in the main gate, signaled the arrival of Martín's family. Lupita, with Martín Jr. in her arms and the help of Dogie, descended from the truck and into their new home. Both looked strung out and overwrought, but Lupita, anyway, looked very glad to be there. Martín Jr.—or "Junior," as he was soon christened ("*Yoonyor,*" they pronounced it)—met his mustachioed father for the first time, and, tossed a foot or so aloft, promptly burst into tears. This delighted Martín, who thanked the Virgin it was not too late to make him into a man.

There was celebration for the next several days, as all Martín's friends and acquaintances came by to greet the newcomers. It was thrilling for me to see this change in Martín: his eyes, if possible, were even more animated than before, his step lighter, his diligence greater. But through it all Carlos and his friends must have realized something I did not: that the arrival of Martín's wife would fundamentally change life around the workshop. The man runs the family in Mexico, but one domain still belongs to the woman: the household. Its operation is her responsibility, and it soon became clear that Lupita had not expected to find herself managing a hostel. She exercised her traditional right to clean the place up and, sensing the pressure, the boarders began one by one to leave. Martín just shrugged—he wasn't to blame, and there wasn't much he could do about it. The first of us to go was Timoteo, who over the past few weeks had become reacquainted with friends who worked at a downtown office building, where he, too, might get a start as a janitor. We also said goodbye to Ismael, who had a relative in an apartment building across town where he would be able to crash for a while. That left only Carlos, Victor, and me.

It was Carlos's Uncle Cándido who came up with a solution for us. After church one Sunday we went to visit him at his tiny, wood-framed duplex. If Carlos could be regarded as the American newcomer and Martín as a medium-term resident, Uncle Cándido was the old-timer. Arriving as a *bracero* in the 1950s, he had worked all over California, mostly in the fields but also in an auto body shop, until it was discovered six years ago that his kidneys were failing and he needed regular dialysis. Fortunately for him, the body shop's insurance policy covered him. To comfort him, his wife arrived, with two children, Emilio and Alejandra. They then had two more, born in Los Angeles, Alex and Erica. *"You didn't give them Mexican names?"* I asked him. Cándido shrugged. *"They're American,"* he said.

Breakfast was another strange mixture: pancakes, white Mexican cheese, and scrambled eggs with peppers and *salsa*. Even in a city with a Hispanic population as large as Los Angeles's, it was clear that the road to the American way of life wasn't very long.

"Do you ever think of yourself as American?" I asked Cándido. He shook his head. *"I'm a Mexican, through and through."*
"Will you ever go back to Mexico?"

At this, Cándido laughed. He showed me the marks on the inside of his arms where the dialysis machine was connected and disconnected twice a week. *"If I go back to Mexico,"* he said, *"I will die."* A poor man could not afford dialysis in Mexico.

As the men sat around the kitchen table drinking coffee after breakfast, Cándido shared an idea he had for us. *"Around the corner,"* he said, *"is an apartment building run by a man I know. I have talked to him about you. He says if we can come up with the deposit, he will wait a month before requiring your first month's rent."*

"A place of our own!" said Carlos. *"But uncle—"*

"I will lend you the money for the deposit," said Cándido.

The building manager, as it turned out, also had a friend who was a small trophy manufacturer and needed a trainee engraver. Pay was minimum wage, but Carlos snapped it up. Victor found part-time work with a friend doing construction for an Anglo teacher who was fixing up his house. And two other young Mexicans with jobs joined us in the small one-bedroom apartment, to help make ends meet.

It was a turning point. As I had found with Alonso in Texas, the employers of these Mexicans were not interested in hiring me. Even when they had openings, it was easier for them just to hire another Mexican: why take a risk with a white guy, willing for some strange reason to work for so little pay—among Mexicans, no less! It sounded suspicious. And sitting around the apartment all day alone was not my idea of a good time. So with handshakes, several sheets of addresses in rural Mexico, and some good memories, I prepared to return to Phoenix.

To my surprise, the airport limousine service I called the evening of my departure told me they didn't service our neighborhood. The cab fare, I knew, would be exorbitant, so I tried another. Forty minutes before the flight, however, they hadn't shown up either. The neighborhood apparently was worse than I thought. So I rang up Dogie on Cándido's phone. He was there in ten minutes, and I made my plane. In L.A., if you're Mexican—or with Mexicans—I guess you rely on your friends.

Chapter 4

Phoenix to Florida at 25 MPH

WHEN I RETURNED TO the orchards outside Phoenix, it was almost Christmastime. Routine and regularity were now a way of life at camp: the trimmed-down labor force meant work every day for every man except the sick or injured, followed by evenings of exhaustion and lassitude. Though some of my former students inquired about more classes, much of the momentum had been lost. Also, education had gained an enemy: a black-and-white television now presided over the living room of the ramshackle old house, establishing a claim on the men's leisure time. Every night thirty or forty eyes fixed on the fuzzy picture of Phoenix's weak UHF Spanish-language channel, catching up on *Leonela*, the Venezuelan soap opera, or other dramas like *Weddings of Hate* and *You Are My Destiny*.

The prospect of five days' break at Christmas—now less than two weeks away—was a further distraction. It promised a chance to blow off some steam, a break from oranges, and, for a few, even brief visits home. Most men could hardly wait. But a core of workers was impatient about vacation for a very different reason: they wanted to earn more money. Heavy rains had made work impossible several times since I had left, as soggy orchards swallowed ladders, tractors, and shoes. Besides, they felt, when you came this far to work, who needed Christmas vacation? Some of these ambitious men were preparing to head to Florida, where the wages were lower but where longer hours made up for it, where the citrus season lasted not only till May but well into the summer, and where, they had heard, jobs were still available. The talk of travel was contagious—without my friends there, Phoenix seemed a less interesting place—and I started looking into rides to Florida myself.

For most of the men, there were two choices: form a group, pool your money, and buy a car; or form a group, pool your money, and negotiate with a *coyote*. Unfortunately for me, most of the groups I knew about had a surplus of members already. Cousins, brothers, and buddies all wanted to join in when one or two men announced their intention to leave. I checked with four or five groups who had made it to the money-pooling stage, but none had openings. And even if they had, one man confided to me, members would be worried that once a *coyote* learned I was coming he would get nervous and, like the animal, would disappear without a trace.

Matilde, the neighbor of Fortino and Rebeca, had an idea: *"Why don't you become a coyote?"* she asked. *"One of my husbands did that once. He rented a U-Haul, filled it up with men, and then tied a bunch of bicycles to the back door so it would look like he was moving house. Then he drove to Chicago and let them all go. He made three thousand dollars!"* I had to answer that smuggling wasn't quite my line. But a few days later it did give me an idea.

Twenty more men arrived from Querétaro, the home of many already working at the camp. As was traditional, the orchard became their way station, a stop on the underground railroad: while the next phase of their travel was being arranged, they slept out under the trees, relying on the workers for advice and an occasional meal. Immigration and the ranch owners were aware this happened, of course, but because the new arrivals usually came and left within a matter of days, and because they stayed hidden deep in the woods, there was little that could be done about it.

These new arrivals, however, had unusual difficulties. They discovered that, because it was high season for travel to Florida, three of the area's well-known *coyotes* were already out on jobs. A fourth had a sick daughter he wouldn't leave. I visited the men in the orchard, and was in El Mirage pondering their situation one day when a contact told me of a Florida-based *coyote* who had arrived in town the night before. He was looking for a load of *pollos* to take back home with him, he said. *"Can you arrange for us to meet?"* I asked my acquaintance. He thought he could, and the next night I waited for the *coyote* known only as *La Víbora*, "The Viper."

I was in a booth at *El Sombrero*, the Top Hat bar, when a man walked in, about an hour after the time I suggested. It was a weeknight, late, and we were the only customers. Though curious, I concentrated on my cigarette and tried not to look up; if he were La Víbora, he would know who I was. The man, dressed in dark clothes and a dark cowboy hat, sat first on a bar stool near the door. Though across the room, I could almost feel him scanning, sniffing, deciding whether to remain or to quietly back out. Several minutes later I heard the sound of boots approaching on the wooden floor. I looked up; he had committed himself. He was Hispanic, with a long, droopy mustache and black circles under his quick eyes. Without a word he began to sit down across the table from me, his hat still on; perhaps to see what he was made of, I half-stood as he did so, thrusting out my hand.

"Ted Conover," I said.

The man shot a glance at the bar and looked profoundly uncomfortable. He ignored my hand. "La Víbora," he returned.

I had to stifle the urge to smile. For other people to call you something like that was one thing; to use the nickname on yourself was another. It reminded me of professional wrestling; it was like me calling myself "Thor" or "The Exterminator." Lupe Sánchez had told me of a smuggler he once knew called *"El Vénomo,"* the Venom. How could you take seriously anyone with a name like that? "The Viper"? A small wave of relief passed over me.

The waitress called out from behind the bar, and we ordered two Buds. "Just into town?" I asked after a while.

La Víbora looked at me distastefully. "Where are you from?" was his reply. He glanced over my shoulder, searching for the trap. He was a *coyote*, through and through.

"Here. Or from Colorado, really. I came to teach some classes at the camps. I was thinking maybe we could help each other."

The beers came. La Víbora didn't say anything.

"See, I need to get to Florida for Christmas. But I don't have the bucks. Now, I heard you're looking for some guys to take. And I know where some are. I'll put you in touch, but in return I want to go with them to Florida, for free." The experience, I still thought, would be worth the risk of doing business with La Víbora.

La Víbora took a swallow. "Let's get something straight. It's not me looking for the guys, okay? It's somebody I know— a friend." His pause was long and dramatic. "Now, how many guys is there?"

"About twenty."

"Well, all he got is a pickup. He can't fit twenty in there."

"Camper top?" I asked. La Víbora nodded. "Well, he could take some of them, then. Maybe he'll want to come back for the rest. They got a place to work in Florida—if they don't have all the money, you could work it out with the rancher."

"When do they want to leave? Right away?"

"Right away."

La Víbora took another drink. "I'll need to talk to them. Why don't we go have a chat? We'll go talk to 'em. See what we can work out."

My respect for La Víbora dropped a couple of notches. Did he really believe I would fall for that? Their location was my only bargaining chip. There was no way I was taking La Víbora to the orchard. "I've got a different idea," I said. "Meet me here in the parking lot tomorrow at this time. I'll bring a couple of them with me. We can talk."

La Víbora nodded. Hat still on, he rose to leave; I offered

my hand again just to annoy him, and this time we shook. I watched as he moved toward the door. Even if he cut a deal with the men, there was nothing to prevent him from pulling a knife on me at the last minute, or twenty miles out of town, and making me get out of the truck. I knew he didn't trust me, and that was yet another reason not to trust him. On the other hand, it could be a fascinating ride to Florida, for me the ride of a lifetime: how would undercover illegals negotiate such a vast distance, deal with the unexpected? Travel was stressful, and when people were under stress you could learn a lot about them. I walked to a window of the bar and noted the license number of the beat-up pickup truck as La Víbora climbed in—one more thing I knew about him. Then I drove back to camp, slogged through the orchard, and talked with the prospective *pollos*. It was good to have a possibility, they said; wet, filthy, and cold, they were eager to get out soon.

The next morning I went back to visit with a large pot of hot coffee—and discovered they were gone! Beans, wrappers, and various clothes and utensils were scattered about the mud, but no sign that any of them remained. Wondering if they had moved elsewhere in the orchard, I ran to where a crew was picking and asked Mariano, a relative of several of them, where they had gone.

"The coyotes came last night," Mariano said. "They're probably on their way to Florida now."

"What coyotes? Did they have a pickup truck?" Had La Víbora beat me to it?

"No, I think it was a van. Horacio, what kind of car did they leave in?"

"Two vans," shouted the man two trees down.

"Do you know which coyote?"

Mariano shook his head. Nobody knew. Two men apparently had dropped by the previous afternoon, strangers. No, neither wore a mustache. They returned unannounced in the night. The guys hadn't known what time they would come, or even if they would come at all.

I slogged back to the house, back where I'd started, my attempt at brokerage a failure. Noting my despondency, Mariano came up later that day and told me that some men from near his town in Mexico, who worked at a nearby orchard, were buying a car and soon would be leaving. With no better leads to go on, I set out yet again to see if I could persuade a group to let me come.

The ranch was known as Smith's—an unfortunate name for an orchard worked by Mexicans, as almost none of them could pronounce it—(es-SMEET, they said). Old Man Smith lived down the road from it, in an expansive one-story house. Surrounded by carefully spaced palm trees, and with an American flag waving from a tall pole out front, it bore a great resemblance to the visitors' center at a state park. But he housed his workers in trailers. Since the small trailer park, chiseled into a corner of the orchard, was situated right at an intersection of county roads, plainly visible to traffic, he had surrounded it with a six-foot chain-link fence topped with barbed wire. The purpose, I was told, was to prevent early-morning raids by Immigration; but one couldn't help notice the resemblance to a prison work camp. By the time I arrived that evening, the main gate had been shut. I got out of my car and called to a couple of guys having a cigarette just inside.

"Is Emilio Hernández around?"

After low words to the other, one of them nodded. I parked the car, jumped an irrigation culvert, and passed into the gloom of the orchard that abutted the camp. You couldn't really depend on the workers to be home by sundown: Smith's compound, like the finest colleges in England, had a secret, unofficial entrance, known by all, to be used when the gate was locked. You had to work your way, swinging, up the branch of a grapefruit tree, swing your feet over the barbed wire onto the top of a box spring tipped against the inside of the fence, gain your balance and composure, and then step carefully to the roof of a storage shed and shimmy down its drainpipe. I had done it only once, in the daylight—but it was set up very logically. In a few minutes I was back at the front gate, on the inside. The guys there led me to the trailer of the man I was after.

Two of those in the front room nearly bolted when I entered, but others recognized me: *el maestro*, the teacher, that crazy *gringo* who slept in the barn over at Martinolli's. After a chat, I was ushered into the next room, where a card game called conquián was in progress. Hernández, said a player, was already in bed, and a man was dispatched to wake him while I was offered a chair. We talked some more, and as the room slowly filled with men—five, ten, more than fifteen—I realized just how unusual my visit was. Recognizing me was different from knowing me. A couple of men flat out stared; all seemed interested in knowing just what sort of person I was. The room was almost quiet every time I spoke. I sat uncomfortably until another man, wiping the sleep from his eyes, came into the room.

I felt sorry to have dragged him into the limelight, for the bearing of this retiring man seemed designed *not* to call attention to himself. But Emilio Hernández's shuffling step, bowlegs, skinniness, and downturned gaze belied his importance at the camp. Though I did not know it at the time, he was one of the superpickers, an experienced hand who knew how to find work, keep it, and make lots of money at it as well. Where the money went, no one seemed to know—Hernández, thirty, was a confirmed bachelor with no girlfriend back home and no parents living. And yet by all appearances the money was not spent on himself. He wore one of the green American Army shirts, sold at the swap meet on Sundays that were so popular among the Mexicans, an old pair of jeans, and sandals. We shook hands, though he did not meet my gaze, and then, in two facing chairs, surrounded by the throng, we sat down.

Emilio whisked some of his shoulder-length hair back behind an ear, exposing the name label BOUGHTON, sewn on above his shirt pocket. His seemed a reluctant presence.

"*Are you one of the ones going to Florida soon?*" I asked.

"*Sí.*"

I cleared my throat, introduced myself, mentioned Mariano,

and made my request. Then, on impulse, I took a risk and added something I had omitted from earlier presentations. I wanted to go, I explained, for the experience, the knowledge, the ability to describe their lives and situation to people like the Private Boughton who once wore Emilio's shirt, people who were not generally well disposed toward Mexicans in the States. I would share all expenses, I added.

"*Wait a minute,*" said a voice from behind Emilio's chair. "*It's* you *who want to go?*"

I nodded. A clean-cut man with a light brown mop of hair, a stocky build, trimmed mustache, and freckles was looking at me incredulously. It still hadn't quite sunk in.

"With *us?*" he continued.

"*Sí.*"

He suddenly stood back, looked at the others, and laughed out loud. The idea was absurd! A few of them laughed too, but it died out quickly; all could see I was serious.

"*Do you have a car yet?*" I asked.

"*No,*" said Emilio, "*probably tomorrow.*" There was a long pause. "*But you see, the problem is we are full. So many want to come.*"

"*I see.*" I had expected this, from interviews at other camps, and decided to play my last card. "*Well, look at it this way. Having me along is like having an insurance policy. If the car breaks down, or you have any accidents—if anything bad happens, I can do the talking. If we have to buy anything, or stay anywhere, I can do the talking for you. To get to Florida, you'll have to go through places where nobody will speak Spanish, where people will be suspicious. Having me along might help.*"

There was a pause. "*Can you drive? Do you have a license?*" asked the man behind Emilio.

"Of course."

The two consulted briefly. "*We'll have to let you know,*" the man behind Emilio then told me. I said I would come back the next day.

And the next day I was barely able to contain my surprise—
I had not expected a yes. *"Really?"* I answered, trying hard to
act calm. Perhaps it was the insurance angle: at last a group had
decided it might be in their best interests to have me along.
Perhaps it was simply the thought of having an ally. I wondered
if it could be because, for the first time, I had been completely
candid. Whatever the case, they had gotten a car and would be
able to leave as soon as it could run.

"It doesn't run?"

"Nothing serious," said Emilio. *"A little transmission problem,
a little electrical problem. It should be ready Saturday—tomorrow—
but we were thinking of leaving Sunday."* This was a wise move,
made for the usual reasons—the lower numbers of Immigration
and other police. They would pick me up around dusk on Sunday.
We shook hands.

I could barely sleep that Friday night, and all the next day
I was antsy. Once I had gotten this far with another group, only
to wait hours at the designated rendezvous point and not get
picked up. Saying I could come, for them, had been a way of
getting rid of me. I would not get left behind again. First thing
Sunday morning I got a friend to drop me back over at Smith's.

The gate was open and the car was parked between trailers,
already running. I breathed a sigh of relief as Emilio, packing
some blankets into the back of the car, returned my greeting. I
contributed two of my own to the pile. *"Afraid we were going to
leave you, eh?"* he said, grinning.

"No, no, of course not," I said, noting he did not reassure
me they were not.

I had always wondered who goes to those roadside, middle-
of-nowhere used-car lots, the ones with the colored propellers on
strings, strands of bare light bulbs, big white numbers painted
on windshields—*$399.00!!*—one-room sales offices you'd rather
not go in, salesmen trained in psychological warfare. And more
than once I had wondered what ever became of the old family
wagon, the one Dad bought new when I was a kid, the one like

you learned to drive on, the one traded for something better a few years later. But when I saw the Mexicans' car, both questions were answered.

It was a huge Ford Country Squire station wagon, white but dirty, rusting but relatively undented, probably a '70 or '71. I was pleased the tires weren't bald: on three out of four, the tread was actually visible—what more could you ask? After years of faithful service lugging kids and pets to Safeway store and swim club, it appeared to have come to the end of its career. Alas, it did not look as though it would enjoy a quiet retirement.

The hood was up, and I walked around to notice my anonymous questioner from two days before, the man who had been standing behind Emilio. Today he was more friendly. *"Máximo,"* he introduced himself, smiling and offering a greasy hand.

"How's it running?"

"Ohh—pretty good. Just seems to use up a lot of this stuff." He proceeded to empty a can of bright red fluid into the transmission case. I looked around and noticed an entire case of transmission fluid. Good, I thought—they've prepared.

"Nothing else?"

"No one knows," said Máximo with a shrug, *"but Him."* He pointed a finger toward heaven. We would see.

I imagined a lengthy loading process with so many people— from what I could see, there were seven of them, plus me. But the blankets, the tranny fluid, and a case of motor oil were virtually it—these men, I kept forgetting, traveled light. Most of the others in the camp must have been out picking, for the goodbye committee was small, two or three teenagers looking wistfuly from the trailer door. Slowly the others loaded into the car. I made a move for the far back deck—I wanted to be as unobtrusive, as little trouble as possible—but everyone objected: a seat in front had been reserved for me, alongside Máximo and Emilio. They were the other two with driver's licenses, and also the most experienced travelers. The rest of the seating seemed to reflect a status hierarchy: in the middle seat were Emilio's younger brother, Pedro, their cousin, Arturo, and Chucho. Chucho was almost as old, and experienced, as Máximo and Emilio; but the other two seemed to be barely teenagers. In the far back were Moisés, also about our age, and Pancho, the oldest of the group at about forty. Most of the decisions were made by Emilio and Máximo, I noticed; occasionally they also consulted me or Chucho. But they never asked the opinions of boisterous, impetuous Moisés, or timid Pancho, or the boys. Honored to be sitting as part of the ruling junta, I didn't object.

The wagon bottomed out as we left the fenced-in compound. The car was so heavy—the shock absorbers so compressed—that the suspension was rendered irrelevant. I prayed for no rocks on the highways—one more on my long list of prayers, most devoted to getting us out of town and finally onto the highway proper. My plans for the trip had been derailed so many times that I kept expecting the glitch; I was sure something would go wrong to ruin everything. But the Country Squire, piloted by Máximo, kept rolling, first through El Mirage, then Sun City, and finally onto the entrance ramp of Interstate 17, the Black Canyon Freeway. There, for the first time, Máximo really pushed the pedal down, keeping a careful eye on all the gauges as the Squire rumbled up the ramp and into the light traffic, trailing a cloud of smoke, Florida bound.

Emilio and Máximo were all eyes and ears the first few hours, waiting for any sign of trouble in this machine on which we were depending so heavily. The first fault, apparent within minutes, was with the steering: at anything over fifty miles per hour, the big wagon reeled from one side of the lane to the other, unable to hold a straight line. The sway got worse the faster the car went; at sixty, staying on the road—never mind in the lane—was just about impossible. So fifty, we decided, was the line. It would make for a slow 2,500 miles—fifty hours at least, not counting rest stops. But, with no headrests or seat belts, horrible tires, and sundry mysteries beneath us, it increased our chances of survival.

Our first destination, I knew, would be Flagstaff, in the

mountains of northern Arizona. There we would catch Interstate 40, east indefinitely. Interstate 20, which cut across the top of the southern gulf states, or I-10, which rimmed the gulf itself, would have been faster routes; but Máximo and Emilio were adamant about staying away from the Mexican border. Checkpoints were common down there, they said, and cops in general more on the lookout for a car like ours. Where we were going— through the Texas Panhandle to Oklahoma, Arkansas, and Tennessee—Mexicans were less on people's minds.

As the sun was setting I asked to see a map; soon it would be too dark to read. But they didn't have one.

"Excuse me? No map?"

Emilio shrugged. Máximo shook his head. Twenty-five hundred miles without a map? *"We know how to go,"* said Máximo, in gentle reproach. *"We've done it before."*

Digesting this took me a moment. *"You mean to say, you memorized it?"* Slowly the truth was dawning on me. *"All the way to that little town in Florida?"*

They nodded as if to say "of course." I let this sink in. It would mean no plotting of the next town for gas, no meal or rest planning, no certainty of where we actually were. I was used to knowing those things, to depending on them. The map was my compass. But to these guys the map contained mainly details, and details weren't important. If you got on the highway, remembered the major turns, and just kept going, you eventually would arrive, God willing. Later, in a gas station, I showed them our location on a wall map. That was when I discovered that Emilio, though polite and respectful of the service I felt I was performing, couldn't even read maps, and Máximo understood only marginally. *They'd memorized the route.* I couldn't get over it.

The sun went down and the road curved up, up, into the pine-covered mountains. There was some debate as to whether the white glow we could see between the trees was snow or just moonlight shining on the earth; a chilly, windy pit stop led to the discovery that the ground was, indeed, covered with snow, a foot or two by the looks of it. As they climbed back into the wagon, the younger guys chatted excitedly about the discovery; being from southern Mexico, they had never seen snow up close before. Chucho even brought in a snowball, and it was gaily passed around like a reverse hot potato.

But up in the front seat, things were more somber. Weather was coming in—gusts of wind buffeted the car, and within a short while falling snowflakes could be seen whirling through the headlight beams. Emilio and Máximo had seen snow and knew what it meant to a bad car with bad tires. Emilio, now at the wheel, slowed down and turned on the wipers. I stopped myself in the middle of a question about the forecast: forecasts weren't much a part of life in most of rural Mexico, which had only occasional access to radio, television, or newspapers. We would take things as they came. I decided to forgo sleep for a while and see what developed.

We drove along, slower and slower. Presently a heavily loaded van sped by us, dangerously fast; two of the guys in back remarked that it looked like the van of Roberto Espinosa, one of the El Mirage *coyotes*. This observation served only to remind everyone of the news that had been circulating around the orchards the entire week before: Flagstaff was where Immigration had nabbed twenty-one people in two Florida-bound vans just the previous Sunday—this route was no secret to them. And Flagstaff was now less than twenty-five miles away. We had plenty to worry about.

As the road got icier, Emilio revealed how little he knew about driving in snow. He made the usual mistakes: his feet got heavier instead of lighter on the gas and brake pedals, as though muscle could cure our lack of traction; he would brake when turning instead of before a turn. On one steep switchback, when a skid resulted, he turned the wrong way to pull out of it, and the back of the Squire fishtailed around and into a snowbank on the side of the road. Everyone piled out and pushed the car back onto the shoulder. When we were back inside, shivering, Emilio looked me in the eye for the first time I could remember.

"You're from Colorado, aren't you?" He knew I was. *"Don't you know how to drive in this?"*

He knew I did. The problem was, I was reluctant to drive because of the risks of getting caught. A strict interpretation of the law could land me in jail on the felony charge of aiding and abetting. We had discussed this, and they had agreed not to ask me except in an emergency. But this was an emergency. As I slid behind the wheel, I began to formulate my excuses: if they kept driving, someone—perhaps an innocent third party—was likely to get hurt. Any officer ought to understand that. I eased the big wagon from the shoulder to the road, and on into the blizzard.

The drive from Flagstaff east to Albuquerque, New Mexico, takes about six hours under normal conditions; it took us twelve or thirteen, with the wind gusting and headlights probing the entire way. I stopped there for gas around noon the next day. The snow had temporarily abated, but the wind was blowing hard and cold and continued to shake the car; instead of taking the chance to use the rest room and stretch their stiff legs and backs, the guys in back all just stayed there, buried under piles of blankets. Maybe it was the cold, maybe it was the gaze of the gas station attendant; whatever the cause, they seemed to have gone into a sort of hibernation, talking very seldom, moving around even less. If your bladder could take it, I mused, it was not a bad strategy for surviving a lo-cal, high-mile, long-while drive like this was shaping up to be.

With Emilio pumping the gas, Máximo refilling oil and transmission fluid, and I paying, it was a quick pit stop. Enlivened by the wind and freezing temperatures, the three of us did some talking as we rolled across eastern *"Nuevo México,"* Emilio at the wheel. We were done now, for the most part, with mountains, a plus for our safety but a minus as far as interesting reasons to keep our eyes open. The countryside was desolate, windswept, and patched with snow; fence posts and frosted cattle were the only sights above grass line. It was old country, home to Spanish explorers who rode up from Old Mexico, the first Europeans in what's now the United States. They were the ancestors of Hispanics in much of the Southwest. Tijeras, Pajarito, Santa Rosa, Anton Chico: the towns named on highway signs reflected the heritage, made you wonder what the old Spaniards did when it got this cold.

The Mexicans shivered. The little they joked or horsed around made me realize how much this was an ordeal for them: everyone in the car, except for me, came from a land of sugarcane and avocados. The drive, for them, was nothing more than the unpleasant means to a Florida end—a dire passage to a warm and sunny place where they could work. There was precious little of Kerouac here, no driving-as-spiritual-quest. My companions were there not for the experience but for the possibilities, the money—*the fight*, as the job search translated in Mexican slang. This was a business trip, a decision made about potentials. And, yes, it was an adventure too, but for my companions in the front seat of the Country Squire, that came second.

Emilio, Smith Ranch's fabled superpicker, seemed the most driven. Thirty years old, he told me he had spent almost all of the past fifteen years in the States; Arizona and Florida he knew better than his home state of Querétaro. Between seasons, instead of going home to spend evenings in the cantina, he migrated elsewhere in the States to earn more: often in the fall, he told me, he traveled from Florida to South Carolina to pick tomatoes and bell peppers, to North Carolina for apples, or even up to Maryland for cucumbers. Most Mexicans I had met worked hard, but few so unremittingly. Emilio had a manic drive, what seemed a workaholism. And yet, as I sat next to him, he seemed calm; the desire to work did not translate into antsiness when he was trapped in transit, unable to work. Behind his black handlebar mustache—the biggest in the group—and his jet black hair—the longest—he spoke quietly, unassumingly. He looked more like a hippie, the antithesis of the anal-compulsive, hypercompetitive American achiever. He mystified me.

Máximo was easier to place. He was more a worried, responsible parent. We chatted as the day again drew dark, as Máximo took the wheel and exhausted Emilio fell asleep against the passenger-side door. Though only twenty-seven, my age, Máximo already had five kids. It was his third season in the States. He had arrived this time in September and hoped to return home as soon as possible—probably July, but sooner if he had the money. He was earning for his family, and he pulled out his wallet to show me pictures of his kids. Two of the girls were in their First Communion dresses. There was a tiny boy, held in the arms of a woman whose head hadn't quite made it into the photo. *"This must be your son, Mínimo,"* I said, joking with him. Máximo didn't get it.

"No," he corrected me, *"that's Pedrito. You know what he said when I went back and saw him last summer? He said, 'Daddy, can I go with you to the North next year?' He's only seven years old!"*

The rest were daughters, and Máximo told me about them. There was Piedad, the oldest at twelve, *"and already bossing the others around. But she's a great help to her mother."* Ana, eleven, did well in school when she wanted, but often daydreamed; *"she ran away once, but everyone knew where she was—down by my uncle Rafa's place, where they grind the sugarcane in spring. My wife, Camilia, carried dinner down to her when it was getting dark, and Ana burst into tears and followed her home."* I had no stories of children to share, only of my own sisters, and my parents. We talked a long while and then were quiet; I closed my eyes, and Máximo, thinking me asleep, softly began to sing to himself . . . just a little tune, soft notes in a deep male voice. It was a tender, unmacho thing to be doing. It made me feel good. Slowly, I too drifted off.

A queasy, amusement-park sensation woke me up. I took in the situation as quickly as possible. We were on the downside of an overpass; we were skidding on glare ice; and the car ahead of us was too. Stepping hard on the brakes, Máximo had the wheels locked. As a result, the rear of the Squire kept fishtailing around until, though eastward bound, we were looking straight into the sunset. Then, with a jolt, the rear bumper connected with a guardrail, spinning us back around to forward, and a stop. Máximo looked at me and Emilio; then we all piled out his door, as Emilio's was up against the rail.

We were vastly relieved: the left rear taillights were smashed, and the bumper bent a bit into the crumpled rear fender, but the wheels were clear and it appeared we could go on. Back in the car, the rear-seat hibernators had woken up and were full of questions. Most of them thought someone must have struck us from behind. Nobody was hurt. They stayed awake with us the next couple of hours, and their watchfulness, along with the extremely slippery roads, produced an atmosphere of tension and quiet inside the Squire.

That was why I was so surprised when my observation that Amarillo couldn't be far away provoked a storm of laughter in the back. *"What's so funny about that?"* I inquired.

"Amarillo—you said it wrong!" laughed Chucho, pointing an accusing finger at me.

I knew right away what he was getting at. We had been having a running battle, over the miles, over what I considered their mispronunciation of the names of American cities. In the mouth of a Mexican, Denver often became "Dem-bare," New York "New Jork," Miami "Meeyahmee"—sometimes I had no idea what they were saying. So, continuing in my role as *el maestro*, I had begun to correct them.

But now it was Chucho's turn to get back at me. *Amarillo*, the Spanish word for "yellow," described many things about the Texas Panhandle—the color of wheat, the long dead grass, the soil, the edges of the sunset this time of year. But not the way I had pronounced it.

"Amarillo," said Chucho emphatically (ah-ma-RRREE-yo), *"Amarillo, Amarillo, Amarillo . . ."*

"Okay, fair enough," I said, pronouncing it his way. *"Amarillo it is."*

Rush-hour traffic, such as it was, was slow in Amarillo, and got worse as the snow started again. The roads were so slippery that Máximo slowed to fifteen miles an hour and held at that speed as we left town on a straight shot into the Great Plains. So it continued for a tense hour or more, until the defroster began having difficulty keeping ice off the windshield. Máximo was then forced to slow even more, and four or five times we got out to scrape the ice off with our own fingernails and wallets. Finally, a complaint from the far back concerning a lack of heat alerted us to the real problem: the air coming out of the heating vents was itself as cold as ice. Goddamn Squire! The heater had stopped working . . . and the night and the storm had just begun.

We quickly realized that even a car full of blankets might not keep us warm in the impending freeze, and a movement began among some of the men to look for some kind of shelter. Emilio and Chucho were the first to state their preference for a motel. Most of the others resisted, though, leery of spending any more money than the absolute minimum to arrive at our destination. I stayed out of the argument until it appeared deadlocked, and then suggested it might be less a question of staying warm than of staying alive: we were in the middle of nowhere, without heat, in a worsening storm. I could see his breath as Emilio added his agreement. Máximo crept on silently into the advancing storm, virtually unable to see. The next town, it was finally decided, in the next town we'd see about a motel.

But the next town had no motel—or anything else, for that matter—and, unable to see road signs, we rolled slowly on to the next, whenever it might appear. Sometimes it was thirty or forty miles between towns in this part of the world—and at our speed that was a long time. By the time the first motel sign was finally spotted, about three hours later, the resistance to the idea had dissolved. Outside it was a blizzard, and inside an icebox; lacking gloves, Máximo had wrapped not only his hands but the entire steering wheel in a blanket. The rest of us sat shivering; there was frost on the inside of the windows now too. For obvious reasons I was elected to step into the blizzard and do the talking in the motel office.

It took me a while to locate the manager's door, and, once inside, I had to work hard to remember my poor friends freezing outside and keep it short. The manager and his wife were Iranian, with obscure reasons for being in this godforsaken part of Texas; their room was so warm it seemed they were trying to recreate the desert. I arranged for a two-bedroom for me and "my friend," and thought, on my way back to the car, that at least the weather had done us this backhanded favor: the night was too bitter for the manager to come checking. Seven Mexicans in his motel. Lordy.

A satellite dish brought television channels in a variety the men had never seen. As we turned our own room into a sauna, they lounged around the double beds, the younger guys arguing over the controller and searching for police shows. All we lacked was food: nothing but the odd Coke and potato chip had been consumed since we'd left Phoenix, more than forty-eight hours before. But the euphoria of warmth made up for the ache and edginess of hunger. With three to a bed and two on the floor, we were asleep in no time.

At 6:00 A.M. Máximo again took the wheel. As the others piled in and arranged themselves, he crossed himself and said a small prayer. The roads were still slick, and we needed all the help we could get.

En route to the interstate ramp, we approached a railroad crossing. The warning arms were up, the signals were dark, there was no sign of a train anywhere—but Máximo slowed anyway. He looked both ways.

"*Nervous?*" I asked him, smiling. He shrugged, not comprehending; a few months later I'd discover that I hadn't understood either. Visiting his part of Mexico, I learned that crossing signals, where they existed, were never to be trusted. Many were actually operated by hand, by an attendant who lived next to the crossing; if this person happened to be out back feeding the chickens when the train approached, the motorist was out of luck.

It was that afternoon, near Texola, on the Texas-Oklahoma line, that the windshield wiper motor stopped. The freezing rain, however, continued, and when roadside tinkering failed to provide a solution, we pulled off the interstate and into the service bay of a tiny service station in Elk City. Emilio watched carefully as the old mechanic began poking around under the hood; he wanted to know all there was to know. I walked outdoors into the bad weather and stretched my legs. A broadcast I had picked up on the Squire's AM radio described the storm as the winter's worst; it was our luck to be following its path as it raged slowly east. It was going to be a long trip.

Behind the building I found an old Esso sign in the freezing mud; near the cash register I noticed a cheescake calendar of the sort you see around garages. The model was blonde, and her long hair reminded me that the wedding of a former girlfriend, with whom I had remained close, was to be the coming weekend, in Fort Lauderdale. An invitation had arrived for me at home; I had vaguely considered going. I made some quick calculations: possibly if the weather cleared, and we were able to drive nonstop, we would arrive in Florida in time. I ran my calculations by Máximo. He shrugged; to him, calculations of miles and hours were misleading. We would arrive quickly, he said, *"si Dios quiere"*—if God willed it. It was my turn to shrug—with the snow god directly overhead, the fatalistic view made some sense. *Que será, será*, whatever will be, will be. An expression in his language, not mine.

"Battery's too small," the mechanic announced.

"¿La batería?" Emilio asked me, urgently. The mechanic pointed to the Squire's battery mount. The battery was so small it barely fit in without falling out. I nodded. The ruling junta then held a conference and decided we'd better have the mechanic replace it. The price with the trade-in was not the rip-off we had expected. Better yet, it worked—for both the heating and the wiper problem. Máximo entered the cost on the list of expenses he was keeping on the back of a *novela;* he and Emilio paid for now. It would all be dealt with in time. We took the opportunity to add yet another can of fluid to the transmission and to buy another caseful: lately the tranny had been stubborn about shifting into high gear, and we needed to take advantage of the rel-

atively clear roads to make up lost time. There was an upbeat mood as we swung back onto Interstate 40.

At fifty miles per hour—still our limit—we made relatively good time across Oklahoma. But bad weather struck again south of Tulsa. The semitrailer rigs that dominate many interstates, but that are poorly suited to slippery conditions, were sliding off the highway everywhere. My companions were wide eyed at some of the spectacular wrecks. Gradually, though it was midday, the freeway emptied. We should have pulled off too, but, tired, I was not feeling assertive, and they badly wanted to keep going. Things were at their most slippery, with the worst visibility, when suddenly a stopped trailer loomed ahead of us. It had stalled in the right lane, failing even to get over to the shoulder. Perhaps believing in the relative superiority of our newly fixed vehicle, perhaps thinking there really were no other cars out that day, Máximo spun the wheel confidently and the Squire began to change to the left lane. But at this instant, a voice blurted from the far back: *"Look out!"*

Another semi, traveling much faster than we, was bearing down directly behind us in the left lane; on a road as slick as this, a collision was inevitable. Reacting quickly, Máximo steered us back out of its way, and stepped on the brake in order not to hit the stalled trailer. Under normal conditions, we could have stopped. But on that glassy surface, the locked tires were barely slower than ice skates. The Squire bashed into the trailer's rear bumper.

We were mortified. Everyone stepped out into the wind to examine the damage . . . everyone except Máximo, Emilio, and I, that is, for the front doors would no longer open. We had to climb into the backseat to get out.

The Squire had traveled about a foot beyond the trailer's bumper, mostly underneath, so that the bumper rested on top of the slightly squashed hood. The front fenders were bent, the grille was gone, and glass from the four headlights covered the road. With everyone pushing, we managed to slide it back out from underneath. Using the tire iron as a lever, Emilio set about prying the hood open to see how the engine looked; meanwhile, I ran up the side of the truck to try to intercept and speak with the driver. He was just coming down from the cab.

The Mexicans, traveling in a foreign land and subject to rules they did not understand, automatically assumed it was all their fault. After all they, unable to stop, had slammed into the trailer. I was not so sure. I met the driver as he neared the back of the truck, dressed only in his shirtsleeves. His pants flapped in the wind around his cowboy boots. The blank, strained look in his eyes bespoke a trucker's nightmare of spring-loaded seats, white lines, coffee, and amphetamines. Especially in comparison to the brown-skinned Mexicans, he looked like death. Rounding the back of the trailer, suddenly, afforded the perspective of fresh air and no windshield, he realized his mistake.

Out of initial mumbles emerged words and a sentence: "Oh, gosh, I'm sorry. I thought I was on the shoulder." The truck, as far as we could tell, was undamaged. "I was wondering what happened—thought at first it was just my brakes kicking back." He hadn't even realized he'd been hit.

"*Tell him we're very sorry. We'll pay for everything,*" said Máximo.

"*Tell him not to call the police,*" asked Chucho. They looked at me and the trucker anxiously.

"*How's the car?*" I asked.

Emilio was still peering around under the hood. "*The radiator doesn't seem to be damaged. I don't see any leaks. The belts are okay.*"

Máximo borrowed the tire iron and pried open the driver's door. In the process, the metal tore a wide gash in his hand. But he paid no attention, just climbed in and started the engine.

"*The tires look okay.*" said Chucho.

"*I don't think he wants to call the police either,*" I said. "*Is it okay if we all just leave?*" My companions all looked at each other and nodded. They looked relieved.

"Look," I said to the driver, now shivering and working

hard to keep his slippery-soled cowboy boots steady on the ice. "We don't want to be held up either. It's an old car, and it looks like it still works, so no big deal."

He smiled wanly. "Thanks, partner," he said, shaking my hand and turning to go. "I sure appreciate it." He probably didn't understand why I was doing him this favor, and I didn't plan to tell him. He skittered back up to his cab.

The blood dripping onto the pavement under Máximo's hand was starting to turn to dark ice. One of the guys noticed and handed him a clean sock, which he wrapped around the hand. He began to move back behind the wheel, but I said I'd drive. I didn't want any more accidents. I was angry that we had had this one, but also feeling frustrated at having no one to be angry at. The truck driver probably had been in the wrong technically, but it was hard to blame a guy like that. Máximo should have been driving more slowly—in fact, we shouldn't have been on the road at all—but it was hard to blame him or the group for wanting to get there, and soon. All I knew was that we were lucky. The car still worked, and the police had not come. If they had, the men would almost certainly have been deported, and I, lacking a good place to hide in a blizzard, would have been in up to my neck as well. Máximo scooted over and then Emilio, unable to open his own door, came around and slid to the middle of the front seat, kicking the glass from near the tires on his way. Everyone else climbed in. I drove off my anger.

In Henryetta, Oklahoma, we bought new sealed beams and tape: the connections were all right, and in fifteen minutes we had headlights again. I felt like driving nonstop to Florida myself, like getting this trip over, but two hours later, barely into Arkansas, my eyelids were heavy and I was shaking my head to stay awake.

"*You guys, there's a question I've been meaning to ask,*" I said to Emilio and Máximo. They looked at me, a bit concerned, sensing it might be important.

"*When you travel, do you also eat?*" So—the *gringo* was

hungry! Those who hadn't heard had my question repeated by others who had. There was laughter as they realized what I was getting at.

"*Yes, sometimes,*" said Máximo, smiling.

"*Well, look. I know you're tired and I want to do my share of driving. But I can't continue unless I get something to eat.*"

"*Okay, okay. Look—how about the little old man?*"

"*Huh? What 'little old man'?*"

"*Don't you know him? Oh, I think we'll see him pretty soon.*"

"*Where?*"

"*Up ahead. Just wait.*"

Máximo and Emilio had driven this route so many times, I thought, maybe they knew some old guy in western Arkansas who ran a café, some old Mexican who would feed us. I was annoyed at their vagueness, but glad they had an idea. "*El viejito,*" they called him. I managed to drive for another half hour.

"*There he is! There he is!*" Chucho suddenly called from the back seat as we approached some exits for Fort Smith.

What the . . . What were they talking about?

"*Look! With the beard.*"

My gaze followed Chucho's pointing finger up the pole of a road sign for Kentucky Fried Chicken! They were talking about the Colonel.

"*Colonel Sanders!*" I said. "*Why didn't you say so?*"

"*Cairrrn-ul San-dess,*" Chucho struggled. They hadn't been teasing me—it was just a very difficult name for a Mexican to pronounce.

"*All right—el viejito,*" I said. The little old man.

We pulled into the parking lot. A collection was taken for the impending feast; unfamiliar with this town and state, they waited in the Squire while I walked inside to get two huge buckets of chicken, all the trimmings, Pepsis all around, and about half a dispenser of napkins. Carrying it back out required two trips. Though hungry themselves, they all got a big kick out of watching how much pleasure the meal evidently gave me. Whenever there was something extra, it was passed to me. I was all smiles. Food and mood: the relationship is undeniable.

Things settled down as we crossed Arkansas. The frozen roads and barren vistas gradually disappeared, yielding to greenery and air with just the right touches of fragrance, humidity, and warmth to be the South at its best. The blankets in back were converted into use as pillows. The fourth day dawned over a bridge, with the Mississippi River in the side windows and Memphis on the horizon. Everyone relaxed, with the exception of a brief moment of panic when we were passed by a late-model sedan apparently carrying newlyweds. Torn remnants of toilet paper and streamers fluttered from the aerial and around the bumpers, and words formed with shaving cream had slid down the windows into undistinguishable globs.

"Snow!" gasped Máximo. He pointed to the old shaving cream at the bottom of the windows and looked around at the sky. *"Where did it come from?"* He had developed a mortal fear of the stuff.

"Where? Where?" demanded the others, suddenly alarmed.

"¡Tranquilo! It's not snow!" I proceeded to explain what, come to think of it, is a fairly peculiar local custom. They were perplexed. Emilio's brother asked if it had something to do with the groom's shaving. *"Is it just for men with beards?"*

Right before Knoxville we made our first turn since Arizona, this one onto Interstate 75, southbound through Chattanooga to Georgia and Florida. A filling station map later revealed that we could have saved three hours by turning sooner, taking a southeast diagonal, I-24, at Nashville, but I didn't say anything. Maybe they were ignorant of it, but maybe they were not. The shortest route wasn't always the best, as I was reminded when we exited the interstate somewhere south of Macon.

"¿Qué pasó?" I inquired.

"From here, we take another route," said Emilio.

Máximo eventually explained. *"La Migra knows there are guys coming this time of year. They keep an eye on the interstate—ask Emilio."*

From the somber look on Emilio's face, I didn't have to.
"*So*," he continued, "*we take another route.*"

It wasn't until a few days later, when I got to sit down and really look at a map, that I was able to figure out exactly how we had entered Florida. The route was circuitous, but it worked. It wasn't till central Florida that we rejoined the interstate, and then only briefly; it angled west, toward the Gulf Coast, and we headed back off to south central Florida.

During this stretch Chucho got his first taste of driver education, Mexican style. He had been bugging us to let him drive since the snow stopped, but not till now, I think, had we actually believed we would make it without a minor miracle. Of course, he had no license. But the road was straight and little traveled; and, more important, the three of us drivers were thoroughly exhausted. We parked alongside the road, Chucho and Emilio traded places, and Chucho scooted up the front seat in order to reach the pedals. Smiling broadly, the envy of all those in the back, he revved the engine loudly. The troubled transmission took another step toward its grave when Chucho shifted from PARK to DRIVE with his foot already on the gas, and we peeled out onto the pavement. Máximo placed his hands over his eyes.

Slowly, and with coaching from Máximo, Chucho got the knack of it. Against my better judgment, but trusting in Máximo, I fell asleep; probably against his wishes, succumbing to exhaustion, he did too. A couple of hours later, we both awoke with a start at the skidding and bouncing of wheels. Chucho had gone off the road—not on the right-hand side, but on the left—and was just wrestling the Squire back into its proper lane. We were going very fast.

"*What in the hell are you doing?*" screamed Máximo, red faced.

"*Fucking car won't go straight!*" a shaken Chucho shouted back, stepping now on the brake and easing off the left-side shoulder.

"*Well, no wonder—look how fast you're going!*" the speedometer was just coming down past the sixty mark as he spoke.

"*You said the limit. I was only going the limit.*"

"*But the limit's fifty. Look—there's a sign.*"

"*No sir, no—there's the limit. Eighty-three.*" Chucho pointed at a small sign designating the number of the county road.

"*¡Hijo de la chingada, cabrón! What a fool you are!*"

As word of what happened filtered to the back of the car, Chucho was ribbed mercilessly—even though, I thought to myself, most of the rest of them could easily have made the same mistake. Máximo took over the driving once again. Chucho, red faced, returned to the backseat. If nothing else, his training and gaffe had helped pass the time; we weren't far now.

The central part of Florida, especially in the south, remains separate from the popular and well-known Gulf and Atlantic coasts. Divorced from coastal development, retirement culture, the service economy, and the national limelight, the Florida interior is a world unto itself. Humid, windless, and backwoods, it is a place of rust, old trucks, ceiling fans—real ones, not the decorator kind—and undergrowth, noisy more with the sounds of nature than of men. There are lots of dead things on the highways. The people you notice are often borrowed from images of the Deep South: middle-aged white men wearing billed caps, perspiring women in thin dresses, slow-moving, dirt-poor blacks who—more than any blacks in a city—evoke memories of their enslaved ancestors. It seems a place the civil rights movement forgot to visit, a slow-paced backwater where much, you have the feeling, hasn't changed in a very long time. Acreage producing the third most cattle of any state in the union is interspersed with still, murky swamps, secret worlds into which the "crackers" seem to have special insights. The change in scenery as we descended into the peninsula was dramatic. Expanses of bankless, shallow-watered lakes. Spanish moss on dead limbs. Whole woods of the same tree, the same mists. And, of course, agriculture—behind the alligator "farms," vast fields of tomatoes, green peppers, melons, strawberries, sugarcane, and citrus—which were, of course, the sole reason we were here.

It was a long state, and the last few hours went the slowest.

For the first time since New Mexico, the car radio picked up a Spanish-language station, but, after the announcer's introducton and a few bars of the first song, Emilio angrily switched it off.

"*¡Cubanos, pinche cubanos!*" he said. "*Even country-western is better than that stuff.*"

"*You don't like Cubans?*" I asked, surprised.

"*They'll fuck you over, man,*" said Chucho, in the back.

"*Hey, give me one to fuck over,*" said Emilio. "*Give me one of those black ones with the tits and the long legs, give me twenty dollars.*"

"*Just remember,*" said Moisés in the far back, "*the twenty dollars is for* her."

"*You hear that?*" said Chucho, addressing Emilio's brother, Pedro, in the seat next to him. "*They come to the camps. They come on weekends. Save up a little money; it's worth it!*" As I turned around to see Pedro's reaction, he reddened.

"*Eeehhhh, see, he's thinking about it,*" said Emilio, causing the face to redden even more. Everyone was loosening up; soon we would be there. We were in Florida.

We came to what I gradually realized was a vast region of citrus orchards. The many I had seen around Phoenix were nothing compared to this. It was late afternoon, and many men, tired and sweaty, were visible among them, evidently on their way home. The great majority were Mexicans—in the past twenty years, they, Mexican-Americans from Texas, and Haitians have been replacing a farmworker population that was once almost all American black. Estimates place the number of undocumented Mexicans in central Florida at 25,000 to 30,000 during the citrus season. The guys in back devoted themselves to guessing where in Mexico a given group was from.

"*¡Oaxaqueños!*" exclaimed Moisés, pointing to a group of strikingly short men with Indian features emerging from one grapefruit grove.

"*No, no—they're not from Oaxaca, they're from Michoacán!*" asserted Chucho. "*Look at their hats. Look at those huaraches.*" The same way a New Yorker might discern a midwesterner, or a northern Californian a southern Californian, the Mexicans could place those from other parts of their extremely regional country. I knew the basic formula (the shorter and more Indian looking a Mexican, the greater the likelihood he was from southern Mexico)—it was the nuance that escaped me: the cut of the *huarache*, the turn of a hat, the manner of the individual.

We kept driving. By nightfall we had reached La Belle, our destination. The air was wet and heavy. Windows down, we drove along State Road 29, Bridge Street, the main drag of a town that looked like many others in the South. There was a white courthouse here, Baptist church there, little minimalls, park with a picnic table, motels. Down the side streets we could see well-kept neighborhoods, with lawns and streetlights, late-model American cars parked along the curbs. We continued through a zone of motels that looked rather worse for wear than the others, and soon after turned onto an overgrown lane away from the nice neighborhoods.

The paved road quickly became dirt, pocked with holes. There were no streetlights here, but in the moonlight were visible shacks and trailers of various kinds, standing pools of water, trash cans, stoops. Little looked trimmed or manicured, much was wild. Sitting in chairs on their lawn of dirt were two black men, enjoying a smoke; someone in the back of the car suggested rolling up the windows if we were to continue through *that* kind of neighborhood. But Emilio was looking for something: the house where a friend had lived last time he was here, he said, and possibly a place for us to spend the night. When at last he found it, though, it had someone else's car in the yard, a stereo playing music not of Mexico. Emilio drove out of town about five miles, and then, without explanation, turned off the headlights, slowed, and pulled abruptly up a side road leading into an orange orchard. Here he paused and then slowly, adjusting his vision to the moonlight, he guided the Squire into the orchard. He kept one eye on the rearview mirror at first to see if we were being followed, but then lost himself in the task of getting to a remote place where we'd never be discovered.

Finally we were there—ensconced between two close rows in what seemed the very middle of a vast forest of citrus trees. Emilio shut off the engine. Slowly, achingly, people piled out until, for the first time since the Texas motel and only the second time since Phoenix, the car was empty. It was our fourth day. I looked up and saw the sky was filled with stars. Blankets came out of the car, and flat, protected sleeping sites were sought. The soil, I noticed, was sandy, a change from the more mulch-covered Phoenix orchards. Almost everyone lit up a cigarette, and I joined in. After a few moments of sitting in a road-induced coma, we were snapped out of it by Pedro, carrying a load of oranges in his outstretched shirtfront. Oranges were really the last food any of them would have chosen to eat, but the price was right, they were plentiful, and soon the humid air was filled with the tangy, acidic smell of peels, our dirty hands covered with sticky juice. Some men talked and joked for a while, but eventually we all lay down, the sight of the sky through leaves of the trees competing with the lingering image of white lines on dark roadway, etched in our eyes.

Still lacking a good meal, we drove first thing in the morning to a large industrial plant. The windowless concrete structure was set in a huge dirt lot surrounded by orchards on three sides and the state highway on the fourth; eight-foot chain-link fences ran alongside this exposed flank and met at the center in a set of large gates. We parked near the gates. NO HELP WANTED said a big sign affixed to the gate. I translated it for Emilio, but he ignored me and walked up to the gatehouse. Máximo and I tagged along. The guard spoke no Spanish, and Emilio seemed to be having difficulty getting his message across.

"*Tell him we want to speak with Gutierrez,*" Emilio said to me.

This was, I was about to discover, one of the places where being an illegal alien makes you an insider, gets you past the NO HELP WANTED signs. The man got on the phone, and presently—

after having our shoes and trousers misted with alcohol to kill possible carriers of orange blight—we were allowed to pass. Emilio led the way to a trailer on the back side of the factory. Gutierrez met us at the door, immediately casting a suspicious eye on me. *"He's a teacher; he came with us,"* said Emilio. They shook hands warmly, and Emilio filled him in on the situation.

"How many did you say you were?"

"Eight."

"And him?" Gutierrez asked, pointing at me.

"Well, seven without him. But he'll work."

"You will?" said Gutierrez in English, breaking into a large grin. I nodded, reminded of Máximo's reaction when I said I'd like to travel with them. Only this time, because of the company I kept, I felt more secure.

"Has he done it before?" They nodded, and I did too. Gutierrez raised his eyebrows. "Well, okay. I'll try anything once!" He had stolen my line.

We were to start the next day, picking juice oranges for the large juice concern that owned everything around us. Before then, we would need to buy the items which in Phoenix had been furnished us: gloves (a local 7-Eleven store, ever attentive to its market, had an entire wall-full), canvas sleeves to protect ourselves from thorns, and the full-size picking bags used in Florida (the Arizona kind, I discovered to my chagrin, was the more "humane" three-quarter-size bag), though the last could be purchased from the company and the expense deducted from our paychecks (*"not the way you want to do it,"* Emilio advised me, indicating his distrust of the company). But before that, I discovered to my joy and surprise, it was time to eat.

Gutierrez had told Emilio we could sleep and park behind his house in town. It was a small, comfortable frame affair, up the income scale from the shantytown we had visited, but quite a ways beneath the nice middle-class housing we had seen on our first drive down Bridge Street. The backyard was screened from the neighbors by thick vegetation and sloped down to a small marsh. Emilio drove over the coarse lawn and around the house, parking under a large shade tree. We unloaded, and then Emilio, after taking a collection, went off to market.

"They're smarter than we are," opined Chucho.

"No," said Máximo, *"they're just better educated. The low things in their minds have been replaced by higher ones."*

We were all sitting and lying around the tree, shoes and sweaters off, cigarettes out, relaxing, waiting for Emilio. For once the guys who had been in back were getting a good look at me; I discovered, to my surprise, that they'd been burning with curiosity about me since first we left Phoenix, but had felt constrained from asking questions while we were driving. The subject of conversation was Americans, and I was something like a moderator.

"They are more businesslike. They're organized, they plan things out."

"But Americans don't think about sex as much as we do, right?"

"Well, I'm not so sure about that," I said. *"I guess we probably think about it as much, we just don't let on sometimes."*

"We Mexicans are hotter than Americans," offered Moisés with a grin. Arms bent at his sides, he made a pulling motion to make his meaning clear. Máximo made a face and tsk-ed in disapproval at this disrespect, but others laughed at Moisés's audacity; despite the way I looked and no doubt smelled, they apparently had decided I was a person of culture and learning, from the class of person who, in Mexico, would be likely to be offended by such candid references to sex.

"Except for American women," said Chucho, to more laughs. *"They're pretty hot, too!"*

"Yes, las gringas!"

I was learning a lot. Mexicans seemed to look at American men in much the same way we often look at Germans: they were precise, efficient, somewhat cold, too serious. It was interesting because, impatient toward the end of the drive, that was how I had felt with them—I was pushing the speed to the Squire's limit, not talking, maybe a little angry at how long it all was taking. The impatience seemed very American—but what, after all, was the hurry? Why was I so jealous of "lost" time? They were calling it pretty well.

Emilio finally returned, and in his arms were two grocery bags filled to brimming. His main purchase was a vast quantity of barbecued beef. To go with it there were loaves of white bread, cans of green *serrano* chilies, Coca-Cola, and beer. And napkins, for, as he realized, this was going to be a mess. You could smell the barbecue as he set the bags down on the hood of the Squire, a delicious aroma that made your mouth water. We tore the bags apart and then ate, ravenously, endlessly, filling the emptiness of days of doing without. The result was a long period of silence, and euphoria.

"Did you see your girlfriend in town?" his younger brother asked Emilio.

"Which one?" Emilio said, smiling.

"The one with the big car, the rich blonde."

"Hey, Ted," interrupted Moisés. *"What does this mean in English:* 'Hi, baby, I Moses, you verrry pretty want to come to home with me?"

I told the others, since Moisés apparently knew. There was a request for other English phrases you can use to get women into bed with you, since Moisés swore to them that his worked for that purpose. I confessed, at the risk of appearing a wimp, that I didn't know any.

"But you do know lots of gringas, don't you?"

"Some, and when I see them next, I'll send them your way."

"Just make sure they don't charge!" said Chucho.

It was a day to laugh, to relax and recover. There would be precious few like it in the next weeks and months: Orange picking in Florida was considerably harder than in Arizona. The hours were longer, the rates lower. Pedro, Arturo, and Pancho, the newcomers, would discover that the ladders they were to use were wood, not aluminium, and therefore half again as heavy; the bags were heavier, the air suffocating. In the orchard there would be tensions with the Haitians, Cubans, and other Caribbean immigrants who also did the work, as well as with the few dirt-poor Americans, blacks and whites, that still held on to jobs there. Arizona picking requires a degree of skill and finesse, for most of the oranges were table oranges, not to be bruised or battered; but most of the Florida oranges they would pick were juice oranges, stripped off the tree and dropped to the sandy ground with the greatest speed possible, later to be collected in huge "ten-box" tubs which unlikely tractors known as "goats" would anonymously collect all day long. The work was more machinelike than ever, but there was lots of it.

Gutierrez's wife, who was a kind of unofficial real-estate broker for illegals, would find housing for about half the guys in a project near the shantytown. Of course, federal housing was intended for American citizens, so rent was paid to the Puerto Rican family that it was officially rented to, with a nice kickback to Señora Gutierrez. She found a trailer for the rest of the guys, which lacked windows and a locking door but at least had water in the sink and a sound roof. Until Emilio, Pedro, and Moisés were caught by Immigration and deported, all seven carpooled to work every day. Later Pancho had to drop out; he fell sick with an intestinal parasite that doctors supposed he'd brought from Mexico. Though, given the conditions in which they lived and worked, it was hard to be certain.

All in all, they picked enough oranges to put juice on the breakfast tables of a small city. They would leave Florida at varying times, tired but, by their standards, richer. Except, that is, for Arturo, who developed a taste for consumer goods, including the *putas*, or hookers, that frequented camps on payday. Because he had never had enough money to save, he had a hard time learning how to do it. He went home older and broke.

On that sunny day, though, it was a feast for all the senses. We talked and talked, joked and drank and smoked and slept. Quiet, timid Pancho asked me at one point if I believed in the Virgin.

"*No,*" I answered, "*my family is Protestant.*"

"What is that?"

"It's like the Jews," answered Chucho authoritatively. *"They don't even believe in Jesus."* Pancho looked apprehensive.

"No, that's wrong," I explained. *"Protestants are Christians, we do believe in Jesus. It's just that back in Europe, some Catholics had a disagreement with the Church, and decided to become slightly different."* The Reformation, in twenty words or less.

Pancho was a devout man. He took out his wallet and passed me his plastic laminated picture of the Virgin of Guadalupe, Mexico's patron saint. The pictures were sold by vendors all over Mexico.

"You should have one of these," he said. I asked how many of them did. Five others took out their wallets or reached into shirt pockets and held up their pictures of the Virgin. Only Moisés lacked one.

"If you pray to her, she'll protect you," explained Pancho.

"Yes, she protects us from La Migra!" Chucho joked, to much laughter.

Pancho remained fairly serious. *"I'd like you to have this,"* he said.

I was moved. I took it and looked at it, leaning back as I did against the crumpled right front fender of the Squire, then turning to carefully disengage my shirttail from a sharp snag. Poor car—headlights taped on, front doors unusable, taillights smashed, hood crunched down as though by a wrecking ball— she had been through the war. The truly remarkable thing was that she—we—had made it, somehow squeaking by against all odds. It was more the style of Mexicans than of old American cars. *"Milagroso,"* Máximo had called it when we arrived—miraculous. I knew, by now, that he did not mean it figuratively. And the experience had made me begin to wonder whether he might not be right . . . all the more reason not to accept the picture of the Virgin.

"Thank you, you are very generous," I told Pancho. *"But I think you'd better keep it. I'm afraid you guys will be needing her more than I."*

Chapter 5

In the Land of Avocados

THE WHITE ARROW pitched wildly around a hairpin turn on its descent into Ahuacatlán. The road was a ledge, chiseled into the steep mountainside; a deep valley, a vast volume of air, separated us from the other valley wall, more than a mile away. It was easier to look at those far mountains, golden green in the afternoon sun, than at our own; everything nearby seemed either way above us, up unscalable heights, or far below. Instead of guardrails around the hairpins, there was most often a series of little shrines, of whitewashed brick or stone or cinder block, knee high, with a candle or a madonna or plastic flowers inside, and letters scratched on the outside bearing the name of the deceased: "Raúl Anaya P., 12-5-62." Flew off this crazy height and into the great beyond. His Chevy's still down there because no junk man wants to risk his life winching it back up. You can see it if you get close enough to the edge . . .

The White Arrow was a glorified school bus, painted up, years before, to resemble a regular coach. It had been relegated by the forces of supply and demand to the hinterlands of Querétaro state, just north of Mexico City. From Querétaro City, the capital, to Ahuacatlán, high in the Sierra Gorda, was eleven extremely uncomfortable hours. The bus left once or twice a day, depending. To find its bay at the station, you asked at every counter until you came to White Arrow's: no one else had ever heard of Ahuacatlán. White Arrow, however, serviced two of them, Ahuacatlán de Guadalupe, and Ahuacatlán de Jesús. The clerk asked which I wanted. Barely able yet to pronounce Ahuacatlán by itself (ah-wa-cot-LON), I shrugged in resignation. It was in a high valley, I said, several hours away; that was all I knew. She chose Ahuacatlán de Guadalupe for me and I hoped she was right. Riding the White Arrow required certain leaps of faith.

Another leap had to do with the tires. Because two were bald, two spares were tied to the roof, along with any other cargo that wouldn't fit through the door: trunks, crates, pieces of furniture, sacks of feed, lumber . . . even a casket. *"Is there somebody in that?"* I asked the bus driver, a tired-looking, bewhiskered man, when at last he appeared. *"I believe so,"* he said, flicking down his cigarette and staring at it. I waited for him to say more, but he didn't, just stared. I thought about that tired bus driver, about those bald tires, about that body, dying twice, as the Arrow took the sharp curves.

The first seven or eight hours were through poor farmland that gradually gave up and became desert. Then the desert took on contours: dunes grew out of the scrub-covered flatlands and then solidified into sandy foothills; these in turn yielded to full-scale, arid mountains of considerable grandeur, a landscape evocative of something between the Sahara and the moon. Though, always, something came along to remind you you were in Mexico—dogs, puffed up and dead in the road, their legs stretched stiffly toward the sky. Or burros. We passed four or five of these suicide burros, stationed squarely in the middle of the road, so stupid—or brave—they wouldn't budge unless the bus actually nudged them, would not, in fact, even blink. The evidence all along the way of the fate of dogs and other smaller animals that failed to yield the right-of-way did not dissuade the burros. I stared at two as the bus driver slowed to a crawl and leaned on the horn, finally having to persuade them with his bumper. Seeing my surprise, the old *campesino* seated next to me nudged his friend across the aisle. *"The burros are smarter in the United States, ¿verdad?"* he said to me, with a toothless grin.

I had felt safer on that part of the journey, the journey up: the old school bus engine strained to do even fifteen or twenty miles an hour on the steep grade, with obstacles and the need occasionally to stop and let off passengers conspiring to keep the driver from getting up a good head of steam. Where these passengers went was a considerable mystery to me—there were no settlements in sight at all, not a single house or lean-to. As far as I could tell the darkly tanned and deeply wrinkled old men and women with their bundles walked off into the middle of nowhere. Apparently somewhere in the vast rippled distance, from the deepest creases between parched piles of dirt and slate, water seeped out, and things could grow.

Up and up the bus climbed. The turns got tighter. We passed two shut-down mines which the old man next to me said had once produced mercury. Cut from the rib of one mountain, presumably with considerable effort, was a dirt soccer field, yet who was there to play on it? and if the ball were kicked out of bounds, what kept it from falling hundreds of feet? Near the top of our ascent, a painted sign advertised *"petróleo,"* and one next to it *"leña,"* or firewood, and there it was, stacked in tall cords . . . thick firewood, probably pine—where had it come from? As the Arrow finally wheezed through a mountaintop defile fifty feet deep, I realized we had reached the summit . . . and more. For as we began our descent, the more remote side of the range slowly began to turn green. Tall trees—live oak and eucalyptus—abounded; the ridge tops were rough with shrubbery and woolly with clouds, no longer bare; and sewn between woods on the mountainsides was an uneven patchwork quilt of tended fields. The summit, in other words, was also a sort of grand meteorological fence. On this side, water fell; on the other side, it did not. The land wasn't lush, but people could live.

The high valley we were descending, the Moctezuma River valley, had ancient human origins. When Hernán Cortés arrived in the 1520s, Ahuacatlán (literally "land of avocados") and the valley's other villages had for hundreds of years been home to the Otomí Indians. Though relatively near Mexico City—the ancient Aztec capital of Tenochtitlán, which was the Spaniards' first target—the Otomí were among the last peoples to be subdued by the Spanish conquistadors. Their inaccessibility and their fierceness, legendary in Spanish chronicles of the time, were two reasons, but they also were protected by their lack of organization: where Cortés had effectively paralyzed the Aztecs by imprisoning their ruler, Moctezuma, the same strategy was ineffective in dealing with the tribal Otomí. In the end, it was none other than Franciscan friars (and a large detachment of Spanish soldiers) who, in the 1690s, finally succeeded in subduing the valleys. The natives were forced—upon pain of death—into constructing the first links in a chain of missions that Father Junípero Serra eventually would extend up Mexico's west coast, all the way to present-day northern California. Impressive looking Churrigueresque churches were one result. But a century of pain and death, memorialized by such reminders as the "Avenue of the Massacre" in a town we passed in the bus, and the ruins of cut-stone Otomí temples, in secluded forests unknown to guidebooks, spoke of the cost.

I wanted to go to Ahuacatlán because there was something missing, I had felt, in my travels with Mexicans in the States. That something was a context—the missing pieces of family life, of women, of children, of animals, of town plazas, of *fiestas*. The Moctezuma valley area, including Ahuacatlán, was the home of the men whom I had driven to Florida, the home of Victor and Timoteo, who had accompanied Carlos to Los Angeles, of Mariano and others at the Martinolli ranch—including those who had waited in the orchard while I was looking for *coyotes*. From what I could tell, it was typical of many of the Mexican feeder villages to the States: it had the poverty of southern Mexico, the remoteness that lent an extra Shangri-la luster to the image of the United States, the hardscrabble agricultural base that took kids out of school at a young age, unprepared for any profession but enthralled by a get-rich-quick scheme called *El Norte,* the United States.

Lupe Sanchez had arranged for me to stay with the family of an old friend of his in Ahuacatlán, a former farmworker named Hilario Pacheco. It wasn't only as a favor to me: Hilario coordinated the work in the valley of an agricultural cooperative that the Arizona Farmworkers Union had helped to found. His job required visits to farmers not only around Ahuacatlán, but also in the twenty or so isolated *ranchos* that dotted the valley—and Hilario didn't like to drive the co-op's ten-ton truck on the narrow curvy back roads. Coming from a mountainous place myself, I rather did. And so was born our arrangement.

Again the White Arrow yawed, tilting sharply into the mountain this time, the road passing over a small stream falling down one of the mountain's dark folds. Butterflies danced in a ray of light that illuminated this green recess, entranced perhaps by the warmth, perhaps by the mist. The scene was enchanting, except for the quantity of papers and cans that littered the stream banks. It was trash of the Third World wilderness, a wilderness where people live.

Around the next curve, the bus slowed again; half of the road had crumbled and slid down the mountainside. A crew of men was working with shovels and planks and wheelbarrows of concrete to buttress it up again, among them one Rigoberto Orduña, Hilario's brother-in-law and my landlord for the next four months. He was a quiet, humble, nondescript man, quite gainfully employed by local standards. I didn't know how to pick him out yet . . . but we were getting close to Ahuacatlán.

Soon we reached the valley bottom, and for the next half hour traced the route of the curving Río Moctezuma, hot air rushing in from the advancing night. We skirted a small hamlet, nestled deep in the valley and visible from a distance by the white dome of its large church, and stopped at an intersection on the edge. Few were around to see me descend from the bus, but those that were stopped to watch. No one would be there to meet me, because they didn't know exactly when I was coming. Besides, one could spend a long afternoon waiting for the White Arrow.

I walked up to one older, straw-hatted man on the nearest corner. He looked down, pretending not to see me as I approached, but then at the sound of my *"Buenas noches"* was extremely polite and attentive. Yes, he said, he knew the house of Hilario Pacheco. He would take me there.

Hilario's wife, Lupe, handed six-year-old Juanito a sack full of empty soda bottles and tucked a one-hundred-peso note in his little pocket. *"Four Coca-Colas and an orange,"* she instructed her son, and he left the shade of the kitchen for the hot Ahuacatlán streets. There was to be a guest at the midday meal—an American—and cold soft drinks were to be served. He had a mission.

It was an errand he ran whenever a guest was served—last time it had been the priest—and he liked it because his mother always shared one of the Cokes with him. That was a rare treat. And what sweetened it was that his three older sisters usually didn't get any. And they always complained.

Juanito headed toward the nearest of the three stores in town that had refrigerators—Don Beto's, on a corner opposite the plaza. After the dark kitchen, he had to squint—the sun was bright and very hot. On days like this, Juanito's brown crew cut reflected its blond highlights—though not a blond by American standards, already he was called *"Güero,"* or *"Rubio,"* by many in town.

There were not many sidewalks, so Juanito walked in the dirt road. It was not like in cities of the United States, where a parent would hesitate to send such a small child on errands. In a remote town of less than a thousand people, everyone knows each other. Harm a small boy, and not only were you put in jail, you were ostracized—which is worse. The town's law-enforcement system was its very smallness. Nor was traffic a problem, simply because few in Ahuacatlán had cars. What traffic there was was limited to the highway on the edge of town.

Rather than cars or creeps, what Juanito mainly feared were the pigs of Señora Eustolia, across the road from his family's house. There were five in all, a sow and her brood of four piglets. As with the animals of other widows, or poorer families, they were part of public life in Ahuacatlán. Juanito lived in a concrete-and-plaster house, with corrugated plastic roof and stone walls around its two acres to keep the animals in. But Señora Eustolia had only her two-room bamboo hut. She couldn't very well keep all her pigs tied up, so they just ran free. The pigs seldom got lost, as everyone knew them by their coloring, and, actually, they seemed among the happiest creatures in town. The sow led a sedentary life near the village dump and Eustolia's door, her tiny eyes too small for her body, bristly back as high as Juanito's nose. But the piglets were a marauding gang, snuffling around underneath kitchen windows, lying in mud by the river, on the run when playing or whenever one of the town's sorry dogs found the energy to yap at them. They ran fast, sometimes in formation; and if you were small, like Juanito, they would not change direction for you.

Why the robust pigs of Ahuacatlán were afraid of the dogs is a mystery of nature. Like their cousins all over Latin America, the dogs of Ahuacatlán were among the world's most pathetic creatures. You did not call over a Mexican's dog and scratch it behind the ears—they were dirty. They expected you to hit them. Mexicans seldom caressed them. Back home, when two dogs got into a fight, mothers had to warn you to stay away. But in Ahuacatlán, a dogfight was a reason for celebration. On more than one evening at the plaza, the sound of snarling attracted a throng of twenty or so children. Cheering, they chased the feuding dogs down the street, sometimes throwing stones to intensify things. Juanito saw the old mongrel of his buddy Pedrito lying in the street and let loose a good-size rock. The missile connected with its stomach; the dog leapt to its feet and slunk off with its tail between its legs. That's what dogs were for.

Juanito's kindergarten teacher, Idalia, smiled at him as she passed going the other way. Soon Juanito passed the café where the male teachers took many of their meals. As usual, they were sitting in two groups. There was some kind of war going on between the teachers. It had to do not with the school, but with Mexico. All of them, Juanito knew, were from out of town. As part of their deal with the government, they received their education and credentials in return for agreeing to serve in a remote area for three or four years. But because they were young and bored with Ahuacatlán, and came from several different Mexican states, they found reasons to hate each other. Juanito was glad that Idalia wasn't a part of it all.

Tomás Peña called a greeting to Juanito, and Juanito looked over at the boarded-up little storefront where the Peñas lived. Señor Peña was out front, a long five-gallon gas can resting up on his shoulder, draining into the fuel tank of a government truck. Tomás was watching from the window. Juanito would have been surprised at the sight of an American gas station: big illuminated sign, fuel pumps, bells, air hose coming out of the ground. There was nothing so fancy in Ahuacatlán, or even in Querétaro City. Here, if you wanted gas, you found Señor Peña's house, knocked on his door, and told him how much. His gravity-flow storage tank was in the back; a Pemex tanker truck came around to refill it every six months or so.

Next Juanito neared the plaza, fronted on one side by the huge white domed church, by far the largest building in town. It had taken a long time to complete that church—the Indians, under Franciscan rule, had started it, and mestizos, ruled by their poverty, had finished it. The plaza was quiet, almost all the dark green, wrought-iron benches that encircled it empty at midday. Except one: sitting in a far corner was Zeferino Herrera. Mamá said he was an idiot. He walked around all day without seeming to know where he was going. When he got hungry, he knocked on people's doors; most of the *señoras* would fix him a plate of beans, scrambled eggs, something. When Don Beto gave him batteries, he listened to his transistor radio, held it right up to his ear. Juanito walked quietly up the sidewalk opposite Zeferino, hoping he wouldn't be noticed.

Don Beto, a friendly, outgoing man whose large belly was the subject of many children's jokes, reached from behind the

counter for the bag of empty bottles as Juanito entered his shady
store. It took a moment for the eyes to adjust—the stores never
had lights. Don Beto placed the bottles upright on the counter.
"Four. And what will it be, señorito?"

Juanito placed his order; Don Beto filled the bag and handed
him his change. On the way out, Juanito stopped by the overturned crate of the old crone whom Don Beto let use his sidewalk.
She came down from some *rancho* two or three times a week and
sold roasted pumpkin seeds. They were cheap, even from Juanito's point of view, and he knew his mother wouldn't mind. The
crone wrapped fifty or sixty seeds into a newspaper cone, and her
gnarly fingers picked the appropriate coin from Juanito's small
hand.

The walk back took longer, because the bag now was heavy,
and some pumpkin seeds required two hands to eat. Juanito took
a different route, for interest's sake—around behind the church,
past the high crumbling wall of a disused courtyard. That was
the place where the boxing promoters and cockfight entrepreneurs
set up shop once a month or so, placing a card table by the gate
to charge admission, installing loudspeakers to let the whole town
know they were there, running long extension cords from across
the street so they could string up a light bulb or two and keep
things going once it got dark.

There had been a cockfight just that weekend, and down the
street Juanito stopped where three or four other kids had gathered
around a figure seated on the sidewalk. They were watching Pablo,
who ran the town's best cantina. Pablo was bent over something
in his lap.

¿Qué?" Juanito asked his friend Chiquis.

"One of the roosters," said Chiquis. *"He's sewing it up."*

Sure enough, one of Pablo's hands was pulling a needle and
thread from the direction of the rooster. The rooster had a deep
gash in its stomach, where the razor strapped to the foot of its
opponent had struck home. Usually such a rooster was simply
sold as food, but Pablo had started a small side business through
his surgical ability to resurrect fallen roosters: behind his house

was a coop where several proud birds, each with a scar, strutted their stuff, awaiting the day they would go at it again. This rooster breathed heavily, blinked slowly, beak open.

"*Think he'll make it?*" asked one of the boys.

"*This one, I don't know,*" said Pablo, shaking his head. "*Big cut. But he put up a great fight. I think he'll make it.*" Using his teeth, he tied a knot down by the bird's oozy belly and applied ointment to the sutures.

The smells of the midday dinner filled the remainder of the walk home—corn tortillas cooking over wood fires, gurgling pots of refried beans, sizzling meat in the homes of the more comfortable. A rock 'n' roll hits tape, the kind offered Mexicans in any store with space for the five-foot-tall rotating rack, blared from the window of one house—over the months Juanito had come to recognize every song on that tape, they played it so often—and, from another, came the *ranchera* music that was Mexico's own.

> *I dreamed of money in the bank,*
> *And of driving a Cadillac.*
> *I married a blonde, hoping I'd become a U.S. citizen*
> *—but she turned out to be a wetback, too,*
> *And now I'm back home, driving my burro.*

Juanito turned onto his own street, and looked: good, he thought, no pigs. He hissed at Pedrito's dog, which had returned to the sun but was too deaf to notice, and walked through the gate to his house.

Concrete floor, gas range, long concrete countertop, and room for a table with four or five wooden chairs around it—Lupe Pacheco's kitchen was nicer than most. Poor Eustolia Romo across the road had only a dirt floor, had to keep a little cooking fire going all day long, breathe the smoke when she heated water. She smelled like smoke. How did she feel when the government gas truck came to town, and others lifted their empty propane tanks up to the highway for a refill? Perhaps Eustolia's sons would do well in *"Los Uniteds,"* and send something home to make life easier. Hilario certainly had. Though they had Lupe's brother to thank for the use of the house. He had left for Florida ten years ago, forsaking his inheritance for the chance of greater riches up north. He must have done all right, too, for they never heard from him, never had any word that he was headed home. Perhaps it was just as well—where would her family go if one day he showed up?

On the wall was their old AM radio, tuned to the only station it could be tuned to—500-watt XEJAQ, "Radio Happiness," in Jalpan, down on the plains twenty-five miles away. The announcer was young Miguel Ángel, son of her sister-in-law. Lunch hour was when he always did the requests and dedications received in the mail—often from as far away as Idaho. Lupe was not sure exactly where Idaho was, but she knew they grew potatoes there, and a fair number of young men headed there every spring, her husband's nephew Victor among them. The names stuck in her head, but the places were only vague imaginings—a vast cold treeless land of rich soil with potatoes popping up everywhere. On the edge of the farm, she saw the owner's great house, his beautiful wife and children. Lupe's sister had a friend in California who sometimes sent to Ahuacatlán issues of a magazine called *House and Garden*. That was a fun Sunday morning—sitting at her sister's house and going over the pictures of the kitchens, the children's clothes, the surprising things they ate. Lupe had left Ahuacatlán only once—to have an operation in Querétaro City. It was that operation that had sent Hilario back to Arizona, the place he swore he would never return. They had needed money for the operation, and, in only a season and a half, Hilario had saved it. Querétaro was large and frightening, meshed, in her mind, with Hilario's absence and the experience of being in the hospital. Now she felt better, and was sure she would continue to if she stayed at home.

Lupe was thirty-three, but looked ten years older than an American woman her age. Most of the women in Ahuacatlán did, and it wasn't for lack of skin cream: childbearing started early, child rearing took up most of one's life. And when the husband was away—and in Ahuacatlán they were away a lot, making money—there were husband's duties, as well: taking care of the chickens and cow, managing the money, or lack of it, disciplining the kids, and handling relations with friends and neighbors. Vacations were when she got sick.

Ah, and taking care of Grandma. Lupe's mother, in her eighties (*"nobody's really sure how old,"* Lupe told me, *"including her"*), lived in the second bedroom, the one that opened onto the kitchen. Most of the day she sat there, in the dark, confined by arthritis to a tall, straight chair. The girls attended to her feeding and other natural needs. Now she was out in the kitchen, where Hilario and his brother, Cornelio, had carried her in the chair to get her out of the dark for a while. After lunch, after the dishes, she and the girls would take Grandma out to the patio, to comb out the waist-length silver hair and pick out nits. It was next to Grandma, dressed in her widow's black, toothless and deeply wrinkled and mostly deaf, that Lupe looked positively girlish.

Cornelio, sitting with a glass of milky-white *pulque*—the home-fermented juice of the *maguey* cactus—pulled up a chair next to her. She declined a sip of his drink, and they talked in low tones for a while. She looked worried about something; I could hear her addressing him, *"ayy, joven, ahh, joven"*—young man, young man. Cornelio, who had been drinking a bit, raised his voice: *"Oooh, that's ridiculous, Grandmother. Don't even say such ridiculous things. If my parents were still alive, it would be a great privilege for me to have them in my house. How proud I would be to have my father sitting there. What a great comfort to me! Why, if my father were alive, I would indulge his every vice! If he asked me for a beer, I would send Victor right off to get him one . . ."*

Everyone was listening; Grandma knew it and didn't respond. I looked down at the concrete floor, at the turkey chicks that had wandered in and were pecking at my shoe. Even in a land where the family is intact, where family care for the infirm is a given, the elderly had these doubts. Poor *abuela*, I thought—

though at the same time I thought her perhaps luckier than my grandparents, isolated from young people, from new life.

The silence was broken by the arrival of a laborer from a *rancho* atop the mountain opposite Hilario's home. He carried in his arms a crate of small high-altitude peaches. They were from orchards Hilario had pointed out to me high on the mountain-sides, on slopes so steep that every tree required a stone-rimmed terrace to survive—a project of the cooperative. They were the season's first, and the children cried out in delight—fresh, sweet fruit was hard to come by in Ahuacatlán. Our meal would have a fine dessert.

After receiving the peaches, Hilario sat back down at his chair on the porch next to the kitchen, surrounded by corn husks, and ate a peach without expression. His main work was with the cooperative, but in his spare time, almost as a hobby, he grew corn and small amounts of sugarcane, coffee, and fruit. The sugar-cane was mainly a treat for his kids to munch on—with his machete he had just cut down a single cane, sectioned it, sliced off its hard outer layer, and handed pieces to me and Juanito. We gnawed as Hilario returned to shucking the corn. He wasn't preparing it to be eaten on the cob; instead, the ears would go onto the roof, in a fenced-in area protected from birds, next to the coffee beans, to dry. Later, Lupe would grind the corn to mix daily with lime and salt as tortilla dough. Hilario didn't seem comfortable unless he was working: even in the moments before a meal, he shunned idleness.

He was a slender man, of medium height, fond of jeans and checkered shirts—always carefully ironed by Lupe, and washed, of necessity, by hand. Outside the house he always wore a straw hat, slightly rounder than cowboy style. His was an Indian face, broad with high cheekbones, and black hair, already starting to gray at thirty-eight; but his torso was European sized, long and tapering to a narrow waist. Lupe's face and physique were both European looking, but her skin was Indian dark. In Ahuacatlán as everywhere in Mexico, only a very few—Indians, isolated by remoteness and poverty, or those of European descent, isolated by wealth, privilege, and a desire to stay "thoroughbred"—were not mestizo.

The chickens, a little flock of seven or eight hens, trailed by chicks of various ages, approached and made a run on the kitchen, but Hilario shooed them away. The line between human space and animal space was lightly drawn in Ahuacatlán, due mainly to mild weather, which made doors unnecessary. He then watched with a skeptical eye as they approached Lupe's flower bed. The flowers were slowly being pecked to death, until, the day before, Hilario had taken twigs and small branches from a dead bush with lots of thorns and made a sort of natural perimeter fence. A couple of the tiniest chicks somehow snuck in, but the big ones stayed out. Several of these, I had thought, were some sort of exotic Dr. Seuss breed: their pink necks were completely bald. But Hilario set me straight: it was the work of the crazy rooster, he explained, the mean one with the missing eye and frayed comb—he attacked the hens instead of just stimulating them, plucking out their neck feathers from behind. His wounds he had received in battle with a turkey. He was a nasty piece of work, but we had him to thank in part for this special dinner: earlier that morning his life had ended at the edge of Hilario's hatchet, on the chopping block. We were having chicken with chocolaty *mole* sauce, a local specialty and great treat, given the price of chocolate. Its smell drifted out from the kitchen.

"*Lupe!*" yelled Hilario.

"*Five minutes!*" came her harried reply.

The chickens had another enemy: a nocturnal mountain weasel that the locals referred to by its Indian name, the *tlacuache*. For that reason, every night at dusk they were retired to the branches of the huge tree that spread over the yard. The kids all joined in rounding them up, and then Hilario, or his brother-in-law Rigo, who lived down the hill, would toss them one at a time into the tree's lowest crotch. With a great commotion, the chickens would make their way slowly up to the high branches, using small ramps Hilario had built in places where there was too big a jump. At dawn they came down of their own accord, making the final jump—about ten feet—with a frantic beating of too-small wings and an audible *thump!* as each of their heavy bodies hit the dirt.

Pulque in hand, Cornelio came outside and set up a chair in the sun. That week, his son Victor had returned from Querétaro City with the latest issue of ¡*Alarma!*, the popular pictorial magazine of crime and grisly violence. Juanito and Hilario's daughters crowded around as Cornelio haltingly read aloud an update on the notorious Poquianchis, the sisters arrested for prostitution, kidnapping, pandering, drug sales, et cetera, in Mexico's biggest sex scandal. No periodicals of any kind were on sale in Ahuacatlán—XEJAQ had only hit the airwaves three years before—so for them it was a special delight. Hilario disliked ¡*Alarma!* however, not because of its grisliness but because it was frivolous. Occasionally you could catch him reading a western novel. He sniffed his boredom when Cornelio asked him to clarify a word he hadn't seen before. The word was *cocaína*.

Finally Hilario's daughter Lupita came out to tell us the meal was ready, and we walked past the partition to the kitchen. Soup, a chicken broth with noodles, was already on the table, along with plates of the ever-present corn tortillas. Tortillas, rolled into little scoops, were the primary utensils; the spoons, I had a suspicion, were mainly there as a courtesy to me. Next came rice, the rich brown chicken *mole*, and a small circle of white goat's cheese from a *rancho*, a few short white hairs attesting to its authenticity. A fresh batch of piquant *salsa*, ground that morning in Lupe's stone *molcajete*, was there to be added to anything, but tasted best with the rice. Cornelio twisted Hilario's arm until Hilario consented to try Cornelio's cool white *pulque;* my arm needed no twisting. So many were there that only the males (including, to his pleasure, little Juanito) were seated, with Lupe running back and forth, keeping the stack of tortillas fresh and high, serving and clearing. Her sister-in-law, Rigo's wife, Conchita, stood by with baby Omar in her arms, and Grandma watched from the dark doorway to her room. Lupita pushed the colorful baskets that hung from the ceiling back and forth, on behalf of

Omar, who would watch them for hours. The baskets were not only decorative but necessary for the storage of foods that appealed to crawling bugs. Lupita's older sister, Alicia, shooed out the chickens. Lupe served coffee and lemon tea, Cokes and orange soda. Omar, to his mother's surprise, reached out and caught a basket with his six-month-old hand; when she pried it away, with great difficulty, Omar began to bawl.

"He loves to hold on to things," Conchita said to Lupe, who listened with half an ear. *"His little fingers are so strong, and he hates to let go. It's like he's afraid something will happen if he lets go."*

"Pobrecito cabrón! Pobre cabroncito!" cooed his Uncle Hilario to wailing Omar. Poor little bastard!

"Once he got a hold of my hair," said Grandma from the doorway, to no one in particular.

Cornelio poured us more *pulque.* Lupe presented us with a plate of the dry sugar-sprinkled pastry from the town bakery. Alicia cleared off more dishes, and carried them outside to wash in the tub. Juanito picked at his chicken and sipped his Coke with gusto.

Hilario decided we would take our coffee and peaches outdoors. *"Gracias, señora,"* I said to Lupe as we stood up from the table—immediately feeling silly. Though appropriate at home, it was an elaborate decoration here: people were not thanked for performing their duties. No one ever said it but me. It was just one of many things I had yet to learn.

Cornelio did not share his brother Hilario's strongly Indian appearance, or his reputation for strictness and self-discipline. His hair was wavy, his shirt collar open, his manner relaxed. The three of us sat in the shade of the large tree. Cornelio, to me, was a breath of fresh air; Hilario was trustworthy, sober, and responsible, but Cornelio was expressive and open, willing to discuss and joke about almost anything. I knew Hilario had spent many years in the States, but had not yet succeeded in getting him to talk about it. A proud man, he found his years on "the other side" to be demeaning, I knew. His fervent wish was that Juanito never be tempted, nor compelled to go there. That was one reason he worked so hard for the cooperative: if local agriculture could be developed to the point where it would support a living wage, men would not have to leave Ahuacatlán. That afternoon, though, with the prompting of Cornelio, the warm breeze, and the cool *pulque*, Hilario opened up a crack. I asked Cornelio about his time in the States.

"We left for the North in 'forty-nine, the year father died, no?" he asked Hilario. Hilario nodded. He set down his drink and crossed his legs.

"Cornelio was eleven and I fourteen. Men had left Querétaro for other parts of Mexico for years back then, traveling to earn more money, but the States was still a new idea. In Texas the oil boom was starting, and there were jobs in that and in picking cotton.

"Well, we walked one hundred kilometers, from here to Xilitla, because there was no highway then, no bus. We took a bus to the border, crossed the Río Bravo, and found work in the valley, in Weslaco. The crossing cost us many humiliations—no, not from the gringos, from the other Mexicans—because we were so young and small and had no protector. The border towns can be very tough. We stayed there in Weslaco three years, sending money home to our mamá. And then Cornelio left."

"I returned then because my maternal cousin, Antonio, wanted to sell me his delivery business," Cornelio interjected, somewhat defensively. *"That way I was able to help Mamá from closer by."*

"Then, I was so sick of cotton—you know, they almost never pick it by hand anymore in the States—I was so sick of cotton I went with some friends to Oregon, to work in the onions," Hilario continued. *"I did that for two years."*

Hilario had been deported in 1954, during what I realized must have been the large sweep of illegal aliens—1.4 million of them—known as Operation Wetback. Besides being inconvenienced, he was deeply embarrassed by the episode. *"To be handcuffed, put in a truck, have your name published in the paper—why, they treated me like a criminal! I did not go back until Lupe needed the operation."* Cornelio, still delivering bricks thirty years later, had never gone back.

"*No, I didn't save anything for myself, sent it all home to my mamá,*" Hilario continued. "*Ah, no, I take it back: I did bring home a souvenir . . .*"

Hilario unbuttoned his shirt far enough to show a long wide scar on his shoulder. "*You are lucky to live in a time when beer bottles have twist-off caps,*" he said. "*A guy with a bottle opener in a Weslaco bar decided he didn't like me.*"

I was fascinated, as we talked, to learn of the history of what was for them an *emigration* to the States, of the patterns that had developed over time. Men from Querétaro, they told me, generally went to Arizona or Florida to work. Men from the state of San Luis Potosí, on the other hand, typically headed for California and Texas. And it did not end there. In Arkansas, picking tomatoes or planting seedlings for lumber companies, you found mainly workers from Michoacán; in Kansas feedlots, they came from Michoacán and Guanajuato. To California they also came from Guerrero, to Texas especially from Jalisco. In American cities the distribution of Mexican nationals seemed more random, but this order behind rural immigration patterns lent the phenomenon a completely different face from that presented in U.S. newspapers and magazines. This was less a random tide of desperate people than a traditional economic relationship, grown up over decades, between Mexican "hands" (the term *bracero,* used to describe Mexican immigrants in the early years, comes from the Spanish for "arm") and American growers. It was nothing for them to feel ashamed of, and they evidently did not.

The breeze had stopped, so that we could feel the sun beat down; we scooted our chairs back into the shade of the tree. As Cornelio refilled my glass, I put my little notebook away—research for the day was done. I had to watch out in Ahuacatlán: men's most interesting memories of the States often emerged after a few drinks, which was precisely when it became most difficult for me to remember them. More than once I had to double-check a story the next day.

Lupe called to Hilario from the porch—a local man was there, with a big jar in his hands. *"Honey,"* said Hilario to himself, rising to fetch the man some from the large vat under the porch. Honey was a big money-maker for the cooperative. I used the opportunity to point out to Cornelio a large, ripe pomegranate hanging from a tree across the yard; he agreed that we deserved it, and soon it was in our hands. Cornelio and I sliced and ate our second dessert of the afternoon, the delicious red juice staining our fingers and shirts.

There was a rapping outside my door. *"Slee-ee-pyhead! Ti-i-ime to get u-u-p!"* Waking his American was, it seemed, one of the great pleasures of Hilario's day.

"What time is it?"

"Late! Already very late!" I scrounged around for my watch. It was 5:30 A.M.. The sun had not yet risen; roosters were only starting to greet the brightening sky. In half an hour or so, choruses of cock-a-doodle-doos would sweep over the town—but there had been barely a peep yet from the neighbors' big fighting cock, who seemed the village choral director. I needed a drink of water, badly . . . but the only water at Hilario's house came straight from the river. I groaned.

"Up yet?" said Hilario, cracking the door to get a good look at my puffy face.

"¡Sí, sí! I'm up!" I sat up painfully. Hilario was delighted. Americans acted so superior, but really they were soft. I was the proof. He grinned and gazed. It was not pleasant. *"You can leave now,"* I said. *"Shut the door, please?"* Hilario grinned more widely, and shut the door.

When members of the *cooperativa* weren't staying over, I had a room to myself—part of Rigo and Conchita's little house, fifty feet down the hill from Hilario and Lupe's. Towel over my shoulder, I made my way from there past the chickens to the laundry

basin which both households shared. The donkey brayed plaintively as I approached—my sentiments exactly, I thought. I scooped
a bowlful of cold water from the rain barrel—which sat underneath the extension of a gutter from Hilario's house—poured it
into a small plastic basin, and splashed it over my face. The effect
was devastating, but it opened my eyes. I was changing the car-
tridge in my razor as Hilario came up to wash his hands.

"*What are you doing?*" he asked.

"*Changing the blade,*" I said.

"*So soon? You changed it just last week.*"

"*At the* beginning *of last week,*" I said defensively.

He picked up his old safety razor. "*See this?*" he said. He
indicated the blade, and I knew what was coming. "*Six months!*"
Wasteful Americans!

"*Well, maybe if you changed it more often, you would be more
handsome.*"

"*¡Pah!*" was his reply, emitted as he turned to go toward
the kitchen. "*Breakfast is ready as soon as you are,*" he said, without
turning back. ". . . *as soon as you are done holding everything up!*"
he might have added. Slow Americans! Pah!

My consolation was that Hilario really had a use for me. The
night before, members of the cooperative had filled the bed of
the group's ten-ton, three-axle, ten-speed truck with sacks of
cement. Its destination was the *rancho* of Rincón de Pisquintla,
where villagers would use it to construct a modest reservoir to
store water from a small mountain spring, making possible the
irrigation of otherwise unproductive land. The first hour of driving was paved highway, but the next two were dirt road—increasingly winding dirt road, that climbed high into the remote
sierra. Hilario didn't like to drive, had no stomach for it. I thrived
on it.

Lupe was up, of course, to serve us coffee and simple past-
ries. The coffee was brewed from the real beans that dried on
the roof of the house—but it tasted strange to me, the way real
farm eggs have a different flavor from the store-bought kind.

Alas, I was raised on store-bought coffee, so I opted for the tea she brewed with leaves from the lemon tree out back. Three cups quenched my thirst from the night before, and, with Hilario pacing impatiently beside me, we were off.

It was status to drive a big truck like this in the sierra— good ones were expensive and seldom seen. I felt powerful climbing up into the cab. Little kids waved; I tooted the horn. In the small city of Jalpan, down on the valley floor, we stopped for Hilario to buy oranges—the distributors made it this far, but not up to Ahuacatlán—and then soon it was back off the highway and into the mountains, *rancho* bound.

The road was everything one would expect from a remote mountain road in Mexico—precipitous, curvy, full of surprises: a herd of goats around this bend, a muddy morass around that, a hairpin turn where you would least expect it, totally unmarked. Fortunately, Hilario provided verbal road signs, well in advance. We crept across two streams where the wooden bridges had been washed out. Hilario suggested I was being too nice to the livestock we encountered—if they couldn't get off the road, they were not meant for this world. And if they got hit, well, *"Somebody will eat them soon,"* he assured me.

Ranchos were among Mexico's most remote locations. Typically they had only between twenty and fifty residents; almost never did they have electricity. Many could not be reached by automobile—you got a bus to let you off on a certain creek or ridge, and then you walked. Small mountain springs were often their sole reason for existence. Up these mountains, many had fantastic names: when we wanted to arrange a meeting, Hilario would pay for an ad to be broadcast on XEJAQ: *"Attention, residents of Piglet, Big Peach, The Bats, and Saint Peter the Old! Meeting next Friday at the home of Rafael Ramos at sundown."* Normally one person could be counted on to hear the message, and that person would be responsible for telling everyone else. The residents were generally interrelated, and family feuds had long and sometimes violent histories. Residents of *ranchos*, I had discovered at Martinolli's, often understood the world in different terms from the rest of us. I had asked a *rancho*-born student of mine in Phoenix how far he lived from Ahuacatlán.

"Eight hours," he explained.

"You must get tired of all that driving," I suggested. He looked very puzzled, and asked what I meant. *"Just that, any time you need something, like radio batteries, you have to drive eight hours both ways."*

"No, no," he explained earnestly. *"We walk. Eight hours walking."*

Hilario, in answer to my question, explained that parents in *ranchos* were among the most eager anywhere to get their kids to emigrate to the States. *"They see it as their big chance to get rich,"* said Hilario. *"Their sons come home with fifty dollars, and it's the most money they've seen in their lives. Some parents nearly throw their kids out the door!"*

The mountainsides were bushy, but not lush. Spectacular vistas opened up as we rounded one ridge, then the next. The broad mountainsides were different from those of my home in that they were cultivated—looking across any expanse, you could see the different-colored crops separated from each other by stone fences, dotted with faraway humans in straw cowboy hats and the stout oxen that helped them plow. Clouds obscured the highest points, thinned by the wind as they descended the tableau before us. Nearer the road, a common sight was lines of white boxes set up on stumps or wooden legs, each one striped with a different combination of bright colors. *"Beehives,"* Hilario explained. *"The stripes tell the bees which box is theirs. Or so it is thought."*

"You see that road?" he continued, pointing out a steep grade forking off to the left. *"Padre Cano, the priest, visits all the ranchos once or twice a month. Last summer he told me about something which had just happened to him on that road.*

"It seems the father was coming down on horseback with Don Reyes Alvarado, who lives up there, in Huilotla. They came upon a

fat man and his wife and their infant daughter making their way slowly up the hill.

" 'Good afternoon, young man,' said Don Reyes. The young man stopped and stared and Don Reyes, who finally brought his horse to a halt. 'Well?' demanded Don Reyes finally, 'what's the matter?' "

" 'Don't you recognize me, father?' said the young man, slowly. It was his son! He had been away seven years in the States, getting fatter as so many do there, finding a bride."

I whistled lowly.

"But you know," said Hilario, "it could easily have been the other way around. I have heard many stories of children not recognizing their own parents. Many return only when they hear their parents have died . . ."

"If you want to know more about this, you really should talk to the priest. He is very highly educated—in your country, in fact—and he thinks about these things a lot."

After passing several other settlements, we finally arrived at Rincón de Pisquintla. Only a few dwellings were visible to us, all of them made of wood or cane. Two had metal roofs; the others were thatched. There were a couple of old dogs. The air was wonderful, cool and fresh and full of butterflies. Men came out of fields, clad in *huaraches* and home-sewn clothes, to greet Hilario, and kids were sent to find other men. After a discreet interval wives and mothers asked Hilario for news of their sons in the north—had he heard anything? Hilario said I had been in Phoenix, and probably had more recent news—and then it occurred to me that probably I *did* know several of the men who belonged to these women. Talking with the wives, seeing the babies, the plots of beans and onions, was a revelation: up in the States, I had never appreciated that the men were . . . well, so *important*. On the ranch they seemed so single, and rootless—like random pieces of an unknown picture puzzle you found in a cabinet and were unsure what to do with. Here, suddenly, I saw how they were husbands, fathers, owners—missing pieces that would make a puzzle complete, prettier, a whole picture.

After the wives came younger men, just entering their teens. Approaching with extreme shyness and respect, they asked if I could get them jobs. No, I had to say, I wasn't an owner, I had worked alongside others from this town. *Was there much work?* Some, I said, not a lot, but some if you were patient. "University of Arizona," read the emblem on the T-shirt of one little girl.

By late afternoon we had the truck unloaded, and had been treated to chunks of *quiote*—the fibrous, sap-soaked inner core of the *maguey* cactus, round and white like a slice of pineapple, chewed and sucked on as a pick-me-up. Cokes were served alongside, making the snack a bizarre combination of Otomí and Americana. *Did I like it?* a woman asked. *Tastes a little like wood,* I admitted—if you lied about these things out of politeness, I had learned, you were liable to get another helping.

"*Wood?*" Those who had understood me relayed the answer to those who had not. They thought it was hilarious. "*Wood! Wood!*" Their teeth weren't so good; you could tell when they laughed. One offered me a little piece of wood to chew on, so that I could tell the difference. We laughed about that too.

Rincón de Pisquintla was perched on a hillside; all afternoon I had been watching the colors of the land change as the sun moved across the sky. You could hear birds everywhere; no radio or TV noises diverted your attention from the life around you. But the sun began to set, and Hilario signaled it was time for us to leave. I was so pleased with the place, I wanted to spend the night. And I was annoyed when I started the engine—what a racket it made! how badly it stank!—and even more annoyed when a young man came running up with a big tape deck under his arm. He didn't look like anyone else in town. "*I'm the teacher,*" he explained. He was from the southern Mexican state of Chiapas, on the Guatemalan border, assigned here to do his national service. He had run three miles from a neighboring *rancho* when he heard we were here. "*Can you take me down with you?*" We said sure, and fit him in in front. I was filled with romantic thoughts about living in such a place. But the teacher wasn't. The bus to town—probably another White Arrow—hadn't made its weekly trips for the entire past month, he explained, and he was going crazy. His radio batteries were almost dead! He grasped the device with a fervor that made me realize he considered it his sole link to civilization. *"Boy, am I glad to be out of there for a while!"* he said, smiling broadly.

The engine of the truck whined as I downshifted to keep us on the road. Hilario held tight to his seat and told me to slow down. The teacher asked if either of us would mind if he played his radio. Hilario just looked away, out the window. *"Softly,"* I said. A family of turkeys scattered as the big blue truck bore down on them in the twilight.

"No greater disaster has befallen Ahuacatlán since the conquest," said Father Tomás Cano, transferring his heavy white vestments from his rounded shoulders to a wardrobe in the sacristy and wiping the sweat from his florid brow. He was a tall man, with close-together eyes that gave the impression of big cheeks. He walked through a door to his office and poured himself a glass of water from a pitcher on his desk. A ceiling fan turned slowly, and with questionable effect; it *was* hot in there. I had been waiting since he finished evening mass to get his thoughts on emigration to the States.

"Please, have a seat," he said, pulling out a chair from under a table. There was a white cat on it. *"Ah, Gringo, so that's where you've been hiding!"* He shooed the cat away.

"Gringo?" I asked.

The father grinned a bit sheepishly. *"It was named by some children,"* he said. *"Because of its color."*

"Did you mean that—about no greater disaster?"

"Yes! Though, of course, it is more complicated than that. It is, mainly, a great disruption, bringing with it much bad but also some good." He paused to finish the glass of water. *"That is to say . . . it's, it's . . . say, do you know how to swim?"*

"Excuse me?"

"I said, do you swim? It's late enough that the suds should be gone from the river, and the children will have left the swimming hole. It's so hot in here, there's nothing I'd like more than a swim."

The priest was a man of such importance in Ahuacatlán that I had not imagined he did things like swim. Out of respect, I had kept my sleeves rolled down and my collar buttoned high. But this sounded like a great idea.

"Sure—why not?" I said. He turned off the lights and fan and we exited through a side door. He didn't lock the door, I noticed—most doors in Ahuacatlán didn't even have locks. A tiny side street soon turned into a path along the river. The priest was in no hurry.

"Back to your question," he said. *"Externally, yes—having men leave to work in the States benefits us. They send money home, and now we have better houses, clothing, highways, cars. More people can afford farm animals. The parts of life that you can quantify are better.*

"But how much of life is that? I will say it again: not since the conquest have we suffered such a disaster. And here is why. Seven out of ten households here lack a husband, a father—they're all gone, working somewhere else. Sure, maybe—maybe—their families have more money, but the family! The men come home once a year, they make their wives pregnant, and then they leave again. The wives get so frustrated; 'I married a man, not a letter, not a U.S. Postal Service money order!' one said to me. The children of these families have a character that is colder than normal.

"And, of course, terrible things happen. The men bring home venereal disease, from the prostitutes they have up there. We never used to have these diseases in Ahuacatlán; now—ask the doctor!— they're everywhere. Or, what's worse, the men never come home at all. They take a mistress up there, and get comfortable, and that's the last we hear. I think about two hundred never come home at all anymore. That includes the ones that die: my count is twenty-seven dead in the past twenty years. Yes, they die in car wrecks, bar fights, farm accidents . . .

"That is why I have always said: This is a parish of widows and orphans. It is true figuratively, but also it is true literally."

The priest hopped over a log as we continued our way upstream toward the swimming hole. During the day the wide, shallow parts of the Rio Moctezuma were dotted with women doing their wash, each crouched over large, smooth stones dragged into the river for that purpose. Their laundry detergent—and that of women all the way up the valley—was the source of the suds the priest had referred to; at midday the river sometimes resembled a moving bubble bath. But now the suds had been rinsed down into the Jalpan reservoir, and the river ran smooth and dark. Father Cano sat down a moment to rest.

"You know, I studied in your country for five years."

"Yes? Where?"

"Catholic University, in Washington, D.C."

I tried some English on him, but the priest had gotten a little rusty.

"Anyway, coming from the States, you will understand the desire to get ahead. It is called ambition, and it is a beautiful thing. But it is also the reason so many young people here want to leave. They all want to do the best they can, don't want anyone to be better than them.

"They hear their friends chatting—brothers, older boys who have been. Of course, even if they suffered fiascos up there, the stories they tell are pure adventure. The younger boys see their new clothes, see how girls are attracted. To them it sounds like the Eternal Paradise! And besides, they think, only sissies stay behind. What can one who stays have to compare with a tale of crossing the border, eluding the FBI, even being in prison in the United States! The men take great pride in these things.

"So they leave school early and away they go. And six months, a year, or two years later, when they come back, they are disgusted at what they see. Ahuacatlán suddenly looks to them like a pigsty: livestock in the streets, no plumbing, dirt roads. They are ashamed. And this is the beginning of their inferiority complex—they think

everything there is better. They see Americans as very high, themselves as very low. Of course, though, they can never be Americans, or even pass for them at their age—it's too late to learn English well enough. But many feel stupid because of it. And they are ashamed to be Mexican."

The father shook his head. *"Ay, Teodoro, it's a crazy world, isn't it?"*

"And getting crazier," I said.

"What is there to do, sometimes, but go for a swim?"

"Yes."

The swimming hole was just around the next bend. I was amazed as we got close: here was the Huck Finn swimming hole missing from my youth. The main pool went down about fifteen feet. One side was a wall of stone, with numerous diving-off spots; the other was flat and grassy, with two huge sycamores sprouting from the riverbank and arcing up over the deepest pool. As the priest would soon demonstrate, you could also dive off these.

It was dusk. Far above the rocky side of the river, the highway passed. Apart from the occasional whine of a truck, all was the rushing of the river. Without a word, Father Cano disappeared behind some shrubs, where he modestly disrobed; the next thing I heard was a great splash as his body hit the deep pool, and an *"Ah!"* as he came up for air. I hung my clothes on a tree and waded cautiously into a more shallow pool downstream, getting the feel of the pebbled bottom. This was the best bath you ever got in Ahuacatlán. It was also, I discovered, plunging all the way into the cool, dark water, one of the best swims you got anywhere.

Just down the hill from Hilario's property, enclosed by his same stone fences, was another, newer small house owned by Lupe's brother, Rigoberto. Rigo, his wife, Conchita, and their six-month-old son, Omar, used two rooms of the house; the third, reserved for members of the co-op when they visited, was also mine. Though I ate with Hilario's family, and they were my hosts, I enjoyed Rigo's company. He was younger than I, which I always found

hard to accept, given his family and responsibilities and seriousness. Rigo was home by dark, up before dawn to work on the
government road crew, and preferred to spend extra time with
his family. But one Friday night, when both of us arrived home
later than the usual supper time, I suggested we go out for tacos
and beer, and Rigo accepted.

Tacos are a great Mexican snack custom, as popular in Mexico City—the world's largest metropolis—as in tiny Ahuacatlán.
In a small storefront or at a sidewalk cart, the vendor will toss
four to six corn tortillas (twice as many as tacos you order) into
shallow oil or onto a convex grill, to warm and soften them up.
Then the customer chooses the meat filling—usually different
cuts of chopped beef—loin, sausage, tongue, intestines—posted
on a piece of paper or chalkboard, done up in different sauces
(barbecue, and so on). The vendor spoons a line of filling into
each tortilla, sprinkles it with tasty, parsleylike *cilantro*, folds the
tortilla in half, ladles in a little homemade hot sauce if you like,
and nestles it side by side with the other soft-shell tacos on a
small plate. A beer or soft drink from a bottle is almost a man-
datory accompaniment. Around the counter the customers, usually men, may not know each other, but they talk. Going out for
tacos is a great way to avoid eating dinner alone.

Rigo and I sat down in a small *taquería* just down a side
street from the plaza. We called our orders over to the *señora*
behind the counter, and helped ourselves to Modelo beers from
the refrigerator case. Screw-off tops were just arriving in Mexico;
we used an opener hanging from the refrigerator door by a string.
The beers weren't too cold—they never were in Ahuacatlán—
but they were beers just the same. Rigo, a man of few words,
began as his distant and polite self, but started to loosen up as
the beer, foreign to his system, took effect. Little Omar's cold
was taking a long time to go away, wasn't it? Had I noticed the
feathers returning to the necks of the hens since that rooster got
the ax? That shallow trench he was digging was for plastic tubing,
to bring river water from Hilario's house down to Conchita's
kitchen, to help her with cooking. For nine hours a day on the

road crew, he was paid 900 pesos, or just under three U.S. dollars at the time. I did some thinking about this. How much were a pair of jeans? I asked. Twenty-three hundred pesos new, he said— or about half a weekly salary. Decent meat was very nearly as expensive—a big piece for dinner, if you could find it, cost almost a day's salary. That's why he didn't go out much, said Rigo. Did he ever think of going to the States? I asked. No, said Rigo, he wasn't the sort.

It was then that two couples came through the saloon doors of the little *taqueria*, catching everyone's attention. The women, apparently in their late teens, wore high heels, nylons, nice dresses, and makeup, and they had their hair down, brushed till it was light and bouncy. The men, also young and handsome, wore boots, designer jeans, and carefully ironed long-sleeved shirts. One of the shirts was the army surplus variety popular with Emilio Hernández and others I had known up north, though starch and ironing gave it a very different look. The taller man, in the army shirt, also wore a gold chain around his neck; he was brown haired, clean shaven, and had an engaging smile. His friend had dark, curly hair and a mustache. They nodded at me as they seated the girls and walked to the counter, and I nodded back.

I looked at Rigo; these folks obviously weren't his type at all. Next to them, he looked a perfect country mouse. Next to him, they looked like big-city playboys. But appearances could be misleading.

"Hello. How are you?" asked the taller, clean-shaven one, leaning against the counter. His accent wasn't too bad.

I smiled at the good effort. "I'm fine. And you?"

"Oh. I am—" he looked at his companion "—we are fine."

"Yes," said the shorter man, "fine!" Both of them were grinning widely now.

"Just-come-here?" asked the taller one, haltingly.

"Not long ago," I answered, to looks of puzzlement. Damn, I thought, what was an easier way to say it . . .

"Yes," I said.

Rigo, shifting uncomfortably in his seat, interrupted quietly. *"Ehmm, I'll be going, Teodoro."* He pointed to an old clock on the wall, somehow still working. Eight o'clock. *"It's getting late."* He held out three crumpled one-hundred-peso notes, a third of his daily salary; I could earn that in a few minutes back home, I thought to myself; it wasn't fair. I waved him off. *"It's on me. You're my host."* We shook hands and Rigo made an unobtrusive exit. A certain tension left the air when he did. I walked to the counter to pay and then, when the men beckoned, joined the young foursome at their table.

"My name's Teo," I said.

"Yes, we know." Of course—by now the whole town, as well as a dozen *ranchos,* knew about the *gringo* from Arizona staying with Rigo and Hilario. *"I'm Jesús, and this is Victor."*

"Ah, Cornelio's son?" He nodded, and we shook hands again. I glanced toward the women, expecting them, too, to be introduced, but it was not to be. There was a momentary silence—when men had the floor, women were silent, and introducing women, as well, apparently was not done.

He had learned his English in Idaho, explained Jesús, the tall one. Victor, a distant cousin, had gone too, but wasn't quite as quick with language as Jesús. They had been going every year, to the same ranch, for five years, leaving in April and returning in October, just in time for the soccer season. The Ahuacatlán team, *Los Tecolotes*—the owls—were state champions, Jesús said proudly. The two looked to be in their early twenties.

It was great, finally, to meet more guys my own age. *"This is a parish of widows and orphans,"* Father Cano had said. The Arizona and Florida citrus harvests emptied the town of nearly all its able-bodied men from fall to early summer. What was left in the spring—it could as well have been a time of war—were mainly boys, the elderly, and women, all of whom watched them go and awaited their return. The exception were these guys, who went to Idaho on a different harvest calendar. There were twenty or so left in town, from what I had heard. Jesús and Victor stood up to take their dates to whatever came next—but suggested we meet the next evening on the plaza. I agreed, and we shook hands yet again.

The rhythmic thump of basketballs sounded from several streets away; basketball, the sport of choice in the sierra, was going in full force when I arrived at the plaza. The rugged terrain of the Sierra Madre Oriental made soccer or baseball very difficult; carving out a flat spot big enough for a field was a major undertaking. Half a basketball court, however, was a reasonable alterative even in a *rancho*—there was, in fact, a *rancho* league—and a full-length court was well within the reach of a village like Ahuacatlán. The cement court constituted half the plaza; down two steps, along one sideline, the tile began and you could safely stroll with your newborn or grandfather. Two strings of bare bulbs, left up by popular demand after the last fiesta, crisscrossed the entire plaza and made basketball possible well into the night.

The players tended to be young teenagers—a boys' game was going on at one end of the court, and a smaller girls' game at the other. Those with some cash at their disposal wore store-bought sneakers, but a great many played with astonishing control in their leather, rubber-tire-soled *huaraches*. Presiding over all this activity, at the high end of the court, were an older group of young men. They still played basketball among themselves, but were too dignified to join the melee of the kids.

As I cut across the plaza to meet the men, I was intercepted by another young man, woman on his arm, baby in her arms, whom I recognized as a *tractorista* from Smith's.

"*José, ¿qué húbole, what's going on?*"

"*¡Teodoro! ¡Welcome to Ahuacatlán!*" We chatted briefly, and then he told his wife about me. "*Teodoro worked in Arizona near where we do. He is a college professor at the University of Arizona. Also, he makes films. He is very famous!*"

"*Uh, well, mainly I write books,*" I elaborated.

"*That too! Wonderful!*" He continued to elaborate on my background, most of it imaginary. Apparently it was prestigious, in a way, to have an American friend, and he kept patting me on the back and speaking my praises. Finally I ceased trying to correct him—why fight it?—and we talked about why he was there. He had sprained his ankle in the orchard, he said, and, since he hadn't come home between seasons last year, he decided he would finish the season early. Through connections he had secured a "Tourist" decal and fake papers for his Oldsmobile, and to his delight had succeeded in getting it through Mexican customs for only a one-hundred-dollar bribe—unheard of! He now joined the ranks of a select few Ahuacatlánians with cars next to their little homes. The license plates were a key, of sorts, to their owners' double lives: Arizona, Idaho, Texas, Florida, they read. José asked his stylishly dressed wife, in front of me, what she thought about having a car, and she dutifully replied it was *"muy padre"*—pretty neat. Of course, in the Mexican countryside, women were almost never permitted to drive; many men, upon returning to the North, even built little stone walls around their cars to make sure they would stay in "storage." But José was a good provider.

"The best thing about being back," he continued, *"is that my daughter is getting used to me."* As if to demonstrate, he lifted the infant from her mother's arms—but the baby immediately broke into tears. José laughed uncomfortably and returned her to his wife.

"Sweet little thing! I met her for the first time last week. In just that time, she has stopped crying when I come into the room." I supposed that was good news, if it was true. José had indeed been gone a long time.

He and his wife continued their promenade and I returned to the guys watching basketball. Jesús and Victor introduced me to some of their friends: Concepción ("Conce"), Rogelio, Elihu, and Tiberio. Other, younger men were hanging around the edge of this group, but apparently were not worth introducing. As I would learn later, this was the core of the Idaho group, the coolest guys around Ahuacatlán now, the soccer players, the prestigious dates, the young bucks. The men at their periphery all aspired to be accepted by them, to be taken along to the North. But it was a select group, and there was only room for so many. Again, I began to explain myself to Jesús's friends, but as they listened I realized they already knew.

A light rain began to fall, and there was a suggestion we all walk over to Pablo's cantina, the main gathering place for men in town. I nodded and fell into stride with the others.

Pablo's was a bare-bones kind of place. Two entryways opened onto the street. There was no sidewalk, no swinging doors: when Pablo's was open the doors were lifted from the entryways and stashed somewhere in back; when he was closed, they were fitted back into place. There was a front room and a back room, both with yellowing plaster walls. The front room contained a table and chairs for card games, a jukebox, and Pablo himself, appearing especially short behind the large plaster bar. The back room contained a pool table, and a tiny partition in the corner, behind which men peed into a hole in the floor. Strung over the table were wires and counters for keeping score; a pool-cue rack was on the wall. There was a rush for the rack as we entered: only one cue was straight and had its leather tip. For fifty pesos Pablo handed over a box containing the balls.

As Jesús racked up the balls, Tiberio put a coin in the jukebox and selected some numbers in the *cumbia* style. *Cumbia* is a *salsa* rhythm popular in southern Mexico and much of the Caribbean; to dance to it, you shuffle forward in little steps, hips tilting suggestively, head and upper body very still. To all this, Tiberio always added a wide grin—and the sight of him dancing around by himself, doing the *cumbia*, always made that grin infectious. Conce bought beers all around.

I lasted two games without being eliminated. A couple of the group's young admirers watched me from the shadows, but the other players—Conce, Jesús, Tiberio—paid no special attention to me. They were all still quietly checking me out, waiting for me to reveal myself. Would I be like the bosses they had known? Was I cool, okay to have around? Would I add a degree or two of prestige to the group, or be too much of a peculiarity?

Was I a threat? I knew that Americans, myself included, had difficulty appreciating the way we came off to Mexicans. This was in large part because no country on earth makes us feel weak, or backward, or disorganized, or corrupt. I could appreciate that any American in a less-developed country would have to watch his step, never taking on superior or condescending airs, never expecting special treatment while at the same time hoping to be treated as an equal. So it was with me in Mexico: my American-ness was something I could not deny, and yet it was important not to lord it over them.

Whether they were courting favor or simply being hospitable, I don't know, but nobody in the bar would allow me to pay for my own drinks. Long before the beer in my hand was empty, someone would tap me on the shoulder and point to a fresh one on the bar. Sometimes I knew these people, sometimes I didn't. More than once that evening there were two beers lined up for me on the bar, and behind them Pablo's smiling face. *"Pablo, tell them I appreciate it, but I could never drink all this beer!"* I pleaded. He said he would do so, and then turned around and poured me a tumbler of his special *aguardiente*, a powerful color-less spirit distilled locally from *maguey* cactus juice. Sip it, I said to myself, to survive you're going to have to sip it slowly.

Pablo's place was largely without decoration, save for a few bottles of spirits up on shelves on the wall behind him—inter-spersed with cans of four or five sorts of American lager, perhaps brought to him as gifts—a few calendars of the genre known in Mexico as *"sexy,"* and four long rattlesnake skins stretched on the wall above one of the doors to the outside. Jesús, taking a break from the table, came over to buy another beer; this time, it was my treat. I noticed a colored sheet taped on the wall behind him as he waited for the beer. It appeared to be a page torn from *¡Alarma!* the grisly tabloid. *"¡POBRE SANCHO!"* cried a two-inch headline. Beneath it was a photo of a naked man, hands covering his privates, rushing from a house. *"Husband comes home and the sancho gets his due,"* said a caption at the bottom.

"Who's 'poor Sancho'?" I asked Jesús. Others near the bar

heard the question, and started laughing. *"His name isn't Sancho, it's 'Señor González,' "* offered one man, provoking a storm of laughter. I could see that Sancho seemed to be a sort of running joke.

Jesús explained. *"Around here 'sancho' refers to a pet,"* he said. *"Say you have a little piglet, or a turkey or a rabbit, and a child likes it. The child pays lots of attention to it and the piglet becomes tame. The parents let it into the house—it's like a member of the family. Then you say to a guest, 'Don't worry about that pig— he's sancho.' Get it?"* I nodded.

"Okay, well, around here, we have a problem. The husband leaves, and sometimes a neighbor man moves in—with the man's wife, you see? Then he *becomes sancho, because he's kept, he's looked after, he's her pet."* Jesús looked at me to see if I followed. *"We call him sancho, but another name is Señor González. You know why?"* I shook my head. The men around the bar laughed. *"It's a saying around here:*

> *Tu conoces Señor González*
> *—el entra cuando tu sales.*

> [You know Señor González
> —he enters when you leave.]

The story under the picture on the wall described, vividly and in a highly moralistic tone, what happened in one rural household when the husband came to find a "Señor González" in bed with his wife.

"We act as though it's funny," said a man at the bar, *"but when you* sanchear *someone around here—make him a cuckold—it's very serious. Why, just up the river in Escanelilla, a man left for Florida and his wife had twins by a sancho who moved in. When she heard he was coming home, she got so scared she drowned both babies. Of course, she went to jail. But then the husband came home and found out anyway. Since he couldn't kill his wife, he killed the*

sancho. Who could blame him? Now both husband and wife are in jail."

The others standing around shook their heads. Being cuckolded, in Mexico, was very serious business. The longer I stayed in Ahuacatlán the more I realized it was perhaps married men's greatest fear upon leaving for the States. Having "Pobre Sancho" up on the cantina wall was a good way to be able to laugh and talk about it, just as we tell jokes about herpes or killer Tylenol or the space shuttle. And in their stories, perhaps, there was an oblique warning for me. When a young man from a sexually "promiscuous" country came into town for a while, it had to cross people's minds.

The jukebox stopped, so that suddenly we could hear the sound of the rain, now falling hard on the dirt road outside. The pools of water forming in the road reminded me of a rainy walk down a paved street in Phoenix with Carlos. *"I think the main difference between Mexico and the United States,"* he had said to me then, *"is that when it rains here, the roads don't get muddy."* From out of the Mexican mud, moments later, entered Jesús's younger brother Vicente, dripping water but smiling. Vicente was lean but slightly shorter than his brother; crooked teeth and an acne-pocked face made him less attractive. Unlike Jesús, there was a hungry look in Vicente's dark brown eyes. He was unusual in Ahuacatlán in that he traveled alone, never taking others with him to the States. Word was that he had been fired from the potato ranch in Idaho for sleeping in the field; most recently he had worked in Monte Vista, Colorado, in the sugar beet harvest. We shook hands and he joined a card game of conquián taking place on a low wooden table—the cantina's only table—in front of the jukebox. But before long he was back at the bar near me. I interrupted his order for a beer and discreetly slid him one of the two unstarted ones in front of me. I could no longer count the beers I'd drunk; Vicente had downed at least two so far.

I was curious about Vicente; I had never met a lone wolf in Mexico. Mexicans at home, generally, were not shy about speaking of work in the States—but with an introspective, private man like Vicente, you had to be careful how you broached the subject. Fortunately, one of the younger teens at the bar did it for me.

"*So, Teodoro, will you travel back home with Jesús and the others?*"

"*I don't know, Serafín. I really haven't given it much thought,*" I said.

He was just making small talk. "*Well, if you do, you'll need lots of dough!*" he said. "*I heard four hundred dollars!*"

"*Stupid!*" Vicente suddenly lashed out. "*When Teodoro goes over the border, he doesn't need to pay the coyotes. He's an American! He just walks over the bridge. He only pays bus fare!*

"*Besides, you don't need four hundred dollars. If you know the score, a hundred is more than enough. Fifty is enough!*"

The boy was chastened, and said nothing more. But he had made an opening. I knew Vicente didn't like to talk about his famous solo travels, but given the topic of conversation, and the level of alcohol consumption, it was worth a try.

"*Fifty?*" I said. "*How do you do it?*"

Vicente took a long draft. "*From here to the border,*" he said to me, back to the young man, "*the buses are only twenty. And if you don't have that, why, just hitchhike to Querétaro or San Luis Potosí. There you can hop a freight to the border, to Ciudad Juárez and El Paso.*"

I had spent a long time riding freights in the States, and had seen Mexican hoboes from the windows of Mexican passenger trains. But I knew nothing about them. I watched and listened to Vicente, fascinated.

"*At the border, you cross like everybody else. You walk or swim. Cross at a town, not in the middle of nowhere. Then hop another freight north.*"

In border towns, I knew, that was easier said than done. Immigration was always in the yards, checking every train and every car; they even stopped trains a few miles out of town, to see if anyone had hopped on as the freight left the yard.

"*And La Migra?*" I asked.

You just had to know where to ride, said Vicente. I did know where to ride, I said, and so would the Migra. No, no, he replied, then you don't know where to ride. Vicente rode where they didn't expect him to. He rode, for example, on top of the axles underneath either end of a boxcar, or atop the auxiliary air tank underneath a flat car. I took a notebook from my pocket and he sketched diagrams showing me where.

"Are you crazy? There's nothing to hold on to under there. You know what happens if the train's moving and you slip?"

Vicente nodded. He knew. A man he'd met once in Eagle Pass, Texas, had fallen, and he, Vicente, had witnessed it. He had seen a man die. He drank some more beer. *"You know, when you're under there, and it's nighttime, you see sparks,"* he said, the aggression gone from his voice. Vicente had stopped looking at anything particular in the cantina. He was looking somewhere into the past. *"The train changes tracks, or passes over a switch, and sparks fly out. They land on you, but they're out right away. They don't hurt."*

What a life, I thought, to be out there like that, alone. I had met a young Mexican once, in Bakersfield, California, who crossed the trains in a yard by crouching down and scooting underneath the cars. American tramps never took that risk—a train could jolt into movement at an instant and cut you in half. It was a thrill to take those risks, but also, something happened to you when you did. When you saw men die, get mangled that way, it damaged you a little bit too. The line of beers waiting for me on the bar was down to three; I passed Vicente one, and we drank up.

Eventually I looked around me. The jukebox was silent, the pool game had wound down, and Pablo wanted to go to bed. Somehow it had passed midnight. *"Buenas noches, señores,"* he said, turning off the lights and collecting beer bottles. We stepped out into the street, humid with the mist of the shower, noisy with the sounds of water dripping off roofs and trees. The rain had stopped. I had no further obstacle that evening than navigating my way home.

"¿Estás bien?" asked Jesús, a blur in front of my face.

"Of course, of course, I'm fine," I said. *"See you later."*

"Remember—soccer at two P.M. tomorrow. We leave the plaza at one."

I paused. That's right—the next day was Saturday. *"Sí,"* I finally replied. *"Sí."*

The paving stones of the streets around the plaza were wet and slippery and, in the darkness, impossible to see. I stumbled over them, my way lit only by the stars; it was a relief to reach the muddy but even footing of a dirt road. In nooks and crannies along the way I was vaguely aware of young couples, smooching against walls or railings, denied the comfort of a Chevrolet, practicing foreplay with their feet on the ground, their privacy the night. Daytimes, it was often hard to tell who was with whom; but on weekend nights couples were everywhere.

I turned left at the stone wall marking the side of Hilario's property. They swung a gate across the main entrance after hours to discourage entry; I would go in the small side gate. If, that was, I could find it. Large, big-leafed trees hung over the small alley I was on, obscuring all light, and the paving stones reappeared underfoot. I ran my hands along the wall like a blind man, searching for the gate. All of a sudden, I touched not wood but bare flesh—a warm stomach, an arm! A breathless, half-squelched cry came from the girl I had bumped; I leaped back in alarm.

"¡Perdón, perdón!" I muttered, circling the young couple unsteadily, still sober enough to be embarrassed. Two rocks tumbled from the wall before I found the gate. Then at last I was in.

I relieved myself by one of the big trees near the wall before entering my room—by common understanding, the outhouses were for sitting only—and noticed, as I did, the round forms of the chickens safely on their branches, outlined against the stars. I wondered to myself what those mountain weasels really looked like. Light came out from underneath the crude wooden door to my room; I pushed it open with a squeak. There on the middle of my bedspread sat a large furry spider, three or four inches across, the same one that was always there when I forgot to turn off the dim overhead bulb. As usual, I coaxed it onto a newspaper, opened a window, and tossed it out onto the street. Ah, I thought, laying down under one thin blanket, home in Mexico.

That Saturday, the Owls beat the Wolves 2–1, Jesús and Tiberio each scoring, as I watched from the stands. Jalpan's field was all dirt, with the boundaries marked in lime, and everyone left the stadium hot, sweaty, and dusty . . . but with big smiles. "*¡Que vivan Los Tecos!*" cried Tiberio from the window of Jesús's family Renault, as we sped from a tiny beer store to the Jalpan reservoir with two six-packs of cold Corona to find some shade and cool off. Though not officially for swimming, the murky reservoir served that purpose when the long dugout canoe we found and were paddling capsized; there was also a distance contest for walking on our hands, and the involuntary baptism of some younger guys from Ahuacatlán whom we ran into as we were drying off. Dinner at a local bamboo-walled restaurant followed, and after that an unsuccessful search for a party at the nearby town of La Purísima.

The next weekend I was called in as a substitute during the last fifteen minutes of the Tecos' game. A fortnight later the same thing happened, and a week after that, I got a spot on their relay team for the province's annual "Marathon of the Mountains" footrace. Other outings cemented my friendship with Jesús, Tiberio, Conce, and Victor: an afternoon spent drinking the excellent *pulque* of Doña Rosa, a tough Ahuacatlán widow; flirtatious visits to the office of Elisa and Elena, young social workers sent from Querétaro City to minister to mountain folk two days a week; more nights in Pablo's cantina; a tour to see the annual milling of sugarcane at Pepe Pacheco's, where a horse tied to a beam walked endless circles around Pepe's grinder and dried cane husks fueled a fire that warmed wide evaporation tanks. The rapping of pebbles against the windowpanes of my room was the invitation to another outing, and the days flew by.

Jesús in particular loved to talk about his experiences in the States, usually in the form of anecdotes. Learning English was one of his main preoccupations, and many of the tales concerned the obstacles he'd encountered along the way. One day several of us were seated around the *huarachería* of Tiberio's brother Ignacio, watching him and his assistants cut and sew the leather for sandals.

"*Teo*," asked Jesús, "*how do you say it when a girl is wearing perfume? What do you say to her?* 'I like your smell'? *Is that it?*"

"I like the way you sm——?"

"*Yes, yes, that's it,* 'I like the way you smell,' " he interrupted. "*Well, you know what I said to my girlfriend there one night?*"

Jesús had dated a number of American girls, none of whom spoke Spanish. I shook my head.

"*We were driving in the owner's car—that old Cadillac he gave us—and she smelled good, so I took her real close, like this, and I said, 'Baby, I like the way you stink.' *"

I burst out laughing, and Jesús explained it to the others: in Spanish, you use the same verb for smell or stink, and Jesús hadn't appreciated the difference. "*Did she explain it to you?*" I asked.

"*Yes, but she was mad!*" said Jesús. "*You know, she taught me some other words too.* 'Be nice,' *she used to say—that's when we were in the car, and, well, you know . . .*"

Tiberio made the appropriate body language to describe what they had been up to.

"*Ooh, but we made some big mistakes up there. Remember, Tiberio, in the Burger King? They asked if we wanted everything on it.* 'Yes,' *I said,* 'but no mustache.' 'What?' *she asked.* 'No mustache,' *I said. I thought I was saying* 'mustard.' "

Another time he had suggested to his girlfriend a dinner at the Pussycat—"Pizza Hut" he had meant to say—and yet another time, he had asked the foreman if he could borrow the "fuck you" from his trailer.

"What?" said the foreman.

"The fuck you," repeated Jesús, a bit nervously—he knew the phrase had a bad meaning, but thought it also meant "vacuum." The words sounded identical to him. So did "eyes" and "ice." These confusions had gotten him into lots of trouble, he said, offering extra explanations to the others in the room so they would understand what he was telling me.

One of the most rapt listeners was a middle-aged man squeezing rivets into straps of leather for the *huaraches*. *"Ay, English,"* he said. *"They say it's the hardest language in the world."*

"No, Chinese is the hardest," offered Ignacio, also middle aged. As these men debated the point, I realized something extraordinary was happening here: these older Mexicans were listening closely to men barely into their twenties. Age was the traditional determinant of who listened to whom in rural Mexico, older men seldom having time for younger men's stories (neither having time for women's)—but here, emigration to the States and the experiences it brought had the town turned around. The young guys were heading out, earning in a week up north what their fathers would toil months for. They returned to constitute a higher class of men, wealthier and more experienced, if less wise. Father Cano was right: in ways both subtle and obvious, emigration was setting Ahuacatlán on its head.

"English is a thousand times harder!" the older man continued, now rather heatedly.

"That's not so!" countered Ignacio. *"Chinese has thousands of letters, and difficult sounds. Who do you know that speaks Chinese?"*

The debate was escalating to an absurd degree: Ignacio and the old man had put down their work and were now yelling. The younger guys were murmuring that perhaps I ought to offer an opinion and put a stop to it—but I didn't want to take sides. Finally Tiberio stood up, interrupting them, and asked if we knew the joke about learning Chinese. Nobody did.

"How long did the Russian say it took to learn Chinese?" he asked the room. There were shrugs. *"Five years,"* said Tiberio.

"How long did the American say it took?" Again, shrugs. *"Four years."*

"Okay, how long did the Mexican say it took?" Sensing that a punch line was imminent, men started smiling. *"He said 'ten years,'"* offered one. Tiberio shook his head.

"The Mexican said, 'When's the test?' "

It was a masterful move; in their laughter the older men forgot the squabble. Jesús nudged me. *"That's the reputation we Mexicans have—everything 'mañana,' right?"* I nodded.

Soon we stood up to leave, but as we did Tiberio directed a question to Ignacio, something about when the cash would be ready. *"Next week,"* his brother replied.

Other talk of money, of pesos and dollars, of Rogelio, a bank teller, being able to arrange a favorable rate of exchange, filled the air as we walked to Don Beto's billiard hall. I wondered if they were planning to buy something, and asked as we walked through the saloon-style doors into Don Beto's.

"No, no, it's for El Norte—for the trip, and the coyotes," Jesús explained.

"Do you plan to leave soon?" There was a hollow feeling in the pit of my stomach.

"Probably next Sunday, or the one after," Jesus replied. *"The fields in Idaho will be all melted soon, and work will start again. And the Owls play their last game next weekend. But Tiberio and Conce are still rounding up dollars."*

I played a horrible game of pool, completely preoccupied by the idea of them leaving. With my friends gone, there would be little reason for me to stay in Ahuacatlán. But what an adventure to go with them! There was every reason, from my point of view, for me to accompany them north—but would they take me? I waited until we'd had a couple rounds of beers, and then, my courage up, I took Jesús aside and broached the subject. He was not the least bit surprised, I don't think; knowing why I was in Ahuacatlán to begin with, he probably expected it. Still, he said he would have to check with the others.

The next morning I set out to find him at home and learn the group's decision. But news travels fast in Ahuacatlán: crossing the plaza in the mid-morning, I ran into none other than young Serafín, whom Vicente had told off in the cantina. *"So, you're going with those guys up to Idaho, eh?"* He looked at me jealously; it was his life's main goal. *"Well, maybe,"* I replied—I really didn't know. But he must have thought I was hedging, for his sake. *"No, I know you are. I heard it!"*

He was not the only one. Ignacio accosted me from the open window of the *huachería* as I passed, waving me in. He wanted to make me a special pair of *huaraches*, he said, custom sized to my feet, with softer, better leather than the ordinary—*"the perfect shoes for crossing the desert."* I was thrilled to hear this—maybe it really was going to happen. He traced my foot on a piece of paper on the floor, explaining that he wanted to do it because I was going to the States with his brother; maybe I would look after him a little.

I walked on, stopping at the local *Conasupo,* the government food store, to buy some canned tuna for Lupe. The mother of Jesús and Vicente, Raquel Rendón, ran the one-room store, and when she mentioned that she, too, had heard I would be going, I knew I wouldn't need to continue on to find Jesús. I was thrilled. But she looked pensive. *"Ah, Teodoro, Teodoro,"* she said, *"they're leaving again."* She leaned forward on the counter and shook her head.

"What is it, Señora?"

"They're leaving again, and now their younger brother, Armando, wants to go too—before he even finishes secondary school." She sighed. *"We have eleven children, the father of Jesús and I. Only three are boys. Of course, at their age, they're independent. But their father and I try to tell them not to go. There's no future in it! It would be better if they stayed home, studied for a career. Jesús is very good at fixing cars, and his father arranged for him to have an apprenticeship at a shop in Querétaro. But he had no patience. To do these things, you have to sacrifice! But they're more interested in adventure."*

I didn't feel she was trying to get me to change their minds; rather, their leaving was something she just wanted to talk about; and her opinions, I figured, were something I ought to listen to. She continued:

"I suppose the experience of being over there is good in some ways. If they get into tight spots, they have to get themselves out.

Here, they can always turn to one of us, to a relative. And they have learned some English. But you know how it is—when they go, they usually go with a group of friends. Since they can't speak English, those are the people they're always with. So in some ways, they don't learn any more than if they had stayed here.

"They do come home and tell us stories. Did you know Vicente was arrested in Texas last time? He spent a month in jail, but he told me it wasn't that bad. There was a big room where he could talk with all the other guys. They talked about sports and things like that.

"Their father and I make enough to get by, so we're not like lots of parents—we don't expect them to send us money. What they earn, they can spend. But we keep telling them it's important to save it. If not, what do you have when you're done? Nothing! You're just older.

"I wish them well, but oh, sometimes I'm frightened when they leave. It is next week, right?"

I nodded.

"Well, there's nothing to be done. God bless you, Teodoro. Look after them in your country." She finally smiled, and handed me a lollipop from a display on the counter. For the road.

We met on the same corner where the White Arrow had dropped me off, that first day in Ahuacatlán, four months earlier. Jesús was wearing boots and jeans, a snap-down shirt with the sleeves rolled up. Slung over his shoulder was a white *costal*, the woven-fiber carry-bag of the sierra. Conce arrived in his trademark sleeveless T-shirt, straw cowboy hat casting a shadow over his face. Tiberio wore sneakers, as usual, and his *Tecolotes* team soccer shirt. Victor was there, and two others I had met from *ranchos*: Plácido and Rolando, both highly experienced, in their thirties. I was somewhat surprised by the presence of two others: Marín, one of the core group's hangers-on, a fifteen-year-old with big feet who must recently have been promoted; and Inocencio, a small Indian with a big smile who worked part-time at the sandal shop.

The group gravitated toward the cauldron of *chicharrones*—intestine stew—that was gurgling in front of the butcher shop, which faced the highway. Jesús and Victor bought small platefuls, though it was only midmorning. (For me, the time was never right for eating *chicharrones*.) Everyone looked a little jumpy, a little nervous, and small talk helped pass the time waiting for the White Arrow. But something about the scene was strange. Jesús had ten siblings in town—where were they? Plácido had a wife and four children—why weren't they there to see him off? Why were there no parents around, no buddies? Instead of calls of *bon voyage* or *buen viaje*, there was, it seemed to me, an ambivalence. The men were leaving on a rite of passage that shook the town to its core. Even if they could expect to benefit financially, friends and relatives could not be glad to see them go. And the men themselves, though excited about the adventure ahead, were once again leaving home (the two youngest for the first time) on an uncertain passage, an outlaw trip across the border and into a foreign land. I recalled that work, and the search for work, were nicknamed in Mexico *la lucha*—the fight. There was a good reason for that. We sauntered toward the open door of the White Arrow when finally it arrived, a swagger masking the uncertainties beneath.

Chapter 6

Coming into the Country

AS THE WHITE arrow retraced the winding road to Querétaro,
Jesús was losing a battle to keep his eyelids open. Again and again
they dropped, their slow, fluttering fall interrupted only by the
shock of a swerve or an occasional pothole. A long stretch of flat
road and the bus's calming drone finally succeeded in closing
them completely. Jesús's jaw relaxed, too, and, mouth open, he
slumped down in his seat, head against the vibrating window.

A sharp bump jolted him back to semiconsciousness. He sat
up and blinked.

Conce looked at him from across the aisle, amused. *"Hombre,
¿qué pasa?"* he asked *"This is the* beginning *of the trip! Why so
tired?"*

Jesús gazed back at him, not quite focusing. *"Ooo,"* he moaned.
"I was up late with la costilla." La costilla translates "the rib"—
slang for a woman, a girlfriend.

"María Elena?" asked Conce, turning sideways in his seat
to stretch his long legs. María Elena was the mother of Jesús's
first child, a two-year-old boy.

"No, the other one," said Jesús.

"Aaah, Evangélica," Conce replied, smiling. Evangélica was
a very pretty, petite young woman from a *rancho* near Ahuacatlán

who had been smitten by Jesús during his most recent stay. We had met, though none of Jesús's friends knew her well. Nothing more was said for several moments, until Jesús revealed: *"She's meeting us in Querétaro."*

Conce sat bolt upright, wide eyed. *"What? Alone?"* Jesús only nodded. Conce leaned back against the side of the bus and stared at him in disbelief. I couldn't see what was so unusual—she was going to see him off? So what? But Conce knew what it meant when a woman from their area traveled out of town, alone, to meet a man. *"You're going to bring her with us? Across the border? The whole way?"*

Jesús nodded again. And now I was staring too.

"She took the bus at four a.m.," Jesús said. He turned to me. *"Her family would not permit it,"* he explained, *"but she wanted to very much. Last night she said 'Take me.' I said I would. She left her rancho yesterday. Her family thought she would spend the night with her sister in Ahuacatlán and would return today. But she had a little suitcase, and her sister figured it out. They got into a big fight."*

Conce whistled and shook his head, again leaving the impression that this was very grave. *"But I still don't see—what's the big deal?"* I asked.

This time Conce explained. *"You don't know the sierra,"* he told me. *"If a man takes a woman without asking permission, without marrying her, then her whole family—her father, her uncles, all her brothers—may come after him, may even kill him. If he's up in the States, maybe they'll even find him there."*

Jesús looked a little pale. *"Maybe this time I'll stay two years,"* he said. *"Then I will have earned more money, more time will have passed, and her family will be a little less upset."*

The bus whined on up the hill. Besides his child in Ahuacatlán, Jesús, I knew, had another in Monte Vista, Colorado, by a Chicano woman. A third child, I supposed, could be expected within a year in Idaho. Fathering children and "having" women remained closely tied to masculinity in rural Mexico. It often did not seem a happy connection.

Word soon spread down the seats to the rest of our group,

and by the time we arrived at the station in Querétaro City, all eyes were searching for Evangélica. But Jesús had prearranged a rendezvous at a far end of the platform, and only Conce and I were asked along. She stood behind a tile-covered column, almost hiding, wearing a royal blue chiffon dress and clutching a small white purse—her Sunday best. Dark brown hair fell over her shoulder, setting off a complexion the color of coffee ice cream. Her eyes were large and brown, as dark as her hair. Even in high-heeled shoes that matched her dress, she was scarcely five feet tall; standing near Conce and Jesús, each nearly six feet, she looked even smaller. She and Jesús embraced, and I could see why he had been tempted. Conce, too, was staring at her.

"Where is your suitcase?" he asked. She shook her head—no suitcase. It was as Conce thought. *"Then these are your only clothes?"* She nodded. *"¡Ay, caray!"* said Conce, turning away and rolling his eyes. Jesús, finally realizing what his friend was getting at, looked at her straight on, with outstretched arms. *"We're going to walk across a desert!"*

"But all you said," she protested, *"was that we were going to America!"* In a nice place like America, obviously, you had to look your best. A lump formed in my throat. The men had seen the world, but the women never left Ahuacatlán—or, in her case, the *rancho*. She had no idea.

We made a quick huddle. Two hours remained until the bus left for the border—enough time to walk into town and buy Evangélica what she needed. We regrouped and headed toward the shopping district. Several stops netted Evangélica jeans, a jacket, and a pair of sneakers. Others, meanwhile, stocked up on *novelas*—Mexican-style comic books, good for passing the time— and food for the road: two roasted chickens, fried potatoes, a can of hot *serrano* chilies, and hot corn on the cob, smothered in mayonnaise and paprika. Also, we picked up Eduardo, a tall, curly-haired Ahuacatlán native also known as "The Wood-pecker." He worked as a government mechanic in Querétaro, but had heard a lot about the States and was eager to try his luck. With the Woodpecker, the group total was eleven.

Evangélica was very shy, speaking only to Jesús and then only in low tones the rest of us couldn't understand. Conce, so concerned at first about her presence, now appeared to regret his initial behavior toward Evangélica. Perhaps he had come on too strong. *"Are you angry?"* he asked her, as we crossed a plaza, Jesús talking with someone else.

"No," answered Evangélica softly, *"just scared."*

We returned to the bus station, which had grown so crowded we were unable to find any seats. In resignation, we gathered against a wall in a little semicircle. *"Where are all these people going?"* I wondered out loud. Jesús looked at me as though I ought to know. I looked more carefully. The passenger profile, I suddenly realized, was almost exactly what it had been in the Nuevo Laredo bus station on the border, where I'd waited with Alonso. The passengers were almost all men, young to middle aged, and evidently from the countryside. They, too, were bound for America. *"Why else would a group of campesinos travel together like that in their working clothes, carrying all those bags?"* said Jesús. *"It's like this every night."*

On his instruction, no one in our group was toting more than a small shoulder bag or knapsack—that was important for the desert, he had said, as well as for dealing with the police . . . something I would understand later. At 10:00 P.M. the emigration began, with a mass movement from the terminal to the platforms of the seven different coaches that were making the trip to the Texas border. That left a smaller group—maybe fifty people, including us—for the two 11:00 P.M. coaches to Tijuana, Mexicali, and points on the Arizona border.

Our specific destination was Sonoita, a tiny town across the line from Lukeville, Arizona, 1,600 miles away. Our bus—a Yellow Arrow this time—finally rolled out of the station around 11:30, headed first west to Guadalajara and then north up the Pacific coast to Mazatlán, Culiacán, Hermosillo, and *la frontera*. It was a big coach, with reclining seats and a rest room; the eleven of us occupied eight double seats, across the aisle from each other.

We were half-starved from having waited so long to eat the

aromatic chicken dinner, and now dug in ravenously. Most Mexican food had come to seem bland to me without the hot little peppers, but when I rubbed a sleepy eye with a finger that had been dipped into the can of them, I quickly realized there were still things to learn about Mexican food.

"Yow!" I cried, as the pepper juice began to sting my eye. Something salty was the best cure for too hot a pepper on the tongue, but I had no idea what to do about juice in the eye. Fortunately Evangélica, peeking back at me through the crack between her and Jesús's seats, knew a good mountain antidote. She turned around, leaned over the seat back, and offered me one of her long pigtails. I stared at it dumbly.

"Take the end of it and rub it on your eye," Jesús advised. I resented him making this joke while my eye burned, but Conce too was nodding.

"A woman's hair is the best cure," he confirmed.

So I took the pigtail and rubbed around my watering eye with the hair ends beneath the rubber band. It still hurt. *"Rub it some more,"* commanded Jesús. I did, and Evangélica nodded approvingly. It felt a little better.

The next day we helped pass the miles with the small stack of *novelas* we had bought in Querétaro. *Novelas* are the main form of recreational reading for millions of ordinary Mexicans—akin to the junk novels Americans consume, but much briefer and even more popular. The intelligentsia disdains these novels, with their supposed "vocabulary of only some 300 words"—but they are some sort of indicator of the interests of the everyday Mexican, as well as, perhaps, an aid to literacy in a country that lacks it. They are set up like comic books, with glossy covers, drawings, and newsprint pages in color, the characters' lines printed in balloons over their heads. The dialogue includes the slang of everyday life, and the themes of the little dramas are equally popular: police intrigue, romance, westerns, Biblical tales. I was somehow not surprised, as I riffled through them, to find an entire series entitled "Wetbacks: True Tales of the Braceros."

Emigration to the States, in fact, figured importantly

throughout Mexican popular culture. In the *ranchera* songs devoted to the exploits of *braceros,* in Mexican films (fully one-third of those produced over the past ten years dealt with intrigues of the border and life "on the other side"), in the attention newspapers gave to anything having to do with Mexicans in the U.S.A.— the permeation of the emigration theme into Mexican life was complete. I looked at the numbers of the *novela* series. "Better He Never Had Gone" was one title; the cover showed a stern American Immigration agent waving his finger at a downcast Mexican. Inside, an attractive young couple were forced by tragic circumstance to seek their fortune in the States. They made plenty of money; but due to her weakness and the influence of "loose" American friends, their marriage fell to pieces and she was killed in a car wreck. "Hell on Earth" detailed the tragic misadventures of two brothers who crossed and were variously exploited by employers, falsely accused of crimes, and beat up by police and their cellmates in American jails. The cover of "I Want to Earn Dollars" promised "all the intense drama generated by ambition and greed," but the story delivered mainly an exposition of the awesome computerized efficiency of the Immigration and Naturalization Service. (Agents of the American *migra* generally were feared and respected in Mexico; Mexicans always looked puzzled or disbelieving when I described the lack of seriousness with which they were taken by many Americans.) Jesús, Conce, Plácido, Tiberio, Rolando, and others who knew what it was really like didn't have much use for these *novelas,* but the Woodpecker and young Marín and Inocencio—and I—devoured them.

Friday morning dawned on me with thoughts of chicken leftovers, but no sooner was Jesús up than he threw the remaining half-eaten carcass out the window. I protested as I saw it hit the pavement below and crash into pieces. *"What was wrong with it?"* I asked. *"It's Friday,"* he explained, with a tone of uncharacteristic piety. *"No meat—only fish."* Thus we began to get out when the bus stopped in stations along the way and search for food, or else wait for vendors to offer us things through the windows. If the bus drivers permitted it, occasionally vendors would also board the bus. They were usually boys, selling Chiclets or Cokes or their mothers' *burritos*, wrapped in paper and carried in buckets. Now and then one would simply stand in the aisle and sing a song at the top of his lungs, passing the hat afterward. The bus drivers were most permissive toward the handicapped beggars, present in almost every station, who passed out picture cards of the Virgin with an explanation on the back such as "I AM DEAF AND MUTE. THIS IMAGE OF THE VIRGIN COSTS 20 PESOS. PLEASE RETURN IT IF YOU DO NOT WANT IT. GOD BLESS YOU." They came in thin plastic envelopes, and enclosed was a tin crucifix on a string. All of us bought these cards, and, imitating the others, I hung the tiny crucifix from the ashtray of the seat back in front of me. It was Mexican travel insurance.

As we entered our second evening of travel, the coach left the coast, heading directly north toward the border. By now it was filled almost entirely with men in their twenties and thirties; a few more had gotten on in every city along the way, and some had even been turned away for lack of room. Around midnight the bus was waved to the side of the road by men with flashlights. We came to a stop by a small, two-room building with lights on inside. A uniformed man climbed up the bus stairs.

"*¡Pasaportes, tarjetas turísticas, identificación!*" he cried. Everyone stopped talking. Another uniformed man, with side arms on his belt, climbed in and stationed himself at the door. I glanced across the aisle at Tiberio and Conce; their faces wore the sort of look you see on a person about to have to deal with someone who can screw things up for them, someone in power: a school principal, a supervisor. Most of the men were handing the official their military service card; I got out my tourist card. We watched as he approached, turning to give extra scrutiny to one of the emigrants-to-be who had boarded with us at Querétaro. The man had a large amount of luggage stashed on the shelf above his seat. As Jesús had explained when he instructed me to pack light, luggage could be taken as evidence that you were planning to stay away a long time. Cops would accuse you of plotting to cross the border. Of course, there was no Mexican law against this, but few rural Mexicans knew the law, and if the cops came up with some pretext for arresting you, you had to pay them off to keep them from doing it. This was a Mexican customs stop, also known as a graft opportunity. The policeman ordered the man off the bus.

Seated right behind the offender was Eduardo, the Woodpecker. Our jaws were tight as he, too—apparently implicated by the same mass of luggage—was ordered off the bus. The policeman seemed uninterested in me, or in any of the others in our group; he continued his slow walk to the back of the bus, sending two other men into the little building outside before he was done.

We talked lowly when the policemen left, but there was not a great deal to discuss. The only question would be how much Eduardo would have to pay. Jesús had explained previously: they would threaten him with detention if he didn't cooperate, say they would tell the bus to go, leave his belongings on it. More severe, physical methods of coercion could follow if that didn't work. It was worth your time to barter with them over an amount, but not to refuse to pay.

Red faced through either embarrassment or anger, the Woodpecker eventually returned to the bus. The damage had been only 750 pesos—two and a half dollars at the time. He could live with it, he supposed. The only consolation was that another of the detainees, a Guatemalan, had got it worse. When the man could produce neither a Mexican draft card nor immigration papers, he had been ordered to strip. Sewn into the cuff of one of his pant legs was $150; the police found it and kept all but $10.

I nodded. I had done an article on Central American refugees in Mexico. For them, customs inspections were truly a thing to dread—because almost invariably that's where they were separated from all their money. Many were en route to the United States, but the problem was that Central Americans already were Mexico's illegal aliens. I had been to the southern border to interview people and watch them wade the Río Suchiate, and was startled by the many similarities between their situation in Mexico and that of Mexican illegals in the United States. During harvest season in the cotton, banana, and coffee plantations of southern Mexico, there was seldom a problem, for they could be hired even more cheaply than Mexican laborers and, it was said, they worked harder. Out of season, however, Mexicans had no need for them, and when they were discovered during customs checks on buses, the demands of customs officials became exorbitant. It was an interesting form of immigration control: in the States we shipped immigrants back to the Mexican border, causing them the loss of a few days' work and whatever it took to pay another *coyote*. In Mexico officials simply extracted a direct payment. It was an odious practice, but it saved both sides time and probably money.

For hours the bus traversed the vast Sonoran Desert, a cold black space with no lights; the horizon was marked by the line where the twinkling sky yielded to pitch darkness. Though cramped, the dimly lit bus offered warmth and security, a sense of enclosure. With extended travel through such a large, indeterminate space, I had almost ceased to anticipate a stop; but those who recognized our destination, the little border town of Sonoita, jerked the rest of us out of slumber, and after a scramble to collect coats and sacks, we were down the steps and into the night. The coach turned left, to trace the border the rest of the way to Tijuana, and left us in a cloud of warm, acrid diesel smoke.

A frigid north wind reminded me that the desert didn't stop at the border; only Mexico did. The desert was a seamless continuum ranging from perhaps 500 miles south of here all the way north to Oregon. It was probably very nearly as cold that evening down where it began in San Luis Potosí as it was up north near the Bitterroots. Bisecting the expanse was the arbitrary line of the border, the only conceivable reason for the existence of the little town, the x-axis of its location. The y-axis, as we would see with daylight, was a little stream running roughly north to south, a thin green corridor along which a few livestock grazed and *los mojados* lounged before undertaking the crossing.

My problems with Alonso in mind, I suggested to my companions that we remain separate when in public places on the border. Entering the bus stop café, I sat apart from the long table where I knew most of them would take a seat. But Victor, Marín, and the Woodpecker forgot; they walked up and plopped themselves right down at my table as though they had known me for years. In response to my hissed protests they laughed, said I was overcautious and a worrywart, and ordered coffee.

The existence of a twenty-four-hour café—unheard of in most of Mexico—was a reminder that we were close to the States, and something of a comfort to me. But apparently we were there only to brace ourselves against the cold, for with the first light of Saturday, a couple of hours later, we were outside, briskly following Plácido down the road toward a bridge that spanned the stream. From the end of the bridge railing, a narrow footpath curved down to the stream. The thin, lush floodplain was a welcome contrast to the desert's severity. We walked single file through shrubs, trees, and grasses for a half mile or so, until we were a comfortable distance from town. In the dim light we silently passed several groups, large and small, of sleeping people crowded under blankets on the ground—earlier arrivals. Already awake and grazing were a few cows and goats, the other inhabitants of the riverside park. Skirting their numerous piles, we came to a knoll and there built our morning warm-up fire.

The presence of other beginners saved me from having to ask naive questions about what came next. Plácido, the senior member of the party, explained to Marín that the main thing to do was wait—the *coyotes* would come to us. There was competition among them, so we would hold out for a good price. Most would want to take us all the way to Phoenix, and would charge up to two dollars for every mile of the 150-mile distance. But all we needed was a 15- or 20-mile ride out of town, a drop-off in a remote area away from the border patrols originating in Lukeville. From there, I already knew, their custom was to trek north through the desert, into Organ Pipe Cactus National Monument and then the Papago Indian Reservation. The Papagos traditionally had been able to supply a second ride—transportation the rest of the way to Phoenix—for a reasonable price; this way, we could expect to save about one hundred dollars apiece.

Plácido, thirty-three and the father of six, was the most experienced Idaho hand. He could claim eight seasons working in the Northwest, and as many desert crossings. A sweaty man, he did not much resemble the others: his black hair, parted way over on the side, stuck to his forehead, his shirts always looked too tight, and his pants were never quite up. From his face—usually expressionless, especially around the eyes—and his corpulent build, the name (meaning "placid, serene") seemed to fit. But Plácido was neither slow nor relaxed, and, when it came to important decisions, everyone looked to him.

Until the *coyotes* arrived, Plácido visited with the senior members of other groups waiting in the park. As they woke up, different groups would send envoys over to us, or Plácido would mosey over to their camps, to see who they were and what they knew about the local situation. One group of ten men, he reported, was from Michoacán; another group of four from Sinaloa. Another group that disappeared with the dawn had been from Nayarit. About all that was new in Sonoita, he had heard, was that the Federal Judicial Police, Mexico's main national police force, had recently opened a branch in town. With all I had heard about bandits and con men along the border, I thought this would be good news to the others. But they seemed, if anything, more worried by the presence of the so-called *judiciales*. *"When the judiciales come to town,"* Jesús explained, *"official bandits replace the unofficial ones."* The other groups reported a number of *coyotes* in the area, and gave a description of one suspected to be a snitch for the *judiciales*.

The morning passed slowly, and one by one the *coyotes* made their appearance. I never noticed them arrive; they just seemed to slip into our area, so that instead of seeing Plácido resting on the grass, I would look up to discover him and Rolando and possibly Jesús huddled with a stranger. I was curious about how their discussions went, but it was important for me, at the delicate negotiating stage, to maintain a low profile, to not be noticed at all, if possible. Even if they assured the *coyote* that I was trustworthy, not a risk, the *coyote* might up the ante, or refuse to go.

Different *coyotes* appeared: a short, flashy man sporting mirrored sunglasses and jewelry, who brushed off a tree stump with a handkerchief before sitting down; a nervous-looking, slightly overweight kid in sneakers and jeans who claimed to be representing a friend; a tall, aggressive, denim-dressed man in the cowboy mold; and an old farmer type, in floppy hat and baggy pants, who asked many questions about us before even suggesting that he might be able to barter for a ride. The conversation with him seemed to drag on for hours, because he matched the description of the suspected informer. Plácido and the others expertly offered even less information than he offered them: it was the original Mexican standoff. I admired their skill in this, and that of Mexicans generally; though at other times, when I was trying to find something out, it would drive me crazy: Mexicans, if they so desire, are maddening experts at not coming to the point.

The tall cowboy-*coyote* was the only one to give me any trouble. *"And who is this gabacho?"* he demanded, before even stating what his price might be. Plácido was about to answer, but the man came right up to me. *"Hanging out with all these Mexican guys . . . an informer for La Migra, perhaps?"* He wore a wide belt with a silver buckle; the points of his cowboy boots, a couple of feet from where I lay on my stomach, were also covered with silver. I sat up.

"We heard you *were the informer,"* I said.

"Who told you that?" he demanded. He took the bait easily; he was not too smart.

"Oh, just some guys down the road. Who are you if you're not the informer?" From my experience with La Víbora back in Phoenix, I felt that the best way to get a *coyote* to back off was to ask him about his profession.

"None of your business!" he replied, swearing lowly as he turned. By evening we still hadn't settled on a *coyote;* according

to Plácido, all of them wanted too much. We were faced with a night out in our little meadow, the eleven of us huddling under three blankets near the embers of a fire. It wasn't only the cold that made it unpleasant: the word from the other border-crossers was that thieves had been making regular raids along the stream banks at night, knowing their victims carried cash. All night we shivered, from cold and nervousness. The only one unconcerned, from what I could tell, was Evangélica, lying slightly apart from the group, curled up with Jesús in his big parka.

The nervous teenager returned the next morning and conferred again with Jesús and Plácido. After twenty minutes Plácido left with him, to negotiate directly with whomever it was the kid represented. He returned half an hour later. "Twenty dollars," was his good news, "twenty to La Nariz." La Nariz means "The Nose," a descriptive local nickname for a strange rock formation half an hour east of town, just across the border. I expected a cheer to go up from my fellows, all still thawing out around the fire from the previous night—the offer was an amazing ten dollars cheaper than the next best one. But they only nodded: getting the ride wasn't a surprise, just a matter of time.

We would rendezvous with the *coyote* in the desert that night. In the meantime we had to reprovision ourselves with food and water for the crossing. Conce and Tiberio took up a collection, and Jesús and I fell in behind as they walked down the stream toward Sonoita.

It was a Sunday, and the sleepy border town was as buzzing as it ever got—with American tourists. It was arresting to be still in Mexico and see Americans everywhere—in sleek sedans, in lumbering RVs, or on foot, wearing shorts, carrying shopping bags and cameras, looking a thousand miles from home. As we turned down a dirt street toward the grocery store—already packed with border-town Americans who shopped here to save money— we passed an American family of four, the parents portly, the kids fat cheeked and sticky faced from candy. The street was empty except for the four of us and the four of them, and I saw the parents shepherd the kids to the side of the street as we approached; I could tell at once they were scared—but there was nothing to fear. As they neared my friends all looked to the ground, in traditional deference to the more powerful. The parents stared resolutely ahead. Only the children and I caught each other's eyes, neither of us afraid to look.

We passed, closer for that uncomfortable instant than most Americans and most Mexicans would ever come. And it struck me again what a fascinating place the border is. They had crossed south, to spend money. We would be heading north, to earn it. Nowhere on earth did such a developed country border one so poor. In that superficially dull town, all that was different came into strong relief: rich and poor, light and dark, content and hungry, mild and spicy, ahead and behind. Here, Mexicans and Americans caught brief, sun-squinted glimpses of each other; the paths of two nations intersected, however lightly, and continued on their separate ways.

We bought what was needed—flashlights, food, gallon jugs of water, a pair of pliers for pulling out cactus spines—and then, laden with grocery sacks, we walked back streets to the streamside, trying to maintain a low profile. I had checked: there was nothing wrong, in Mexican law, with crossing the border to the United States. But experience had taught me that the fewer people who knew about it, the better. The path to the stream, unfortunately, passed right by the rear of the Federal Judicial Police headquarters, but we saw no one through the dirty windows, and passed on toward our little oasis.

As camp came into view, we saw six men lounging around with the rest of our group. The tallest of them looked up as we approached, and a flash of recognition crossed the face of Jesús, at my side. The men, it turned out, were from Quirambal, a high *rancho* three hours by foot from Ahuacatlán; they had left Querétaro the morning after we had. Jesús and the others walked up and shook hands, and then introduced me—but the men already knew who I was. The tall one, Genaro, was their leader. From dusty cowboy boots to wide leather belt to felt cowboy hat, he was dressed in black. The younger ones, less talkative and less polished, seemed to have carefully imitated his dress, three of them to the point of having spray-painted black their straw cowboy hats. When we learned that they, too, were headed to Phoenix, Plácido offered to cut them in on the *coyote* deal to La Nariz. There was safety in numbers, I reasoned, and economies of scale when dealing with *coyotes*—but perhaps he was just being neighborly. They eagerly accepted, and we celebrated the arrangement by settling down in the shade and drinking the still-cold case of beers we had brought from town.

In the late afternoon, when the sun was lower and the air around us cool and humid, we began to prepare for departure. The two-day desert crossing would require at least a gallon of water per person, and a lot of food. Empty plastic gallon jugs were scavenged to augment the ones we had bought; we filled them at a farmer's house down the road. Next we took belts, cords, and even plastic bread bags, rolled the long way and knotted, and threaded them through the plastic handles of the jugs to provide a better means of carrying them. To each person were distributed bags of flour tortillas, chunks of cheese, boxes of sweet Mexican cookies, fried pork rinds, pieces of cured meat, home-cooked chunks of candy, a couple of cans of tuna, tins of sardines, and, of course, cans of chilies. Plácido and Genaro directed this effort. As they did, it became clear that Genaro—charismatic and outgoing—was more the natural leader. When he and Plácido discussed the route we would take, we saw that he was also more experienced: he had crossed the desert here nine times, by his own counting. Slowly Genaro came to make decisions for the entire group.

The Mexicans had a very different style for managing groups than Americans do. There was no explanation of how far we would have to walk to meet the *coyote*, no questions or answers concerning how long it would take. Leaders made the decisions and the others followed. Broad consensus making was not a part of it; as the moment of departure approached, nobody checked around and asked, "Everybody ready?" Rather, Genaro bustled around, eager to go, waiting only for the moment when enough people were on their feet. And then he just walked off up the stream.

Striding briskly, single file, the rest of us hurried to keep up with him. Evangélica, the day before, had put on her new jeans, tucked the bottom of her dress into them—and added to her newfound freedom of movement by replacing her pumps with sneakers. She and Jesús took up the rear. Within a quarter mile, the stream had sunk down between the walls of a red-sanded arroyo—a miniature canyon—leaving us in shadows about fifteen feet beneath the level of the surrounding land. We moved fast along the muddy earth, and a rush of excitement carried me as I realized we were finally beginning: we were on our way to cross the border. It was a reenactment of the earliest form of human travel: migration, for purposes of survival. For this most critical part of the journey, we were resorting to our feet. I was glad to be with experts.

Shepherds stepped aside on the narrow bank or peered down from the rim of the arroyo as we passed, all taking the time to get a good look at us. Among them, Jesús swore he saw the face of the nosy, elderly farmer-type whom we had suspected of being a police spy. But no one else did, and he couldn't be sure. It was not, in any event, a good omen.

The arroyo disappeared and we climbed back into the light of the setting sun. We had been walking about forty-five minutes. Ahead, seated by a tree, was the teenager who had arranged our ride. He rose and led us five minutes up a small tributary of the stream to a dense stand of short evergreens. There, he said, we would wait until dark. I was nervous and suspicious, but everyone else seemed to think it was a good time to relax a bit. The area around the stand of trees was dry and seemed deserted; they talked freely. Conce had been saving a couple of joints for a special moment; they now were lit and passed around. It appeared we were going to have a bit of a wait. Inocencio, the young Indian, apparently was thinking several days in the future; as Tiberio pulled out his wallet to show me a picture of his last girlfriend in Idaho, Inocencio asked him about a Social Security number.

"*Ah, here—I have three,*" said Tiberio. "*Copy whichever one you want.*" Two of them were scratched on a scrap of paper; the third was embossed on one of those metal replicas of cards you can order through the mail. Inocencio borrowed my pen. "*I bought it from a coyote in El Mirage,*" said Tiberio of the card. He believed it to be his own number, though of course it was not—just another *coyote*'s scam. I had seen a man selling other fake documents once, at the Sunday swap meet. The birth certificates and resident alien ("green") cards went for $50 to $200 apiece. But Social Security numbers, really, could be had for free. I remembered the well-publicized case of the plastic wallet sold by Woolworth's in the 1970s. Inside was a sample Social Security card, with a sample number printed on it. The Social Security Administration, a few months after the appearance of the product, reported that 33,000 people had paid in to the nonexistent account. Such contributions, of course, were of great benefit to the system: Mexicans could pay in, but they couldn't get anything out.

"*I also have a birth certificate,*" Tiberio boasted, carefully removing and unfolding another piece of paper from his wallet. He passed it to me delicately, this important document in an unknown language. Others watched as I read.

"CHURCH OF JESUS CHRIST OF LATTER-DAY SAINTS," it said across the top, in curving, ornate letters. "Certificate of Baptism." It had Tiberio's name printed on, was signed by an "elder" and a "bishop," and was dated two years earlier at Aberdeen, Idaho.

"*It's from the Mormons,*" I said. "*Where did you get it?*"

"*El patrón,*" Tiberio explained—the owner of the ranch, in Idaho. "*He's a Mormon. He baptized all of us.*" He nodded toward Jesús, Plácido, Conce, and Victor, all of whom were watching.

"*But you're Catholic!*" I protested.

"*Yes,*" Tiberio conceded. "*But it made him very happy. We all did it. On a Sunday.*"

"*In the swimming pool,*" Jesús added.

"*What? What swimming pool?*"

"*The swimming pool of el patrón,*" Jesús explained. "*He dropped us in.*"

"*And said these prayers.*"

"What prayers?"

"Who knows?" Tiberio shrugged. *"He was very happy."*

"The whole family is Mormon," Jesús explained. *"They're very strict—they don't drink or smoke. We can never be seen drinking when they're around."*

"But the son—" said Tiberio *"—the son likes tobacco, that kind you chew. '¿eSkoal?' "* He pronounced it fairly well. *"Sometimes he asks us to get it for him. In return, he won't tell his father if he finds a beer can. Though he still gets mad.*

"After our third year here, he gave us a car—a Cadillac, sixty-seven. He was buying a new one. Before that he always had let us drive it around. It's in Phoenix now." They left it there, I knew, whenever they went home, and then drove it back to Idaho upon their return each spring. I smiled at the thought of the guys piling into a millionaire rancher's used Cadillac and cruising up to Idaho. Inocencio's eyes were wide as he heard the tale; you could see him envisioning this supercar. Only a Corvette might have been better.

The night grew older, and we did not eat dinner, nor did anyone mention it: a sure sign that the real traveling had begun. The chatting continued, the little conversations about so-and-so back home, such-and-such in Idaho, replays of the Owls' last soccer game of the season—they had finished third in the state this year. They would have placed second, apparently, except for Tiberio's miss of an easy goal. He looked exasperated as somebody brought it up again—an incident he would never hear the end of. Suddenly those nearer the *coyote* began rising to their feet, and my heart leaped . . . our turn. After three or four hours of waiting, it all seemed very sudden. Within fifteen seconds we were off again, single file.

The land quickly turned to scrub desert as we left the tiny stream. The earth was white and powdery, the shrubs thin branched and small leaved, in scattered clumps that made the path circuitous. All was black and white under the quarter moon. I put on my jacket as we walked—the wind had begun to blow. We walked for ten minutes, stopping at a depression in the desert floor. *"Here we wait again,"* said our guide.

We sat down, lay down, waited. My ears were pricked for any sound: for some reason I expected some kind of setup, an ambush. Tales of betrayal and robbery were legion along the border. But nothing happened until much later, when we heard the soft purring of a motor arriving in wafts of the wind. Everyone stood up, even our guide uncertain of which direction he ought to look. Then there was the more definite click of a door opening, and we hurried toward the sound.

An old pickup truck had backed into a clearing one hundred feet from our little crater. The driver lowered the gate as we appeared, and, without a word, we all climbed in. Genaro and Plácido conferred with the driver and the guide, and then Genaro climbed into the cab with the two *coyotes*. Plácido came around to the back of the truck, now weighted far past capacity, slammed the gate, and struggled to cram himself in amongst the fifteen of us already there. *"They say they'll collect at the other end—at La Nariz,"* he answered Jesús.

The driver shifted into gear and then, ever so slowly, began to roll forward. The headlights were off, and he leaned way out the window to negotiate his route around the shrubs. For fifteen minutes we rolled softly through the desert, the hum of the motor a comfort after so many hours of silence. Nobody said a word. We went a little faster when a vague dirt road materialized, braked to cross the ledge of pavement at the edge of a highway, and finally accelerated as the driver steered into the eastbound lane. After ten minutes of driving, the headlights came on. I breathed a small sigh of relief as we hit 45 MPH or so, the effect of the cold wind diminished by the sardine closeness of all the others. None of us could move, at risk of pushing someone over the edge of the truck bed.

Something behind the truck caught Plácido's attention. I, facing forward, watched his face until light reflected off his eyes and the cab window told me there was somebody following us.

Plácido nudged Jesús. Several of us turned around to stare in the direction of the approaching vehicle.

That it was gaining on us did not concern me at first; we weren't going that fast. But then I noticed that it was coming up on us extremely fast, and that everyone was watching. The driver must have been worried too—you could hear the engine strain as he tried to accelerate. But the old truck was moving as fast as it could, and within seconds the headlights in the distance were following us by only twenty feet. Then a row of high-intensity lights exploded from the roof of the pursuing vehicle, making it impossible to see at all. It sped up alongside us—a pickup truck, but small and souped up, with the cab crowded and two men in back. The passenger window was cranked down, and a man with a long arm held out a revolver. *"Pull over!"* he yelled at the driver. The driver kept going. The two men in back held up rifles. *"Pull over!"* they screamed. The driver drifted to a stop.

In a matter of seconds the four men had hopped from their truck and surrounded ours. I half expected some movement from my companions, a rapid scattering out into the desert, but no one stirred. The tall man with the pistol opened the driver's door, hauled him out by the shirt, and whacked him on the side of the head with the gun. He fell to the road.

The men with the rifles trained them on us. *"Stay right where you are!"* shouted one. *"We will shoot if you move."*

Genaro and the guide were ordered from the other side of the cab and around the front of the truck by a short, round-faced man with a submachine gun. The tall *pistolero* questioned all three of them. *"Where were you going?"*

"Home," said the driver. I noticed, for the first time, that he was also a teenager. The tall man punched him in the stomach, and he doubled over.

"Where?" he demanded of the guide, who held his hands over his head. *"To our farm,"* said the guide. The tall man's elbow landed near his ear, and he fell onto the pavement.

"Don't lie to me! Were you taking them for money? Are you drug smugglers? Answer!"

None of them did, and they were struck this time with fists. The tall *pistolero* placed the barrel of his revolver against the driver's temple and ordered him back into the old pickup. *"Follow them,"* he directed, sliding onto the seat next to him and pointing to the other gunmen. Genaro and the guide were loaded into the back of the fast pickup. We did a U-turn and followed the truck in the direction we had come. Through the back of our cab we could see the silhouette of the tall man and the driver, pistol against his head. He drove slowly.

Plácido was close to me. *"Who are they?"* I asked.

"I think they're judiciales," he said—the Federal Judicial Police.

"They are?" That was astonishing to me—I thought they were some sort of bandits. *"But why? What did we do?"*

Plácido shrugged. *"Maybe the coyotes didn't pay them first."*

"The coyotes have to pay them?" You had to pay if you were going to smuggle, even though you violated no law; it was probably considered a normal expense of doing business. No wonder these *coyotes* had offered us the budget rate.

"But how did they know we were there? Where are they taking us?"

Plácido shrugged again. I remembered the old man we had suspected of being an informer.

We arrived again in Sonoita, its streets empty and dark. The two trucks parked next to a building which I immediately recognized as the Federal Judicial Police headquarters. I was a little relieved to see they were official, and not common criminals— naively relieved, as I would learn. Under gunpoint, we were ordered to leave our gear in the back of the truck and climb stairs up the back of the building. The tall gunman, waiting on a landing at the top, told us to stand against the walls of a large, empty room. It was dimly lit by a single bulb. My heart was pounding. The faces of the men were stony, those of the young guys and Evangélica terrified.

I didn't know how I looked; all I was sure of was that the police had not yet realized there was a *gringo* present. The lighting was part of the reason: neither moonlight nor their forty-watt bulb really illuminated my pale skin and blue eyes. I also credited my dress: a baseball cap, with a hooded sweatshirt pulled over, hid my hair and cast a shadow across my face. But my best disguise was simply the company I kept—I had been around the group so long that they treated me like one of the gang. And who in a thousand years would dream that a *gringo* would be crossing the desert into his own country?

Apparently thinking all three to be *coyotes*, the police kept the driver, guide, and Genaro across the room from the rest of us. Then, one at a time, the driver first, they directed them into an adjoining office. The fourth, the tall cop, stayed in the big room, his revolver trained on us. Through the thin partition we could hear nearly everything.

"*Who do you work for?*" a voice demanded.

"*Nobody,*" came the reply, through the wall.

"*Don't lie!*" There was a sudden exhalation, the gasping of a blow to the stomach. "*It will be much worse if you lie.*"

The "questioning" of the three lasted nearly an hour. We winced as we witnessed with our ears the beating of the driver and his friend. But fists were clenched and eyes glared as Genaro's turn came up and he was pushed into the office. The interrogation was curt and desultory. First we heard accusations, then Genaro's denials, punctuated by louder accusations. Finally, after a long silence, the words "*¡Ay, Dios mío, Dios mío!*" came through the wall—oh, my God, my God. His relatives from Quirambal, dressed in black, trembled as the torture continued. "*¡No! ¡Por favor!*" They stared hard at the floor, tense, and we listened. There were thumps and bangs from within the room. "*Señores, ¡por favor!*" The tall cop watched us. There was a sputtering, coughing, and gasping—evidently Genaro was having a hard time breathing. I prayed the Quirambal guys could keep themselves under control, for their own sake.

After what seemed hours, Genaro hobbled out the door, hands cuffed behind his back, hat missing, face and shirt wet, clearly shaken. It was more than sweat—his shirt was soaked,

and stuck to his chest. *"Tehuacanazo,"* said Jesús, standing next
to me. He was grim. *Agua Tehuacán*, I knew, was Mexico's popular carbonated mineral water. *Tehuacanazo*, I would later learn,
was the slang term for a torture, popular among the judicial police,
which involved holding the seated victim's head back, covering
his mouth, and then pouring the fizzy water up his nose, through
which it entered his sinuses. The torture was so common and so
ghastly that almost everyone in Mexico knew what *tehuacanazo*
meant. From his age and imposing presence, they had probably
figured Genaro to be the leader.

Three others from Quirambal went in next, one at a time.
I swallowed hard when I realized I was next in line. They were
going around the room. The tall cop came up to me. I continued
to look down.

"You! What's your name?"

"Teodoro."

"Where are you from?"

"Colorado."

"What?"

I paused. There was no way out. *"Colorado. Over there. On
the other side."*

The cop brusquely lifted the bill of my cap. He stared at my
face. *"Identificación."*

I took out my driver's license. Fortunately, I had also had
a business card printed in Spanish the week before, identifying
me as a journalist and naming the press syndicate to which I had
been sending articles on Mexico. *"I'm a journalist,"* I said.

The tall cop abruptly called to the others, and they came out
of the office. They asked me questions—I was crossing the border
to write a magazine article, I lied—and then conferred among
themselves. I was directed into the fluorescent-lit office, and then
into a chair. The tall one came in and closed the door behind
him. I braced myself. One of them picked up the phone on the
desk, waited a long time for someone to answer, and then apol-
ogized to them. They were calling the *comandante*, who had been
asleep. The *comandante* had to come down. Apparently this was

serious. They decided to do nothing further without him, and so, for half an hour, I sat.

I took in my surroundings. On the floor were the black hats of Genaro and his young cousins, dusty, upside down. They had gone in wearing those hats. On one wall was a long gun rack. It held at least ten different kinds of rifles and automatic weapons. I recognized M-16 and AK-47 machine guns, and an Uzi sub-machine gun—they could not have been standard Mexican government issue. The others I could not identify. It was a small arsenal. The cops had me empty my pockets onto the desk. They flipped through my notebook. It was full of slang you could not find in a dictionary—words I was trying to learn, many with sexual connotations. They thought these were funny, and asked why I had written them down. It was a relief to see them laughing, though I did not trust their sense of humor; they derived too much pleasure from suffering. The notes, I explained, were simply to help me communicate with people in their own language. While we waited, they taught me a couple of new words.

The *comandante* arrived, a clean-cut, surprisingly young man with puffy eyes and a mug of coffee in his hand. The *judiciales* were not local kids—they were trained at a national academy, recruited from across the country. He took off his coat, sat down at the desk, and looked at the contents of my wallet.

"You say you are a journalist?"

"Si, señor. Of the Inter-American Press Association."

"And what were you doing with these men?"

"Writing an article on what it is like to cross the border."

He paused. *"Who besides us knows you are here?"*

There was something menacing about the question. I decided it would be best if everyone knew I was there. The more people that knew, the harder it would be for them to dump me in the desert with a bullet in my head.

"Well, my editor in Miami, who sent me on this assignment. And then there's another editor in Phoenix, who was going to pick me up tomorrow on the other side. And my wife and kids in Denver—I called them this evening. They all expect me in the morning. They

were a little worried, you know." I laughed. I had even made up people.

"*Mmm. And what will you be writing in your story?*"

"*Well, nothing, I guess, because I couldn't cross the border. If I didn't cross, there's not really a story in it, is there?*"

The *comandante* shook his head.

"*They won't be happy, but I'll just have to tell them—this wasn't a good idea. It's too dangerous. It's against the law, after all—though I didn't realize that before.*"

The *comandante* looked at me. "*No story, then?*"

"*Of course not.*"

They asked me about the *coyotes*, and I explained adamantly that they were wrong about Genaro. To the best of my knowledge, I went on, drugs had nothing whatsoever to do with the trip. As far as specifics of route and financing, I pleaded ignorance, not wanting to contradict anyone else's story.

Finally the *comandante* left the room with the tall one. A few minutes later, the tall one came back and looked at me.

"*You can go.*"

I rose, reassembled the contents of my wallet, and walked out of the small office. In the large, dimly lit room where they waited, I knew my companions were watching me. I wanted to tell them what had happened, see what I could do for them now that my cover was blown . . . but the tall cop had opened the door, was standing by it. In my last glance into the room, I saw Evangélica, huddled against Jesús . . .

Outside it was even darker. Until I reached the highway I remained nervous that it was some kind of ruse, that they were saying I could go, but didn't really mean it. Then finally I was relieved, but a sickened feeling lingered in my stomach. They were all still in there, and I felt like a traitor for having been released. I walked a few blocks down the highway, to the bridge over the stream, descended to the banks, and then circled back around behind the police station. Quietly I skirted its dark side, and then crossed a street to an alley which afforded a view of the back door. And there I waited for them to come out.

The windows of the headquarters were open, and male voices drifted out. There was yelling, what sounded like insults and demands, and periods of silence, but at least no more of the telltale gasps and moans, no cries of "¡Ay, Dios mío! Oh, my God!" It was cold; I guessed it to be three in the morning. After another hour they all filed out, still at gunpoint, and climbed again into the truck. My heart began to pound again: where were they taking them? Where would I go? After five minutes, the tall cop came out and collected money from each one. Jesús paid for Evangélica. Then the cop returned to the building, and they waited.

I was sorely tempted to whisper out to them, even to sneak over and climb in too. Otherwise, I well might lose them for good. But if I were caught again, I knew, they would not go easy on me. For what seemed hours but was probably only thirty minutes, they waited, crammed as before in the back of the smuggler's pickup. The smuggler and guide apparently were still inside the headquarters. Then at last the building's lights began to go off, and the *comandante* and four *judiciales* came out and locked the door. They appeared not even to notice the group in the back of the pickup, just walked to their cars. The *comandante*'s was a large, powder blue, brand-new Oldsmobile Cutlass. At the last moment, one of the cops stopped his car alongside the truck, rolled down his window, said a few words, and then drove off. As the dust settled, one by one my friends descended from the pickup truck, stiff legged and tentative, looking around, as I had done, for the trap. But we were alone. As they headed for the street, I came up behind them.

We stopped and had a huddle. The Quirambal men looked bruised and unhappy, and kept to themselves. But the others wanted to know what had happened to me. And then Jesús described what had happened to them.

"*After you left, they didn't beat anyone else.*" Tiberio patted me on the back. "*But they accused Tiberio, Conce, and me of planning to smuggle drugs. We said no, but they said we were, and we were probably carrying money we made from it, and so they told us to take off our shoes. They found the money of Tiberio and Conce in their socks, and mine in my pants. They took half of it, and said that was the government fine.*"

Tiberio took over. "*Then the fucking bastards said we'd had enough trouble for tonight, and they offered to drive us back wherever we were going. Of course, we didn't believe it, but what choice did we have? We had to go climb back into the truck. Then that tall bastard came and got twenty dollars apiece, the amount they found out we were going to pay the driver. And then we waited. And then those bastards left. The last thing they said was, 'Oh, you're still here! Well, sorry, our shift's over and we've got to go home. Good night!' Son of the virgin whore!*"

At least, I thought, they had left Evangélica alone. We walked to the main highway, but instead of turning right toward the stream, they headed left.

"*What's going on?*"

Jesús pointed to the town's main, American-style motel. "*We're going to go see how much they charge.*"

The price was twenty-five dollars for a one-bed double, an exorbitant rate for Mexico—but this was the border. It was hard to believe that, having just been robbed, the guys were willing to shell out that much money. But then, it was hard for me to believe what had just happened. And everyone needs a break now and then: when the night clerk finally agreed to allow three to a bed, they accepted. Victor, Tiberio, and I took showers and then crashed on the bed in our room. It was, alas, somewhat narrower than a normal full-size. But the room was warm, and no one paid any attention. No one even had the energy to remove the bedspread. We just lay down on top of it, and slept until midafternoon. Then the full group went out to a café for breakfast.

Genaro rose gingerly, one hand over his left kidney, one on his back. He had not wanted to talk about what had happened to him, but someone had finally pried it out of him. While handcuffed, he said, he had been made to close his eyes so that he would not know when they were going to punch him in the stomach. After being punched, and doubling over and falling to the floor, he had been kicked in the stomach and back. All this preceded the *tehuacanazo*—the charge-water torture. *"Lucky we hadn't eaten dinner, eh?"* said another of the Quirambal men wryly. He had had a pistol held against his temple and a can of Mace inserted in his open mouth, though neither had been discharged. The same cop that did that—a short one, nicknamed *"El Chino"* for his Asiatic features—had also struck his brother open handed against both ears at once. The boy was still having trouble hearing.

Genaro, for once, was not laughing. He was angry and humiliated and sore. The description of his torture had not been necessary to understand how he had suffered. His cries were my most vivid memory of the night before: a man from the *ranchos*, a man who thought nothing of all-day mountain walks, who crossed the desert as a way of life, who lived hours from a doctor, a man as strong and tough as Genaro did not cry out for God unless he hurt bad. I hated the *judiciales*.

With Genaro finally on his feet, we were ready to go. There was still some space between the sun and the western horizon, but we had decided it was necessary to take advantage of the light: we were going to walk the entire way. It would add a day and a night to the trip, but there was no other choice. We were reprovisioned and extremely wary. There would be no *coyotes* this time—they could not be trusted, and we could not afford to get caught again.

With Plácido back in the lead—restored to that position by Genaro's injuries—we again struck off up the stream. No one, I noticed, paid the slightest heed when we passed the stand of trees where we had waited earlier. That was behind us. Ahead would be a very large desert, a hostile place jealous of moisture and motivation; there were many enemies on the road to the United States.

Because the stream meandered back and forth in huge curves that sometimes even took us opposite from the direction we wanted, we made many shortcuts, most on the advice of Genaro, at the end of the line of walkers. Usually the shortcut entailed scrambling out of the arroyo, over rocks and loose sand, grabbing for roots or anything else to steady you, and then walking across flat land to meet up with the stream somewhere else. Occasionally someone would climb a tall tree—there were a few, as we were still close to water—to try and spot the most direct route. It was a tiring way to travel, and always a relief to return to the moist, cool streamside. Human footprints mixed with goat prints on the sandy bank.

As the sun was about to set, Genaro directed us to leave the stream again and climb the north bank. At the top we found ourselves on a parched field—an onion field, by the looks of it, lying fallow. There was a light breeze we had not felt in the arroyo, and I paused to cool down and watch it scatter straw over the empty furrows. The field was wide but laced with deep fissures as though it were dry way, way down. Carefully we picked our way across these, having to work hard to move over the loose soil. Then Genaro, finally climbing out of the arroyo with the help of his townsmen, hissed us to the ground.

"*Why? What is it?*" Jesús whispered back. Genaro pointed across the field. Following his direction, we focused far away and saw . . . cars. Two of them, moving rather fast, apparently traveling a good road.

"*La frontera,*" came the reply. It was the border, and the border highway. I gulped, realizing we finally were there. *Los Estados Unidos*—home—and yet, from this angle, it did not beckon as usual. For the first time, I could almost see America as a foreign country, full of mystique and danger. A new feeling had been superimposed on my old one in the course of my Mexican odyssey: Was I home, or had I arrived someplace else?

With the sun casting long shadows, and nothing behind us to prevent a silhouette, we were obvious, standing tall on the field. But crouched down, guerrilla fashion, it would be harder to pick us out. We moved ahead, lowly and slowly, taking advantage of a dry irrigation ditch for as long as it ran, and then of a barbed-wire fence that had had a wall of tumbleweeds blown against it. Slowly, across a landscape of browns and golds, we approached the highway.

We stopped again fifty feet away, and waited for a faraway truck to approach and depart. Then, when it had disappeared, we abandoned our single-file formation and sprinted across the road, en masse. Immediately we were faced with another barbed-wire fence, triple stranded; two men stepped on the middle wire and lifted the top one, making a hole for the rest of us to slip through. It was still light enough to make out rocks and small cactuses and other obstacles, but discerning the strands of wire was a little harder. Another two hundred feet and we were faced with a third fence, old and loose enough to push down and walk over carefully. Now we were on the side of a hill, climbing. To my amazement, yet another fence presented itself minutes later: barbed and four stranded, it had, in addition, vertical wires joining the strands every foot or so and was strung extremely tight. Nobody knew for sure which was the border fence, but this one got my vote. Though only four feet high, it was very tricky to cross. Straddling it, three people including me got their pants caught and pricked their thighs; one of the Quirambal men, slipping through, went too fast and got his black jacket hooked. Scared to stop and sort it out, he kept going, the result being five long white slashes down its back where the insulation was revealed. Evangélica was literally lifted over by Jesús and Tiberio. We had just become *alambristas*, Mexican slang for our sort of wire jumpers.

Now we moved fast, Plácido setting a stiff pace and nobody talking. The American side of the border was hilly and uncultivated; I guessed we had entered Organ Pipe Cactus National Monument, which had the border as its southern perimeter. As we walked, the organ-pipe cactuses grew taller and taller, eventually towering way over our heads, twenty or thirty feet apart. Interspersed, and splaying in every direction, were the long, thin *palo verde* cactuses; prickly pears and barrel cactuses were the main hazard to our feet, especially those feet clad only in *huaraches*—about half of them. But mostly the surface of the desert was clear and flat, sometimes pebbly, sometimes rocky, sometimes sandy.

After about an hour, we stopped so that those who had them could get out their flashlights. Genaro and Plácido conferred about the route. Genaro pointed toward the northeast horizon, and a jagged line of mountains just visible against the darkening sky. It was hard to say how far away they were—twenty-five miles? They, or more specifically the gap between two of them where there was a pass, were our immediate destination. To have as our object something so vast and dark and distant set the imagination swirling. As the procession rose to its feet and continued, I wondered how many others were thinking about those mountains, now just a shadow—would we be able to see them in the light? What lay in that dark, indeterminate space between us and them, what obstacles, what enemies?

I fell into step two people behind Conce, who kept a flashlight pointed at the ground in front of his feet. There was a time lapse between the moment his light illuminated the ground and the moment I arrived there, and I tried to adjust my eyes and brain to the delay, tried to remember where to step. The large group lent confidence—a sense of momentum, purpose, and capability. For at least another hour and a half we walked, the desert surface rolling slightly, rising always, leading us to the mountain. Then a water and cigarette break with everyone squatting around in a circle, flashlights off, the sliver of a moon, stars, and cigarette embers the only light. The smell of tobacco smoke was reassuring. But the break lasted no longer than a cigarette, and soon we were back on our feet, trekking hard.

A yelp came from the back. Young Inocencio, ignorant of the desert, had been swinging his arms a bit too enthusiastically and had attracted the barbed spines of the jumping cholla cactus. The cholla were probably our worst enemy among the plants; their luminous clusters of needles grew mainly at a height between one's shoulders and knees. The slightest touch—sometimes, it seemed you didn't even have to touch, but simply come close enough for them to leap onto you—the slightest touch and their microscopic barbs implanted themselves in skin, clothing, shoe leather, anything. Any further movement after that, and larger barbs worked their way in too. Inocencio had batted the back of his hand against a cluster of four cholla pricklers, and they were in deep. His friend Marín had donned a glove and was about to try to pull them out, but Genaro stopped him.

"You can't touch these with anything soft," he explained, shining his flashlight on the pale hand. *"They'll stick in gloves too."* Unfortunately, the pliers we had bought were in the pocket of Plácido, up front, and this required immediate action. Genaro handed me the light, picked up two rocks, and told Marín to hold Inocencio's fingers. *"This is going to hurt,"* he told Inocencio, who nodded. Then, using the rocks as pincers, Genaro got a grip on one cluster at a time, and pulled. The spines yielded reluctantly, releasing the skin at the last possible instant. Inocencio flinched, but said nothing. His hand was torn and bloody, but the spines were out. We moved on.

I was getting tired, and was impressed by how the Mexicans kept up the pace. I thought of Mexican nourishment: weren't Americans much better fed? Milk, fresh vegetables, and red meat—that's what I had been raised on, and Mexicans had little of any of them. But, even on camping trips with backpacks, I couldn't ever remember having pushed it like this. I didn't think my American friends and I—even with European hiking boots and the finest clothing—would have been able to do it, not without eating, not for so long. How could you explain it? Was it simply will? Growing up accustomed to hardship? Was it fear? My mind was slowly numbing due to lack of blood sugar, and it was only vaguely that I realized Genaro had speeded up from the tail end of the expedition and, barely even puffing, had passed me on his way to the front. I slowly came to my senses, and shook the sleep from my head. If Genaro could do it, in his condition . . . I forged ahead.

We marched on over a rise and there, on the far side, beneath a low outcropping of rock, came upon the delicious sight of the leaders unshouldering their sacks and dropping their water jugs. Relief! Mine fell to the sand like lead when we reached them. Cigarettes came out and lighters clicked, and the men from Quirambal built a small camp fire, for it was cold if you weren't walking. A few of the group stayed up to watch the fire burn itself out. The majority, though, lay down, jackets on, side by side, and with a blanket thrown over us for warmth. I saw the fire flickering on the rocks and on an organ-pipe cactus before I closed my eyes, and in the first seconds of sleep was reminded of the large, furry spider that used to climb on my bed when I left on the ceiling light in Ahuacatlán. This was tarantula country! I sat up and took a sleepy look around me, at the scattered rubble under the rocks, the decomposing trunk of an organ-pipe cactus, the broken branch of a cholla, the white, sandy dirt: shouldn't we put that fire out? Then again, I thought, you could grow old fast trying to prepare against everything. As Mexicans appreciated, that's what prayers are for. I lay back down and said one.

It seemed only three or four hours later that we were up—the sky was barely turning light. Plácido responded to the grumbling by reminding us that, outstretched and in the open, we were easily visible from *La Migra*'s patrol planes, which flew during the day. A warm-up fire was out of the question for the same reason; we were reduced to watching the steam of our own breath as it rose and dissipated in the cold air. Someone broke out a loaf of bread and some slices of cheese, but, to my surprise, only a few partook of this skimpy breakfast. The rest, it seemed, were impatient; they moved to walk: it was not yet time to eat.

The sun rose quickly into a cloudless sky as our file continued toward the mountain with the notch. I was tired, but daylight made the going easier: now, at least, I could see where I was stepping. We wound our way around cactuses and dry shrubs, the ground mostly even except for where showers had washed a channel in the desert floor. The higher we climbed toward the mountain, the deeper these channels became, until they were regular arroyos. When we stopped it was always in an arroyo, for there we cast no shadows, could not be seen. But other creatures enjoyed these refuges too, and, upon descending to their sandy floors, you had to look carefully for desert rats, spiders, and snakes. We had seen all three by our second rest of the morning; a young cousin of Genaro's, who came upon the rattler, expressed great disappointment that it had gotten away before he could find something to knock it on the head with. The Mexicans were at home in the desert.

There was no path, no obvious route, but several times we came upon wrappers from Mexican products—*Alas* cigarettes, *Chiclets* and *Canel*'s gum, a pair of spent and corroded flashlight batteries—that showed us others had passed the same way. The space around us was wide and empty, but there was never a sense of loneliness or uncertainty: we knew where we were going. Those with experience were committed to getting us there quickly and alive. It was an entirely different sort of trip than any American might make: we weren't there for outdoor exercise, or for education about the environment; this wasn't a game. Somewhere nearby, I knew, thirteen Salvadorans had perished on a crossing in 1980. They had entered Organ Pipe Cactus National Monument on the Fourth of July weekend, with the same plan as ours but without the experience. Dressed in city clothes and carrying suitcases, they expired of thirst on a day when the temperature on the desert floor was estimated at 150 degrees. Moments before their deaths, they poured cologne, deodorant, and even their own urine down their throats in a last-ditch effort to survive. People crossed for work or to escape war, but never for fun.

The walk became steep as we finally trod upon the very skirt of the mountain we had seen from afar, the vegetation subsiding almost completely.

"We should climb this fast," said Jesús, coming up alongside me, Evangélica in tow. *"There's no cover at all."*

The file disintegrated as the slope steepened more, each person picking his own line up the crumbly surface. My heart pounded—normally a person slowed down for a climb. But, even in their smooth-soled cowboy boots and homemade *huaraches*, the men from Querétaro climbed like mountain goats, scampering up and leaving me behind in a light rain of pebbles. Climbable slope narrowed to a strip only a foot or two wide toward the top, with rocks on each side—calling this a pass was generous—and here I took a breather, turning around to survey the land we had crossed. Visibility was good on that clear day, and I knew that somewhere across the arid expanse below ran the highway we had crossed the evening before. But for the life of me, I couldn't pick it out; United States or Mexico, it all looked the same.

Hawks rode the thermals in front of me; some at a lower altitude than I, so that I could see their backs. Vultures circling would have added drama, but there were none, never had been in all my desert travels. Perhaps it was a good omen.

Sweating and wary on the top, we enjoyed the breeze and view for just a few seconds before beginning our descent. Ahead were a couple more mountain ridges, but beyond them it looked flat. We were about halfway down, skidding and sliding in a small cloud of dust, when the faint buzz of an airplane became audible.

"Run!" cried Genaro, down below in the lead, waving his arms for us to follow. Nothing was visible, but it could be soon— and so, then, would we. The dust cloud became larger, our movements reckless and desperate, and we strove for the bottom. There were no trees or cactuses at all on the small slope, and only when I arrived on nearly flat ground at the valley floor did I realize Genaro had jumped into an arroyo. Stooping low under the trees along its rim, I shot in with the others.

As fate would have it, Genaro's cousin, at this same moment, finally found his snake. It was coiled in the sand about six feet from him, rattling, its lair having been suddenly invaded. Everyone froze; the buzzing of the aircraft grew louder until finally it appeared, nearly overhead, through the thin leaves of the desert trees. No one moved until the sound had passed, and we could again hear the snake. Then Genaro broke a dead, scrubby tree in half, came up behind the boy, and lifted the snake with the end of the stick. It slipped off, hissed, and rattled some more. People laughed nervously. Genaro forked it up again, which seemed to me a bad idea until I saw that this time he had it—in the air the snake was powerless. Genaro kept turning the stick to keep it that way. His cousin bent to pick up a large rock; Genaro nodded, then flung the viper down and began to beat it with the stick. Fazed, the snake stopped hissing, and the boy, from about three feet above, dropped his stone on its head. The snake lay twitching. Another drop of the stone, and it was dead.

Genaro picked up the body with his bare hands. We all stood close to examine it—the pointed head, the little dip between the eyes of a pit viper. After it was passed around, it was handed back to the boy who had killed it, who in turn passed it back to Genaro. *"No thanks,"* said Genaro. *"I already have one."* He pointed to the snakeskin band on his hat. *"It's for you."* The boy grinned to himself.

No one could answer my question about whether the single-engine prop had been an Immigration plane or not—*"they're never the same,"* said Jesús. But, after all the excitement, everyone agreed that it was finally time or a meal. All packs were untied, jacket pockets were emptied. It was mostly shady where we were, but still hot—a good time not to be walking. A good time to be eating. Despite the leaders' warnings to save some, we ate nearly everything we had brought, and then lay back—our stomachs full and round, like a snake's—to let it digest.

I got up after a while to watch the boy from Quirambal skin the serpent. Using Genaro's knife, he cut off the head and tail and then slit the body lengthwise, to one side of the tough white stomach scales. The long tubular stomach itself produced a handful of tiny white bones toward the snake's tail—probably part of a desert rat that had wandered too close several days earlier. The snake, too, had enemies, among them the sun, birds of prey, and us.

Reluctantly we returned to our feet, and the desert. The sun was at its highest, and as we walked in the trough between two shimmering mountainsides the temperature rose alarmingly. When we stopped for water the wind was too hot, like the breath of some great animal. Only three people, I noticed, had any water left in their jugs. But there was nothing to be gained by worrying, and gratitude was due when the wind stopped, gratitude for the long sleeves that covered my skin.

My concern over what seemed a long detour in the wrong direction melted into affection for Genaro when we arrived at an abandoned well. I later found this well on a topographic map of the area; Genaro had simply been shown it years earlier by another crosser, and remembered the spot. Inocencio, light and small, descended dark steps on the wall of the well to the water level, some thirty feet down. From there he refilled the empty water jugs we dropped and carried them back up, two at a time. As the sun fell low in the sky, we once again found ourselves on the flat desert floor, having crossed over two more mountains. Feet were heavy now, and the going slower. We became aware of a highway in the distance, perhaps a quarter mile away, and began to walk a line midway between it and the mountain range, heading toward a little bump of a hill separate from all the others.

When we were near enough the small hill to see two huts partway up, Genaro and Plácido stopped. Two envoys, Jesús and Plácido, were selected to go on alone, toward the huts. These dwellings, I later learned, were part of the Papago hamlet of Gu Vo; we had crossed into the reservation. Topography had been our only map. The walking, now, was almost over—it was known that the Indians could arrange transportation the rest of the way to Phoenix. To keep inconspicuous, the rest of us waited for our emissaries to return.

The two came back at sunset, to report they had set up a ride for the next day; in the meantime we would have to wait it out. Jesús suggested that I simply hitchhike the rest of the way to Phoenix, an option unavailable to them. It would be good for me—I would save $200—and, though he didn't say it, it might be good for them, since they wouldn't have to explain me to the *coyotes*, whoever they turned out to be. But I demurred: having come this far, the money wasn't so big a deal, and I was by now fairly confident of my disguise—hooded sweatshirt, baseball cap, and, if necessary, Victor's very ethnic-looking woolen *serape* to drape over my shoulders. I wanted to go all the way, I said, and there was no objection.

The night was very, very cold. When it was dark we crossed

the road we had paralleled and circled a hill until we came to a
thicket. There we lay down—though, because I was dawdling,
I almost didn't get a place under the blanket. I had to resort to
the tactics of latecomers, simply lying down on the compact row
of bodies and hoping two of them would part to create room for
me. When finally I did scrunch in, it was amidst all the butt-
fuck jokes that always accompanied the front-to-back, spoonlike
sleeping arrangement. More guys fit under the blanket this way
than any other, and more surface area was warmed by other bodies
than in any other arrangement . . . but it seemed even Mexicans
were embarrassed, in their way, to be this close. That evening
the pressure from people on either end, trying to get in under
the edges of the blanket, made a slot in the middle extremely
uncomfortable. I got a muscle cramp from someone's knee press-
ing into the back of my leg, and then felt an overwhelming need
to urinate. Either one of these problems might have been tolerated
alone, but together they called for action. I squeezed out and into
the freezing air, did my business, and then tried to get back in.
But the slot had closed up, and my pleading evoked only sleepy
grumbles. I tried to burrow in under the legs, but came away
with a face full of dirt and a semiconscious boot in the ribs.
Frustrated and freezing, I got up and paced around.

From somewhere in the distance came the howl of a pack
of real coyotes. It was a haunting, indeterminate sound, a succession of wails that arrived unsteadily, as though carried on a breeze—
but the night was still. It was hard to pinpoint the source, until
finally I decided the pack must be moving. Would they know we
were there, have smelled us? Coyotes don't attack people, but
their calls were filled with foreboding. The pack circled 270 degrees around our camp, crying out sporadically, just when I would
have guessed they'd left. For warmth and comfort I collected a
few branches and built a small fire.

At first I felt guilty when I heard steps behind me: Plácido,
certainly, would not approve of a fire so close to a town. But I
turned around and saw it was Jesús and Evangélica, coming over
to join me. The little fire was almost out but Jesús, to my great

relief, dragged over a couple of big logs and suggested we really get it going. It had been too cold for him and Evangélica to sleep too. I rejoiced: so the cautious, stoical Mexican was human after all! We had it roaring in no time, and soon were joined by several of the others—a certain minimal level of comfort, apparently, was more important than the possibility we'd be detected by *La Migra*. Lying on the dirt, I arced my body forward to keep as much of it as possible close to the flames. Soon I was asleep.

We were ready for the Indians long before I suspect they ever got out of bed. Shortly before dawn we were on our feet, brushing the dust from our clothes, kicking dirt over the embers of the fire. The sunlight made its first appearance at the top of a nearby hill, and we spent a long hour or two shivering, watching it drop tantalizingly toward us. When it hit our heads and shoulders it felt. good, but by the time it had reached the whole group it was already too hot. We walked to refuge in the designated rendezvous spot, a nearby arroyo.

I was extremely nervous. It would be my first time trying to pass, in full daylight, as one of them. Victor had loaned me his *serape*, for the rustic touch, while sweatshirt hood and baseball cap masked my head. I again was glad for the size of our group— with seventeen, the smugglers were less likely to check each person out. But if they did, it could mean bigger trouble for me than the Mexican cops: either they would figure me as an under-cover Immigration agent, or they would believe my story about being a journalist. Either way, we were in the States now, and they might consider it very possible that I would turn them in, having witnessed all the transactions. I could find myself in an arroyo, permanently, should that happen. Though I had hardly slept, I wasn't sleepy in the least. In fact, I wondered how long my heart could pound at its present insistent, rapid rate before wearing me out completely.

I looked around at the others. They were scattered along thirty or forty feet of the arroyo, sitting or squatting, knees tucked up, heads bent forward, waiting . . . Americans never wait like that, I thought to myself. Most Americans, to begin with, don't know how to wait—they pace, or they worry, they make telephone calls. Never would they sit in a low, dark place, quietly, patiently waiting to be taken up in what fate has already decreed. Only Mexicans, and those from other countries too "uncivilized" to consider waiting an affront. We waited two or three hours.

The Indians stomped up from out of nowhere. Jesús got up from next to me and, with Plácido, spoke briefly to them. They were carrying shotguns under their arms. A dirt road ran nearby, but the Indians had parked somewhere else—we would walk there. Everyone stood up and fell into line, with one Indian leading and the other in the rear. We had to pass by the rearguard Indian as we fell into line; I walked as casually as possible, catching a glimpse that told me only that he was short, fat, long haired . . . and carrying that gun. Seen from behind, the Indian in the lead also looked chubby, except that he was tall. Both were clad in overcoats. We walked faster than I guessed the Indians, by their bulk, were accustomed to. In five minutes we arrived at the edge of a landfill, and were directed into a large ditch. There was one car nearby, a pea-green Nova as old as the one I had driven in Phoenix. The tall Indian in charge explained in English to Jesús and Plácido that it was the only car they had; they would have to take us in several loads to where we would meet the *coyotes*. All of a sudden I realized the Indians didn't speak a word of Spanish—why had I assumed they did?—and that, apparently, they weren't the ones who actually would deliver us in Phoenix. Jesús and Plácido were having a little trouble understanding what I, of course, had grasped perfectly; I hoped madly that they wouldn't turn to me, out of reflex, to ask for help with translation.

The first load was selected by the tall Indian, and left. The shorter one, beardless, remained, nervously looking all around. He tried a couple of words of Spanish out on Victor, who responded as though the guy were an idiot. But the Indian persevered with attempts at conversation, gun tucked in the crook of his arm, trying just about everyone with simple phrases in

English. "What's goin' on? How you doin' today? Where you from?" I prepared to lash out with a spray of Spanish if he persisted with me, but he gradually lost interest and paid attention mainly to a large front-end loader flattening out rubbish way across the dump. I slipped my wallet to Jesús for safekeeping. *"If he gets suspicious, I don't want him to have any evidence about who I am,"* I whispered.

In half an hour the Nova was back, and I got waved in with the second load—five of us, plus the driver. I hunched down in the backseat, my face well out of the range of the rearview mirror. But the sweating Indian seemed at least as nervous as me, and I doubt he ever checked it. One reason was that, apart from us in back, there was nothing to be seen in the rearview mirror—the Nova, traveling up to 80 MPH on dirt backroads, put up a great red cloud of dust. We shot over cattle guards so fast they felt like a single bump, an outstretched snake. Twice the accelerating rear wheels fishtailed out to the side and we gripped the seats, but the Indian had probably grown up on these roads and eased off in time. We passed from the Papago to the Pima reservation, through small hamlets with strange names (Ali Chuk, Pia Oik) and back along unmarked roads to the desert. When we were in a seldom-traveled area of squat scrub pines, the Indian pulled off the road a couple of hundred feet and shooed us out with his hands. Obedient as ever, we unloaded—and, without a word, he pulled out in a noisy cloud of dust.

We were nowhere—there was nothing around. We worried we had been betrayed, abandoned for reasons unknown. But finally Tiberio and Conce, passengers in the first ride, appeared from behind some distant bushes—the Indian had dropped us off at the wrong clump—and bid us in. It was another hiding place. Apparently, the real *coyotes* were going to rendezvous here with the Indians and pick us up. Again we waited.

The desert sky was clear, and the temperature soon up in the eighties. All my clothing made me look sick, like an invalid—and, because of the way I sweated beneath Victor's blanket, I did indeed feel feverish. But it was better than the alternative of being a sore-thumb *gabacho*. I found a little piece of shade and wiped my brow.

"*You're scared, aren't you, Teo?*" said Jesús, sitting down next to me.

"Scared?" Mexicans were not always New Age males, admiring of those who shared their feelings and vulnerabilities. "*No, I'm not scared. I'm just fucking hot.*" I thought that sounded convincing.

"*Well, why don't you take off some clothes?*"

"*You know why not.*" It was my disguise.

Jesús chewed on a piece of hard green grass and sat.

I asked, "*You've been through this a lot. Don't these guys ever scare you?*"

Jesús shrugged. "*Not too much. You just have to pay close attention to what's happening, be ready for anything. 'Ponte buso.' *" "Make like one who's been abused," was the slang phrase: alert, wary, suspicious. "*The money is the main thing. The gun is for that—to make sure we pay, after they do their part of the deal.*"

The guns were both back within an hour, and so were the rest of our group, the final three arriving with both Indians in the last carload. For another hour we waited some more, the Indians standing guard—for us, or against us? I wondered—guns cradled in their arms. When, at last, three more vehicles arrived in a big cloud of dust, my heart could not have pounded harder if I'd just run a one hundred-yard dash. I peered through the pines to see who got out.

The first was a Hispanic woman, middle aged, who might have looked more at home in a Laundromat. She drove an old Dodge pickup truck that had had a lot of body work done but never been repainted. Second was a Hispanic man, fortyish, wearing a polyester sport coat and driving a well-polished Pontiac Bonneville. Third was a sunken-chested Anglo in jeans, dwarfed by a huge four-wheel-drive International Travelall, the epitome of a gas guzzler. In the passenger seat of his car was an olive-skinned, heavy man, with dark, receding, oily hair, sunglasses, and a chain dangling on his chest. He had the aura of a nouveau riche operator, and from the minute I saw him, I knew he was in charge—though none of this was what I had expected. Several hip young Hispanic men were what I had expected. *Coyotes* were always fooling you.

"*Who is that guy?*" I asked Jesús, quietly, of the boss.

"*I don't know—the Indians called him last night. He looks like the one who puts everything together.*"

The four new arrivals and the Indians conferred, and the Indians gestured toward Plácido, who stood up and joined them. None appeared to have the least interest in the rest of us, for which I felt greatly relieved. We were to them another group of wetbacks, the great Mexican export, and nothing more; in this human commerce, they were simply shippers. Plácido returned and circulated among us to collect half the fare—one hundred dollars from each—and we in turn watched intently as he returned to them with that great wad of cash. If they were going to screw us, we knew, now was the time. The olive-skinned man took the money, counted it, and then separated an amount and gave it to the Indians.

"*What's that all about?*" I asked Jesús.

"*Their commission. The Indians called him, so they get a percent. I think it's ten percent.*" That, I figured, would be $20 for each of us, or $340—not bad for a morning's work. Next the olive-skinned man peeled off amounts for the woman and the Hispanic man . . . and things began to happen fast.

"*¡Vamos! Let's go!*" the man yelled to us. He held up four fingers; the woman held up five—the numbers they wanted for their respective cars. Genaro split us up, and we ran to the cars. I glanced at the olive-skinned organizer, but he was off lighting a cigarette—his work was done.

Five people climbed into the back of the woman's Dodge pickup. She threw two large dark tarps over them and drove away. Two others, meanwhile, were busy cramming themselves into the trunk of the Bonneville. The Hispanic man unceremoniously slammed the lid when no feet or fingers were protruding, and opened the rear door. There was room for one person on the floor, across the transmission bump, and for another across the seat. His car filled, he drove away as well.

That left eight of us, plus the Anglo and the boss, for the Travelall. We had to jog right in front of them as we piled in; I kept my head down, waiting in huge anxiety for one of them to grab my arm—say "Hey, wait a minute!"—but I made it inside. Plácido, Rolando, Conce, Tiberio, Victor, and I climbed over the rear seat and into the back deck, where we scrunched down, alternating directions, big fish in a small tin. It was like our sleeping arrangement in the cold desert night, except the compression was involuntary, the chill emotional. Jesús and Evangélica sat in the rear seat, the Anglo driver and boss in front. The engine was revved up, a Doors tape was plugged into the cassette player in front, and, in an instant, the patch of desert was empty again.

Not much of the muffler was left underneath us, and between the engine roar and the music it was almost impossible to hear what was being said up front. We in the back, also, had enough to occupy our attention. Besides the blazing sun coming through the windows—open windows in the front of the big car didn't seem to ventilate the rear at all—we soon realized there was a lot of exhaust leaking through the floor. The eyes of Conce and Rolando, who were especially close to the source, reddened and began to water; Rolando began to cough and wheeze. But we were packed in so tightly, and the risk of getting up seemed so great, that no one complained. Unable to bear the heat any longer, I took off Victor's blanket and Tiberio's sweatshirt and used them for pillows—if I were caught now, I decided, I would just run.

The drive was long and unpleasant. When finally we stopped, it was to let the olive-skinned man out. I sat halfway up and recognized the intersection, inside a wealthy quarter of Phoenix. At the driver's beckoning, Jesús moved into the vacant front seat. We pulled back into the traffic, and presently the driver turned off the radio and tried speaking to Jesús. "So, where you guys from?"

"From?"

"Yeah, where you from? You know, what's your home? *Casa*, home?"

"Oh, we from Querétaro."

"Quer-ert——" The driver had difficulty. "Yeah, I think I drove some guys from down there last week. Picking oranges, like you guys."

"What?"

"Oranges. You know, pick oranges?"

"Oh. Jes."

"Yeah, I got laid off a few months ago, nothing goin' on, I got a wife and kids to feed and rent to pay, you know?"

"Really?" Jesús had a talent at this; his short response convinced the driver he was being understood.

"Yeah, met Leo—that guy that was here—while back through a friend. I don't like doin' this, but it pays the bills, huh?"

"Oh, right!"

"I don't know, my wife don't like it, but a guy's got to get by. It's like you guys: crossin' the border is illegal, but you do it 'cause you have to, right?"

Jesús looked at him.

"I mean, nobody else'd do the work you're doin'. Nobody *I* know would do it, that's for fuckin' sure. And somebody's gotta get you guys up here. Look, the government says it's okay to give you a job, but it ain't okay to get you there. Man, that's bullshit! Sometimes you get the feeling they *expect* you to break the law. Fuckin' hypocrites, know what I mean?"

Jesús didn't.

"*Migra?* Hypocrit-o?"

"Ohh! *La Migra!* No, no!"

"No, no sir. That's what I say."

The *coyote* knew the way to Smith's ranch just as airport cabbies know the way to downtown. Two of the guys had once worked there; for the others, it was still like a suburb of Ahuacatlán, full of family and friends. Pulling up alongside the orchard midday, I felt a sense of déjà-vu, as though I had completed a great circle—from the orchards, to Mexico, and back. "Goodbye!" said Jesús to the *coyote*, who was still in midsentence. We all piled out as quickly as we could and ran into the orchard, leaving the *coyote* to close his own doors. Through the trees we went, entering the compound in the customary way, over the fence in back. Since the citrus season was winding down, an empty trailer had opened up; we went in and collapsed on the cots. I was thrilled to be back in my own country, relieved to be out of the hands of the *coyotes*. The others, now in a foreign land, still had fear in their eyes, but it was tempered by the sanctuary. We were getting there.

I sat on the wooden stoop outside the trailer door and stared, eyes unfocused, at my feet. The *huaraches* had come off for the first time in days, and it was remarkable now to see the zebra stripes of tan where the sun had shone in between the straps. A cracked fragment of mirror in the trailer bathroom showed my face to be the same brown hue as the dark stripes on my feet; the whites of my eyes glowed in contrast. It gave me a funny feeling to think back on what I had been through since leaving Phoenix, and especially in the past few days. Men with guns? Brutal cops? Night after night without sleep? Rather than sick, I felt strangely vibrant—damn near invincible, in fact, having made it into the States as we had. Only, I wondered a little about myself: where had my caution gone? I had stretched what I thought were my limits: was the knowledge gained a good knowledge? Was it wisdom? Or did some knowledge bruise? What had changed? I had seen a nice sedan, full of air-conditioned white people— owners, like Smith—drive by on the road half an hour earlier. What did I still have in common with people who were . . . like me?

I straightened my neck and looked around. It was getting dark, but there, a few yards away, was the driveway from which I had departed with Emilio and Máximo and company for Florida . . . it seemed like years ago. There was the trailer where I had first met them, feeling as naive as a midwestern Sunday-school teacher in Harlem. Spanish Harlem.

In the orchards, through the chain-link fence, I remembered picking, nearly killing myself with work. The job seemed even more remarkable now, after seeing what guys went through to *get* the job. What American wanted a job so badly? Any job—not just bottom-of-the-barrel work like this. Would you walk thirty-five miles, through the desert, for a job?

I looked deeper into the orchard, to where it got too dark to see. And I remembered. . . .

It was after dinner, a few months before. Sitting outside at Martinolli's, on a different stoop, I had seen Don Bernabé Garay heading off into the orchards with a rifle. It was Lupe Sanchez's rifle, I knew, a Browning bolt action .243; the aging, respected farmworker had borrowed it to go hunting for coyotes—not the smugglers, against whom he held no grudge, but the four-legged variety: in Mexico grease from their fat, rubbed on one's joints, was held to be the best cure for rheumatism. And with the mid-winter rains that had been drenching the Phoenix orchards, Don Berna's need was acute.

I called out as he ducked under the trees, and when his mumbled reply did not sound discouraging, I fell in behind. *Gringos* seemed to hold little mystique for Bernabé. Growers, field bosses, labor organizers, Border Patrolmen—over the course of half a lifetime in the States he had crossed paths with them all. White Americans no longer intimidated him; they barely even seemed to interest him. There was an aura about the man, stemming from his experience and dignity and the vast respect accorded him by others, Mexican and *gringo* alike. He wasn't arrogant, but Don Berna bowed down to nobody. Tagging along behind him down between the dark rows of orange trees, mud pulling at my shoes, I remembered feeling like a little kid.

After about twenty minutes we emerged onto the clear, flat desert. There it was brighter and colder; the orchard's musty, woodsy smell had yielded to sweet scents of sage and of cactus flowers opened by the rains. Don Berna paused, looking and listening. It seemed half an hour before he even noticed me. *"There were some out this way last night,"* he said. *"I heard them."*

We climbed up onto a little rise and sat down on rocks. Another half hour passed, and I began to feel the cold; I'd left in a rush, without my jacket. Fidgeting and shifting my weight restlessly, I must have made some noise. "*Ssssh!*" he hissed. "*They hear everything. Have you never hunted coyotes?*"

I shook my head. We passed the next half hour silently. The night was completely still; there were no barks, no howls, no hints of *coyotes* or anything else for that matter until a huge owl appeared, swooping around a tall shrub in front of us, the moonlight white on its back and wings and a black shadow tracing its path on the desert floor. The owl was patrolling at about the height of a standing man; you could hear the rustle as it flapped its wings once. It passed again and Don Berna raised the rifle . . . but then, with less noise than the owl in flight, he put it down. Perhaps it was the owl's eeriness in the colorless light that earned his respect, a presence that seemed almost imaginary; perhaps it was respect for another hunter. All Don Berna said was: "*No point killing it now. We'd never see the coyotes then.*"

"*You know,*" he continued presently, "*they're the most suspicious creatures on earth. Sometimes you see them in the orchard, in the early morning or else at sundown . . . but only if you're alone, for two people will always scare the coyote off. Before they leave the trees to cross a road, they look both ways. They want to know if anything's there. And if they hear the slightest noise, the slightest disturbance, they'll go back into the trees. They hate the daytime. And they trust nothing, nobody.*

"*That is why they call those who smuggle 'coyotes' too. They are just like the animal.*"

Another half hour, and Don Berna had stood up to go. I wondered if he blamed me for his lack of success. He exuded competence, capability—certainly, left to his own devices he would have returned to camp with some warm coyote grease to rub on his elbows, hands, and knees. But that night had brought nothing for him, and only a little something I couldn't put my finger on— an inkling, perhaps, of experience to come, a foreshadowing— for me. We had followed the path of dark trees back to camp.

And now I was in camp again. It was like coming full circle—except that I wasn't back where I had started, exactly. I was different, proud of my experience and yet a little worried about it. And things were by no means over. The aluminum door slammed behind Tiberio as he came out of the trailer. He looked barefoot and relaxed, and had changed out of his *Tecos* jersey into a black T-shirt adorned with deer and waterfalls that said "IDAHO." A cold open beer was in one hand, an unopened one in the other for me.

"*How's it going for you, Teo?*" he asked, sitting down and handing it to me.

I wanted to tell him the truth, but the translation job was daunting. It might take hours to explain how it was going for an American in my situation. I popped open the beer, and said it was going well.

"*To Idaho!*" said Tiberio, raising his.

"*To Idaho.*"

Shards of glass littered the front seat of the old Cadillac. The car—wide, yellow, and finned—had been a gift from the farmer up in Idaho, and the setting for the seduction of various *chicas* from the land of famous potatoes ("*Be nice!*" Jesús had been told.) Lately it was more important as a conveyance from the border to Idaho and back. The guys stored it behind a shack across the orchard during the five months a year they were home; this winter, we later learned, some kids had gotten it with rocks. Jesús lightly brushed glass off the damp front seat, produced the precious key, and turned it in the ignition. On the fourth try the old girl started up, to a round of cheers and "*¡Vivan los Tecos!*" The Owls were still in business.

A garage in El Mirage installed a new windshield the next day. And that night the first carload left for Idaho, Jesús at the wheel. I stayed behind with the second carload. Our group had shrunk back to eleven, the men from Quirambal, I discovered, having been taken by their *coyote* to another Phoenix ranch where they had closer relatives. They would look for late work in citrus and then, perhaps, head to Colorado for peach picking on the western slope. Jesús and Evangélica—she had been afraid to stay without him—returned to Phoenix a day and a half later, having driven nineteen hours and slept little. After a morning and an afternoon of rest they were stiff and bleary eyed but still eager to get back north again. It was late Saturday night when I and the rest of those remaining climbed into the Cadillac—perfect timing for avoiding the police. It had been nine days exactly since we left Querétaro. This was the last leg of our trip.

Again, the route was memorized. The highway connecting Phoenix to El Mirage continued on, conveniently, 300 miles to Las Vegas. Within the same early-morning hour, we passed through that symbol of American glitz and glitter and crossed over the gray barren expanse of Hoover Dam and the surrounding hydro-electric works, all starkly floodlit. Next we took a right on Inter-state 15, and it was a straight, boring shot up to Pocatello, Idaho—nearest big town to the ranch. With Jesús on the edge of ex-haustion, I agreed to help Victor with the driving. We stopped only for gas.

Because of the spring melt in the Northwest, and the begin-ning of the farming season, other migrants were on the road too. We knew them by their cars—generally larger, smokier, "pre-viously owned" American cars, packed to the gills and low to the ground. At one gas station we chatted briefly with a group headed north from Los Angeles. The year before, confided one, he had been caught by an Immigration roadblock about an hour north of where we were now: Immigration knew this was a time for travel, and they laid their nets accordingly. We thanked the men and took note, following their route to an older highway that paralleled the interstate for a couple of hours, avoiding the danger zone. And then it was back on the interstate, making miles.

I was in the backseat with four others, asleep and with my head slumped backward, when I felt the Caddy brake and slip onto the shoulder. I snapped my head up, noticed it was morning, and rubbed my eyes. Nobody said a word. I looked around back—

into the flashing lights of a sheriff's car. We had been pulled over.

Jesús, at the wheel, rolled down his window.

"May I see your license?" asked the cop. I looked around me—we were in a small town. Jesús handed him the license, the one he had gotten legally in Florida.

"Where are you going?"

"Where?"

"Where are you going? Do you speak English?"

"Where? Oh, Idaho! We go to Idaho."

"Where are you from? Mexico?"

Jesús played dumb on this question, and the cop repeated it loudly.

"Jes," Jesús finally confessed in defeat. He tried to pronounce the name of his country the American way: "Messico."

"Do you have a green card? Papers?"

Jesús knew what all this was about. There was no bullshitting left to be done. He shook his head. "Do any of these people?" asked the cop, peering into the car. He got no response. "Well, we clocked you at thirty-three in a thirty-mile-an-hour zone. You were speeding. And since you don't have papers, I'm afraid you'll have to come in with us. Follow me, please." Then he repeated it in passable Spanish, so there would be no mistake: *"Sígame."*

Looking straight ahead, Jesús rolled up the window. He looked scared and angry, though emotions other than joy or amusement were subtle on his face. No one else said much, until Conce broke the ice. *"What did he say?"*

"¡Cabrón!" said Jesús. *"Bastard! I wasn't speeding."* I felt he was telling the truth. He and the others obeyed speed limits scrupulously, wanting much more to arrive without getting caught than to arrive quickly. The cop had probably pegged our car as carrying illegals, though why he bothered to stop us, I didn't know. Most local police considered arresting illegals optional, and tended to let them go their way—taking them into custody and transferring them to Immigration meant a lot of extra work.

We followed the patrol car. Suddenly, Jesús had an idea. *"Teo, if they'll talk to you, see if you can keep the car. We'll need it in Phoenix, and you can drive it back."*

"You really think you're going to be deported?" Jesús bit his lip and nodded.

"I'll see what I can do."

The mood was somber as we were led into a holding cell. Just as the officer was about to lock the door, I called to him. *"Excuse me, sir! Sir? May I have a word with you, please?"* He stopped and stared, searching the faces for the one that had spoken English.

I raised a hand. "Over here." He looked at me, befuddled. "Huh? Where'd you come from? What're you doin' in there?" I shrugged.

"Well, get on outta there!"

He took me back to the squad room, where I told my story. I was a journalist, I explained, traveling with them for a story. "What do you plan to do with these guys?"

"Immigration's already on their way," said the sheriff. I would have to ask them about the car, he added. But there was no reason he could see why I was in any trouble. On my request, he directed me to the town café where, guiltily, I filled my stomach and contemplated what to do next. Should I be worried about Immigration? In the opinion of one policeman, anyway, I was guiltless; I decided at least to give it a try. I returned to the station to have another talk with my companions.

"They've called La Migra," I said, when the sheriff let me into the cellblock.

"Ay, cabrón." "Hijo de la chingada." Tiberio said, *"We're fucked."*

"The car," said Jesús, handing me the keys. *"Go get the title to the car. We'll write your name on it before they get here."*

"That won't mean anything unless it's notarized," I said. Then, after a silence, *"Where will they take you?"*

"Are we in Idaho or Utah?" I confessed I didn't know either.

"Well, in Utah, they usually deport you to El Centro, California—Mexicali is the border town. But we'll come back to Phoenix."

"But how will you afford it?"

There was no answer. Their faces were gray, devoid of expression. I had a credit card; I passed Jesús the rest of my cash. *"Call it a loan."* We discussed the things Immigration should and should not learn about our association. I then shook hands all around, embraced Jesús through the bars, and left the cellblock.

Immigration did not arrive until evening. For some of the time, I talked to the deputies. No, they conceded, catching Mexicans wasn't necessarily part of the job. But a big local mine had closed recently, unemployment was high, and, frankly, people just didn't like the idea of Mexicans coming through town and taking jobs. So they helped out Immigration when they could. The jail, I discovered, had five other cells full of Mexicans, and nobody else. The town was Nephi, Utah.

I was nervous about meeting the Immigration officers. "Aiding and abetting" illegal aliens was a felony, and I was treading a very thin line. If they were to learn everything, in fact, the line would evaporate. I counted on the language barrier, our friendship, and my friends' dislike of Immigration to ensure my safety.

The four Immigration agents, all plainclothes, arrived from Salt Lake City with two vans late that afternoon. After introducing myself to the one in charge and explaining that the detainees were acquaintances of mine, I asked about the disposition of the Cadillac. I was referred to the legal officer, a sallow man in a leather jacket. The response was swift: "The car was used in a violation of U.S. immigration law and is subject to impoundment. But before we tell you about the car, buddy, I think you'd better learn about your rights." I swallowed hard as he read me the Mirandas and took me to another room. In trouble again.

They held me for nearly twenty-four hours, and questioned me for three of them. They contacted the INS regional headquarters, their chief counsel in Washington, D.C., and my editor in New York. Finally the legal officer returned. The verdict was in, and it was disappointing news—to him. "We're going to have to let you go," he said. "Not because I want to, but because we don't think we could make the charge stick before a judge.

"But let me tell you something, mister," he said as I stood up, smiling. His thumb and forefinger came together in front of my face. "You came this close."

My relief turned to depression as I walked by the door to the cellblock: the cells were empty. My friends had been taken away. Memories of Alonso getting caught filled my mind—I couldn't stand the thought of another friendship ending that way, in a blank of sudden absence. I hitchhiked to Salt Lake City and caught a plane to Phoenix that night.

Getting back took them all of four days. I was sitting again on trailer steps at Smith's ranch, helping a man write a letter home, when a custom-painted pickup truck with mag wheels pulled up. I jumped up as Jesús, dressed the same as he had been the last time I'd seen him, climbed out of the passenger seat. The driver, a Chicano with leather jacket and mirror glasses, leaned back against the car. Jesús looked exhausted.

"*Where are the others?*" I asked.

"*In a little house. He's keeping them there until I get the money. Look—we have to go around and make a collection.*"

It was a standard *coyote* m.o.: take a group on spec, but don't release them until somebody has paid up. The workers at camp were familiar with it, and mostly sympathetic. Fortunately, it was Saturday evening, and most had some cash left from payday the day before. We passed hats once, and then a second time, and, when that came up short, a third time. An uncle of Jesús kicked in nearly $100; Jesús's brother Vicente, in Colorado, had already sent another $100 by Western Union in response to my phone call.

"*There,*" Jesús said finally. "*Six hundred dollars.*" He and the *coyote* drove away. A short time later the group was back.

They were very tired, but had a good story to tell. After being "processed" near Salt Lake City, they had been *flown* to

El Centro, California, a first for all of them. From the Immigration office to the plane to their release, they were handcuffed together, in a long line. The flight had been chartered just for them—an astonishing and ridiculous expense. The futile gesture of capturing the group, picking them up and taking them to Salt Lake City, flying them to southern California, and transporting them to Mexicali must have cost the government $1,500 at the very least; add to this the group's expenses of $600 for another *coyote*, and the cost of alternative transportation to Idaho—probably another used car—and the price tag approached $3,000 . . . all to keep five Mexicans from starting work on time!

Tiberio apparently had gotten sick on the plane. Evangélica had never witnessed anything so amazing in her life. *"We flew right through the clouds!"* she said enthusiastically. The others mainly looked tired, like they had been through a wringer. The flight had been interesting, but upsetting. They had been on the road, under the most adverse conditions, for two weeks now. More than anything else, they wanted to eat.

Immediate plans were uncertain. There were possibilities: they could stick around Phoenix, maybe work awhile, and buy another car; or they could solicit more money from other relatives in the States and buy a car that way. Jesús worried that if they didn't arrive on time Farmer Edwards would find someone else. On his request I called the man directly, explained what was happening, and asked if there was any chance he might wire them some money as an advance. But Edwards was suspicious and uncooperative, asking time and again who I was. "If they want to work, they're darn well gonna have to get up here themselves," he concluded. "They're good boys, but this can't be my problem."

Plácido, who had made it to Idaho on the first trip, rang two days later, in the midst of these deliberations. Farmer Edwards was getting impatient, he said; they'd better get up there. No means had been discovered, they answered. Finally it was decided that Plácido would come down to pick them up himself. He didn't have a license, didn't like to drive—in fact, his eyes were bad, he had no glasses, and his back hurt. But he did think that other Mexicans working down the road would loan him a car, and so it was decided.

We waited anxious days for Plácido to arrive. When he did, it was time to face up to a problem no one had cared to deal with: with the addition of Plácido to the group, there would be eight people in the car—an impossible number for all but the most desperate travelers. There was only one reasonable solution: I offered to stay behind. This was accepted, but only with a promise to come visit before the season ended.

The day after they drove off on the final, successful leg of a long journey to Idaho, I boarded a plane and flew home to begin writing. Somewhere in the air, talking to the guy in the seat next to me, sipping a cocktail, listening to rock—not *ranchera*—music in the headphones, I thought about another border, the one existing between two cultures in the same country. Like the line at Sonoita, it was invisible, marked by parts of town, railroad tracks and boulevards, places in the heart and mind. I was on that border, I realized, and bound to stay there for a long time.

Epilogue

FARMER EDWARDS first caught sight of me seated in the doorway of the vacant trailer home, enjoying an Idaho October sunset and wondering where everybody was. I had spoken to Jesús ten days before on the phone, had received a map directing me to this place, and had arrived perhaps an hour earlier by car to find . . . nothing.

Edwards approached the way a landowner approaches a trespasser: a little mean, a little wary, with a greeting that was not at all what he meant: "Anything I can do for you?"

"Lookin' for some friends of mine, some Mexicans—Jesús, Plácido, Conce . . . are you Mr. Edwards?"

"I am. You say they're your *friends*?"

Mexicans tended to find it comical that an American would spend his time hanging out with illegals. Americans tended to find it incomprehensible. But I told the farmer about my project, reminded him of the time I had called from Phoenix, and explained about the rendezvous I had arranged with the guys. Once he understood he shared the bad news.

"Well, I'm afraid they left this morning."

"What? You're kidding!"

"You can blame it on me. It was so close to the end of the

season—actually, the potatoes are all in—and they were champin'
at the bit so to get home—you know how it is—that two days
ago I told 'em they could go. Well, yesterday they finally got a
car they'd been wrangling over for some time with the guys down
the road, and they left. It's probably my fault they're not here
for you."

I was crestfallen. I expected I'd see them again someday,
but it had been a long time, and a long drive, and my expectations
had been so high. In my backseat was a twelve-pack of beer, still
cold from the convenience store down the road. The thought of
it made me blue. The farmer didn't seem to know how to handle
my silence and disappointment.

"Um, you uh, you want to come water the cattle?" he blurted.
I nodded vaguely, and climbed into his old pickup truck. A lame
sheepdog jumped in the back, next to a large plastic water tank.
We drove down a dirt county road along the edge of his property,
turning off on a rough trail that led to a corral. "They irrigated
all of this, during the season," said Edwards, gesturing to un-
planted fields on both sides of us. A few potatoes the tractor had
missed were scattered among the furrows. "And that's just a little
bit of it." I had to turn my head to take in all of what he indicated.

The county road had been littered with potatoes for the last
ten or so miles of my drive; to avoid them, I'd had to drive a
slalom course in my small car. As a semitrailer rig full of potatoes
roared by on the road behind us, I saw more bounce out. We
were near American Falls, Idaho, fifty miles north of the Utah
line, and the potatoes made me wonder why there weren't more
Irish out here, alongside Mormon settlers.

We stopped and parked at the corral. The wind had begun
to blow across the treeless fields, and I zipped up my jacket.

"They used to hate it when it got this cold," said Edwards,
of the Mexicans.

"Yes, I know."

The cattle were Edwards's winter project. "They summer
up in those mountains," he said, pointing out a row of hills to
the north. "Jesús and all helped me bring 'em down yesterday."

I jumped out to open the gate of the corral, and Edwards drove in slowly. Within seconds we were surrounded by enormous, chest-high, brown-and-white bodies, mooing and pushing and angling for a position near the round sheet-metal trough, which Edwards had begun to fill from the tank in the back of the pickup.

At about 5:00 P.M. we were through; Edwards climbed back in the pickup and called his wife at home on the CB radio. "Leavin' now, honey," he said. "Okay," she replied presently. He hung up the microphone, but then, as an afterthought, picked it back up. "Bringin' company," he added. "Okay," answered his wife. I was beginning to feel better.

I spent the evening at the Edwards's home. From its modest size, I understood that farmers in the area were more land rich than cash rich. As his wife set the table, I snuck a glimpse of a small swimming pool through the kitchen window—the baptismal pool of which Tiberio had spoken. I felt I knew a lot about Edwards already, but much of what I was seeing confounded my expectation. To Mexicans he was *"el patrón,"* a name which conjured in my mind images of a vast hacienda or plantation. Sure, Edwards was wealthy, but hardly a high roller. His wife set down two big plastic bowls full of potato-vegetable soup, and Edwards said grace. "Nothin' too fancy," said the farmer.

Edwards's son, daughter-in-law, and three-month-old grandson came over after dinner for a brief visit. My friends had briefed me: they had bought chewing tobacco for him, in exchange for his silence regarding their drinking. I felt like I had a secret dossier on everybody. The son spoke Spanish, I knew, which was of great use to his father in running the farm; he had learned it during two Mormon missionary years in Paraguay. I spent the night in a guest bedroom at the son's house, and the next morning returned to the fields with his father. As I helped out with various chores, Edwards warmed to me and became more talkative. I was full of questions.

"Plácido was the first," he said, answering one of them. "One day, I guess you could say he just came knockin'. At first I didn't like the idea of Mexicans—we'd always had regular farm hands around, and local kids to help out with the harvest. But now it seems all the kids are in school or something, and I don't know what happened to the farm hands. Mexicans underpriced 'em, I guess. Everybody was starting to use Mexicans. And so when Plácido came down the road, I said okay."

Every year Plácido had returned with more from Ahuacatlán. Some branched out to other farms but were often mistreated: instead of the paycheck, Immigration would arrive, having been "tipped off" by an unscrupulous employer. Or the living conditions were terrible. But Edwards treated his men decently and that, I knew, was why they loyally returned every spring.

We were driving out across a field to a tractor that had been abandoned in the midst of plowing when a hydraulic line broke. There was no road here; the field was furrowed like a giant washboard, and we crossed it sideways, the truck bouncing violently up and down. Edwards repaired the line, gave the diesel engine a few minutes to warm up, and invited me into the cab. We began to plow.

"That Jesús loved these things," he said, as the steel disks of the plow lifted vast volumes of earth behind us. "He learned most of what there is to know about heavy machinery here. Never looked prouder than in the seat of our trailer rig."

Jesús had boasted to me of the way the farmer trusted him with heavy machinery, some of it worth "millions of pesos." I recalled a postcard he had sent me: it was a prank photograph, of a semitruck with a flatcar trailer, hauling one sole item: a potato as big as the trailer itself. *"Hello from Idaho, of the big potatoes,"* he had written. *"We hope you find yourself in good health. ¡Que vivan los Tecos!"* Long live the Owls!

Edwards swerved slightly to avoid a telephone pole, part of a long string of them, the only things for miles to cut across the horizon. "You ever see 'em eat a pig?" he asked suddenly. "Roast a whole pig?" I said no, and he shook his head disapprovingly.

"Well, every spring—I think it's June sometime—they go buy a pig from Perkins down the road, and they have a feast. They keep that pig for a couple of days, and then they butcher it—right in front of the trailers! Cut its throat, hang it up, and let the pig pump all its blood out. Sometimes before it's all the way dead. It's not the way we do things around here, I'll tell you that. Then they start a fire and cook it on a stick, sort of barbecue style. Thing takes all day."

He shook his head some more, and sort of smiled.

"I tell you one thing, though—they're ingenious. You ever seen anybody tie up a pig?"

Actually, I said, I had, in Mexico.

"How on earth do they do that? How do you get a rope to stay around a pig? Nobody around here knows how to do that."

I explained about the lack of fences in Ahuacatlán, the need for ingenuity. If anybody could tie up a pig, I suggested, a Mexican could. Edwards was admiring.

Finished plowing, we drove the truck to a distant part of the farm, where he wanted to show me the giant potato bins. The drive took about twenty minutes, on dirt roads through land stunning for its isolation. There was nothing around. I had asked Edwards about Evangélica, but had learned little other than that she was a small girl to be carrying what it appeared would be a big baby, and that she spent all her time around the trailer, cooking for the guys and doing their laundry. Edwards had offered no comment at the time, but now he brought it up again.

"You know, I used to see her, that Evangeline, out on these roads, just cryin' and cryin'. I asked my son to find out why, and he said she was just homesick. But I'll tell you something, if I'd been treated the way that Jesús treated her, I'd be homesick too. Did you know they'd all go in to the dances in Blackfoot Saturday nights, and leave her at home? She didn't have any friends, and no way to get around. Why, one weekend my wife felt so sorry for her she brought her home, and they sat around and did sewing together. Neither of 'em knew what the other was saying, of course, but . . . I don't know. It's not right to treat your wife that way."

"Wife? Did they get married?"

I kicked myself the moment I said it. "Well, I assumed they

were married," said Edwards, a note of unpleasant surprise in his voice. "You saying she wasn't his wife? I sure wouldn't have let them live together if I knew she wasn't his wife!"

"No, no! I'm sure she was his wife! I just meant—did they go through another ceremony up here? I was just thinking maybe they went through some other ceremony up here—for Immigration or something."

"Not to my knowledge," said Edwards unhappily. But he didn't bring it up again, and later he resumed calling her Jesús's wife, much to my relief.

Finally it was time to depart from Idaho, to return to home and to work. Edwards and his wife gave me their good wishes, and inscribed to me a copy of the Book of Mormon. It was a loss, having missed my friends, but an unexpected gain to have been able to talk to Edwards himself.

Before climbing back into my car, I took a last walk through the trailer home, trying to picture them all there. Items they had left behind offered clues to their lives in Idaho. On the dresser tops were piles of pay stubs, and lists of dates and hours worked— to be compared, no doubt, with the farmer's own accounting. "11 agosto—10 horas   12 agosto—13 horas   13 agosto— 11 1/2 horas." I saw that sometimes they had worked seven days a week, and up to sixty-five or seventy hours. Under the back porch was a pile of knee-high rubber boots, all covered with dry mud, and stiff leather work gloves. There was an ad torn out of a Spanish-language magazine—it might have been ¡Alarma!— for an aphrodisiac potion. In one room, more delicately decorated than the rest, was a photograph of Jesús stuck into the frame of a dresser-top mirror—it had been *their* room. And underneath it, a spiral notebook with Evangélica's name on the cover. I opened to one page: "*Raquel, I hope you find yourself well and at your husband's side. Raquel, you're already forgetting about me. You almost don't write me anymore. I'll write you right away. Tell Reyna to write me. Send me the other photo, the one where I'm with Jesús . . .*"

Across the opposite page were verses, scribbled randomly: *"I love you. I miss you. Don't forget me."* And *"Evangélica Leal Olvera + Jesús García."* And *"from she who loves and desires you, Evangélica."* It was too private, and too sad; I felt bad about reading more. She would be home by now, close to her family again, no longer scared. If anyone truly suffered because of the whole immigration mess, I thought, it was women like Evangélica, and the wives and kids who stayed at home.

In a room which appeared to be Plácido's was a large water bed—I had listened to it described in detail one night in Pablo's cantina in Ahuacatlán. Few there had ever heard of such a thing, and one man even asked me if it was true. *"But don't you get wet?"* On the floor was a mailing from a psychic in Miami Beach, in Spanish. Drawers and cupboards were empty, save for the occasional bag of *chicharrones* or cookies, a paper bagful of beans. The only things full—and they were packed to the brim—were the closets. They were hung with jeans, long underwear, work boots, jackets, thick shirts—the sorts of heavy clothing required by the cool northern climate. They were a symbol of labor, and a symbol of expectation: No need to take these home. They would be back to wear them next year.

AFTER IMMIGRATION caught him in the back of the bus in Laredo, I never expected to see Alonso again. What a surprise when I walked into the cooperative's warehouse, in Querétaro City, and saw him behind the counter, selling seeds and honey.

"You gave me their address that night in the bus station," he explained, grinning from under a baseball cap that read "PAC-MAN." "You told me to write you there. Well, after they sent me back, I came and asked for a job instead." His timing had been good; the cooperative had had an opening.

He worked for six months, and then left again for Texas. There has been no word from him since; but then, none was ever expected.

. . .

Despite his plan to leave Los Angeles quickly for higher-paying work on a California farm, Carlos remained in the city. He quit the job engraving trophies after several months; after an interim period helping his cousin Martín in the welding shop, he found a job in a "recycling plant." I hadn't heard from him in nearly a year when one day I received a letter, with his return address, written in a scrawling, uneven hand that did not remind me at all of Carlos:

> *Dear Ted,*
>
> *Hi! How are you?*
>
> *I'm sorry I didn't write you earlier, but I had an accident. I don't know how to tell you this, but I lost my hand. It happened at the "recycling." I was cleaning up, and slipped, and my hand got caught in a conveyor belt. The roller broke it totally. Everything happened so fast, I was in shock. I didn't cry, I didn't lose much blood, the ambulance arrived quickly and took me and my hand to the hospital. The doctors did everything possible to reconnect it, but they couldn't save it—the bones, nerves, tendons, muscles, everything was destroyed, and so they amputated it.*

It was his right hand. The script was hard to read because he was writing with his left. The company's insurance paid most of his medical bills, including some costs of rehabilitation. Carlos began attending a course, "in the best computer school in Los Angeles." With his savings, he enrolled simultaneously in an advanced English class.

Learning about computers had been Carlos's dream all along in coming to the States, but until the accident, as he noted, he had been unable to afford it. It had been a sad year: his uncle Cándido had died three months earlier of his kidney ailment. And a "Dear John" letter had come from his girlfriend in Mexico— but at least those had been expected.

> *How to tell you . . . in truth, it was very hard for me.*
> *I felt morally destroyed. But little by little I'm getting used*
> *to my new self. I'm a realist, and I have to go forward,*
> *and fight to survive. It happened in the past, and I live in*
> *the present, preparing myself for the future.*

Emilio, Máximo, Chucho, and the four others I had joined on the slippery wintertime drive to Florida soon consolidated their two households into a two-bedroom trailer home on the outskirts of La Belle. Picking juice oranges was good work, but in their opinion thirty to forty hours a week wasn't enough of it: by the end of the month, they had found another orchard where they could work fifty to sixty.

Emilio soon revealed himself to be a heavy drinker, disappearing with the station wagon on weekends and twice getting fined and jailed for driving while under the influence. The second time he lost his job for missing work, but soon found another in La Belle. After a fall of picking apples in Michigan, he returned to Florida, where he is said to be still. The others say he shows no inclination whatsoever to return to Mexico.

Máximo left for home after five months, having worked hard and enjoyed himself little. He lives with his wife and six children in Escanelilla, a *rancho* near Ahuacatlán. The man who used to pray before driving off on an icy road saved enough money to buy a car, and now operates a bright orange taxi, with lighted sign on top—the only taxi—in Ahuacatlán.

Chucho returned home with Máximo to a wife and four children. Six months later he went back to Arizona to work a season in citrus but returned immediately thereafter. He is one of the best-dressed men in his *rancho*, and often invites male neighbors over to watch or listen to his compact portable television/stereo. At home the floor around his feet is usually crowded with an assortment of marbles, toy cars, crawling babies, and sometimes a piglet. Two large *guayabo* trees grow over the house where his aged mother and retarded brother also live. He speaks constantly of returning to the United States.

. . .

I found Eduardo, the Woodpecker, at home in Ahuacatlán. His friends Jesús, Conce, Tiberio, and Plácido had left for another season in Idaho. But having just gotten married and been offered a job at the local savings bank, he had had little desire to join them.

Over his lunch break, and later at night, in the candlelit cantina when the electricity was out, he told me of what had happened after we parted company in Phoenix. Plácido picked them up, as planned, but everyone was so tired that in Nevada, somehow, they made a wrong turn. *"We got further and further from the highway, until the road turned to dirt and we were all alone!"* said Eduardo, laughing. Because the road they were on was outside everyone's memory of the route, and because they carried no maps, it turned into a twenty-eight-hour detour. When finally they arrived at Edwards's, *"we were so tired that we were worthless. We were ashamed to tell him what happened, so we just said we were sick."*

Irrigation was the main duty of the Woodpecker and the other newcomers. They would walk the ditches morning, noon, and night, placing short plastic tubes between the irrigation ditch and a row of potatoes. A quick suck on one end of the tube would start the siphon action; when the field was saturated, they would pick up the tubes and move on.

A better offer, for the Woodpecker and Victor, came from a farmer down the road, and halfway through the season they moved onto his ranch. He was so impressed with them that he wrangled temporary visas for them for the next season—like gold! When the Woodpecker got married and changed his mind about going, he passed on the visa to Victor's father (and Hilario's brother) Cornelio, who decided he could make much more money by parking his truck and going north again than by staying home and hauling bricks all season. So father and son went north together, crossing the border on a bus—legally, in style.

During the season Tiberio was caught by the sheriff in Blackfoot, Idaho, said the Woodpecker, and deported after being beaten;

Victor was caught and deported twice. Plácido was picked up for driving under the influence, and put up $500 bail to get out. Feeling certain he would be deported if he showed up in court, however, he forfeited the money. Lately he had been talking of bringing his family with him next year.

Evangélica and Jesús moved into the home of Jesús's parents upon their return to Ahuacatlán. (This, according to Jesús's mom, helped to appease her own parents, who had been implying that Jesús's family was responsible for seeing them married.) Two months later Evangélica gave birth to their six-pound, ten-ounce daughter, Nidia, in the hospital at Jalpan. But three months after that, Jesús left again for Idaho. Evangélica, uncomfortable living alone with his parents, moved down the street to the home of her sister and brother-in-law.

Evangélica had Nidia in her arms when I visited. She was as shy as ever, but obviously proud of her baby. The men's opinion about Evangélica was that she had been no fun at all in Idaho, complaining all the time, disagreeing with everything. Jesús, it was said, hadn't *wanted* to take her back north. Evangélica, however, with no apparent animosity, told me that she was the one who had wanted to stay home. It wasn't that she was mad at Jesús, she explained to my surprise, but that "there was nothing to do there" in Idaho, "no other girls," and it was "very cold." The only good surprise had been the television in the trailer—she hadn't known TV—but the shows were all in English.

She worked, as previously, as a nurse in the "county seat," a forty-five-minute bus ride away. Her sister took care of the child when she was gone. I was baffled by her apparent lack of resentment toward Jesús, until I asked others in Ahuacatlán about it. *"You are surprised by what happened to her,"* said Hilario's wife, Lupe, to me. *"But she, Teodoro, was not. When a girl does something like that, she knows the risks. She can't expect any special treatment."* In Ahuacatlán, in other words, it happened all the time.

. . .

Arnulfo Resendiz was not a major character in this story. A quiet, simple, smiling, round-faced man, he lives in the *rancho* of Huajales, just down the road from Ahuacatlán. On his way home every day, on a wobbly old bicycle with broken spokes, he is greeted by Fastidio ("Nuisance"), a very thin, ordinary dog that he keeps and loves very much. Fastidio submits to other dogs the way Mexican dogs submit to humans—he rolls over on his back, puts his tail between his legs, sometimes pees. But, despite constant vulnerability to attack, he is very good natured and full of energy. In many ways Fastidio resembles his owner.

Arnulfo had been traveling with the group from Quirambal when they joined us on the border at Sonoita. Instead of staying with them in Phoenix, he decided to try his luck in Idaho with us, and was in the Cadillac when we were arrested in Utah. Deported with all the rest, he rejoined the men from Quirambal—including Genaro, the leader—in Phoenix, and went to Florida with them, via *coyote*. There they found Emilio and Máximo and the others at work in La Belle, and joined them in the already crowded trailer home. But they were too late to find work and so, borrowing more money, they headed up to Michigan to pick cucumbers.

I talked with Arnulfo in the *huachería,* where he was assembling sandals with Tiberio's brother (the owner), and three others. His co-workers were laughing as Arnulfo related his travels, especially the last part: at the wheel of a pickup truck in northern Michigan, he turned the wrong way onto a one-way street. He was arrested, then taken by the INS to Detroit, Denver, and Ciudad Juárez. At this point, he admitted sheepishly, he finally gave up.

"I was arrested and beaten by the judiciales in Sonoita, deported by La Migra in Utah, and then deported by La Migra in Detroit. All this before I ever found a job! What reason did I have to stay any longer? There was no one left to deport me!"

The others around the *huachería*, all seated on short stools, howled, bent over with laughter. Arnulfo's bad luck had been truly spectacular. But he was more embarrassed than depressed. It was, after all, a gamble. There was something quixotic about the whole enterprise: you went to try your luck, and if things didn't work out, well, what the hell. People might find it funny, but you weren't a laughingstock: all were babes in the woods in the United States. It was a country that could make you feel kind of foolish. What else to do but pay off your debts and try again next year—which, Arnulfo assured me, was his plan exactly.

Afterword

Americans in the Southwest have been aware for years of the unofficial immigration of Mexican nationals, across river and desert. Only in the past decade, with Mexico's economy in shambles and its population expanding rapidly, have Americans—in particular those who live in other parts of the country—grown worried about the larger numbers of immigrants. The Immigration and Naturalization Service has alerted us to a silent invasion of an army of the poor, and passed along the latest statistics: 1.7 million people were caught sneaking over the border in 1986, up 50 percent from the year before. Up to 6 million are estimated to be in the States already. Often they are mentioned in the same breath as drugs that are smuggled across, or terrorists that might try to be. What crosses the border is dangerous; the Southwest is our "exposed flank." There is a nagging fear that we've gone to sleep with the back door unlocked.

In Mexico the migration is less imagined and more concrete. It's something people from the poorest and most remote corners of the republic have participated in for years—at least as far back as 1848, when the United States, through the Mexican War and the Treaty of Guadalupe Hidalgo, acquired nearly half of their country, stranding many Mexican nationals in a foreign land.

Then, as now, migration has been recognized to be a two-way street, of people leaving home for a while, working, and then mainly returning home. The relatively fast pace of American industrialization, coupled with Mexico's economic and demographic crises, has accelerated the movement north. Today, if you are among the majority of Mexicans—those with very little money—working in the United States is not merely something you hear about, but something you might consider. It is one of life's few options.

Migration, to Mexicans, is about taking a chance. Need and ambition combine to propel people north: those who go are usually those most inclined to "pick themselves up by their own bootstraps," those with the greatest hope, energy, and expectations of life. Often they think twice, because the proposition is risky: though you may make some money, you might also suffer the insult of deportation, get hurt or robbed, or, worse yet, find no work. Generally, to go means to leave behind a family—and to a Mexican family is everything. And then there's the social pressure against leaving: *"How many men desert their country in search of dollars?"* asked a recent newspaper editorial.

Emigrants know, of course, that crossing the border is illegal; but crossing does not hang on their hearts as a crime. They realize that Americans with money—*important* Americans—are eager to hire them, as long as that fact isn't broadcast over the radio. Moreover, they realize that the jobs they do are generally scorned, even by poorer Americans. These seem enough to put a conscience to rest.

If the country as a whole didn't want them, Mexicans further appreciate, America would make it illegal to give them jobs. But until recently, while it was illegal for them to *be* in the States, it wasn't illegal to hire them. For thirty-five years our immigration law contained a fundamental hypocrisy:

8 USCS § 1324: Any person . . . who brings into . . . the United States . . . or attempts to transport or move, within the United States . . . or willfully or knowingly

conceals, harbors, or shields from detection . . . any
alien . . . not duly admitted by an immigration officer . . . shall be guilty of a felony, and upon conviction
thereof shall be punished by a fine not exceeding $2,000
or by imprisonment for a term not exceeding five years,
or both . . .

*Provided however, That for the purposes of this section,
employment (including the usual and normal practices incident to employment) shall not be deemed to constitute har-
boring.* (italics added)

That key final sentence explains why, until May 1987, it was
a felony to lend a Mexican $5, but not one to pay him $200 a
week; why you could go to jail for offering one a ride hitchhiking
but not for driving her home after she cleaned your house. It is
why, after working and traveling with Mexicans for a year (in
1984–1985), I broke the law enough times, theoretically, to spend
the rest of my life in jail, while the farmer who hired some to
harvest his crops merely saved a small fortune.

Employers can now be penalized for hiring illegal aliens.
Whether that means they will stop doing so or whether, as many
observers predict, it will simply force the illegal alien to keep an
even lower profile remains to be seen. What is certain is that any
law that treats only the U.S. symptoms of Mexican maladies is
not likely to change the situation much.

Mexicans, in other words, will keep coming. The country's
1984 population was expected to grow by nearly one-half by the
year 2000—the same year that Mexico City, with 30 million people, will indisputably be the world's largest city—and to have
doubled by 2025. Today half of all Mexicans are sixteen years of
age or younger. Already the country cannot employ 40 percent
of its adult workers. Mexican experts quoted in *The New York
Times* say wage disparities make increased migration "almost inevitable."

The future may be of concern, but to date Mexican immigration has hardly been a disaster. Through that "back door" we left unlocked appear to have passed mainly a good supply of hardworking cleaning ladies and lawn men. Mexican labor, according to just about everyone, benefits American business, and therefore it also benefits the American consumer and overseas consumers of American goods. (As residents will tell you, the economy of the state of California—and several others—would likely grind to a halt were all Mexican nationals to disappear tomorrow.)

Like most previous waves of immigration, Mexican immigration leaves some citizens worried that there are becoming too many of "them," and not enough of "us," that we as a nation may drown in the tide of foreignness. But if there is any truism about immigration to America, it is that "they" soon become "us"; and that for two hundred years our strength and vigor have been due precisely to the energy and aspiration of immigrants. This is as true today as it was in the early 1920s, or during the previous century. "The United States," wrote Nathan Glazer in 1985, "remains the permanently unfinished country."

I was not selective about the Mexicans I chose to include in this story—no chapter was censored that included ones I met who were less desirable. These are the guys. They're not perfect, but the majority would make good neighbors; I'd welcome them as mine. I found the illegal immigration monster to be the sort that's less scary up close than it is from a distance. Immigration, you could say, is America's history book. This is the latest chapter, and I am left eager, not frightened, to see what comes next.